How I Became The Gangster of Porn

SuaveXXX

EDITOR: KDR INK
FORMATTING & TYPESETTING:
WWW.DIVABOOKSINCONLINE.COM

DEDICATION

To the greatest woman who ever touch my life, my grandmother, Willa and to my grandmother who passed away before I ever had the pleasure of meeting you. My grandmother, Lydia also to my grandfather, Mr. George Joseph Dugais and my grandfather, Mr. James Pugh and to my Pa-Pa who was the father in my life when my dad wasn't there. To my uncles, Ray Hardy, Charles Hardric and my aunt, Pat and last but not least to my big cousin, Dreta.
I dedicate this book to you all and miss you very much. May you all continue to rest in peace. I will mourn you until I join you…

ACKNOWLEDGEMENTS

Special thanks to my little cousins Shaunta and Avery Ladd. If it wasn't for your blessings and understanding then I would have had to leave out a very important chapter of my life out of this book. Ms. Kisha Green (DivaBooksInc) to whom I would not have been able to complete this project if it weren't for your professional knowledge and know how. My book would have been out on schedule months ago and I would have saved a lot of money if I would have met you sooner, I am thankful to God for placing you in my life. I will recommend you to anyone and everyone who will listen that you are the go to person for those seeking publishing.

CONTENTS

CHAPTER 1

The Gangster is Born

I was born March 31, 1972 just before midnight, which probably explains why I am a night person. I was born in Los Angeles, California at General Hospital. Yes the very one that's on TV every day. I always knew that I would be on TV one day. When I was a little boy, my mother would point to the TV as the soap opera would come on and tell me, "That's where you was born!" I was only about three years old but I used to smile and look very hard trying to see myself or my parents in the hospital on the television screen. Every day as soon as I would hear the music to the show come on, I would stop whatever I was doing and run to the TV standing there pointing, making little finger prints all over the screen.

My mother and father was a beautiful couple. My mother's name is Jean, she is a very light skinned beautiful black woman mixed with Cherokee Indian, but she has hair like wool. She's 5'3 and weighed 110 pounds. My dad's name is Edsel, he is a white dude mixed with Creole and Seminole Indian.

He's 5'8 and only weighed about 170 pounds. He looked more Mexican than anything, and because of that he would get harassed a lot by the police. He would get pulled over and asked to step out of the car and when he did he raised hell and asked "What's the damn problem!" The police would see his olive colored skin and his long straight black hair and commence to whooping his Mexican looking ass. As a result of him being mistaken as a Mexican by the police my dad started to resent any affiliation with people of color.

This in turn started a denial process of his own wife and kids. His father was never fond of him being with my mother. My grandfather would say that the police harassed my dad because he was screwing a black girl and the color was rubbing off on him. I'm the oldest of four children my parents made. It's crazy because my dad has always been somewhat racist. The reason why he ended up marrying my mother was because she is very light skinned and very beautiful. But the marriage did not last long. I can still remember my mother crying because my dad was always beating her black ass.

He would get drunk and do his drugs and show off for his brothers and his friends that would come over. He would play his bass guitar loud all hours of the night. He was a great player. He and his older brother had their own band. They didn't get many paying gigs, so my dad had to break up the band to get a real job to take care of his growing family. I remember we would go fishing a lot out at the ocean right off the pier. My dad taught me how to hunt and fish those were our good father and son moments. I really cherish those memories.

Things were good for a while once he started working. My dad was a machinist and a very good one too.

He would sometimes take me with him to work. I can still remember the smell of the lathes and machine oils.

Soon the partying, drinking came back, and beating my mom. I remember one night being awakened out of my sleep by my mother's blood curdling scream. I was at the most four years old. I came down the stairs one step at a time. When I got halfway down I could see my father over my mother. They were on the floor between the kitchen and the dining room. My dad had both his hands around her neck. I did the only thing a baby could do in that situation, I started crying for my mommy. My dad heard me so he stopped and looked at me with an evil look in his eyes. As he was looking at me, my mother kicked him in his nuts. He staggered back into the kitchen area. Then my mother jumped up, ran up the stairs, swooped me up and ran into my room and closed and locked the door. My mother crawled into my bunk bed with me, holding me and rocking me. I remember holding my mother tight as we both cried ourselves to sleep. My mother was getting tired of it all. My dad had a bad temper, anything that went wrong my mother would get her ass whooped. In turn, she would take it out on us and beat our asses. She would pick up anything she could reach and start swinging it. Anything from race car tracks to plastic baseball bats or even the telephone cord. It was a mad house for a while. It was a vicious cycle. Then my mom had enough of being his punching bag.

One night I was in my bed asleep and I heard banging on the front door. I jumped up and looked out my bedroom as my dad opened it. All I saw were flashing lights and I heard the sirens from the ambulance.

I remember seeing the paramedics rushing into the house and into my parents' room. My little brother, Joey, was crying so I hugged him and I said, "Mommy will be OK brother." At least that's what I was hoping as they hurried my mother's naked body into the ambulance as me and my little brother watched and cried together. That was the first of many attempts our mother made on taking her life. She would take a bunch of pills, get rushed to the hospital… she would come home, my dad would be nice to her, they would make up, and my mother would end up pregnant again. She would have another baby, then after a while he would beat her ass again, and then here we go again. Flashing lights and sirens blaring. Well after three boys and a beautiful little girl my mother finally said that is enough! One day after my dad went to work, my mother packed all of our stuff she could fit into my grandparents' car and we moved in with her mom and stepdad. They lived in a big house in Carson, California. I don't know what was worse, where we left or the mad house we had just moved to because it wasn't just us four kids, and Mom-Mom and Pa-Pa.

It was my grandfather's son Uncle Keith, my mother's older brother, my Uncle Charles, my mother's older sister, my Aunt Pat and her daughter Jasmine; and the twins, my mother Jean and my Aunt Joan, and her 3 kids. Everybody in that house was an alcoholic. One night while the adults were drinking, dancing, and having fun, and my little cousin Ki-Ki that's a year younger than me, watched my grandparents sneak into the kitchen and grab their stash to make a drink. Hennessy was the only thing that my grandparents drank. Top shelf. My cousin and I watched where they would hide the bottles from my, uncles, aunts, and my mother; underneath the stove, behind the skillets by the pots and pans. And at the young age of seven, we were sneaking to grab a bottle. They would put the empties in there too. That's what we would, grab them and we would sip that little corner of the bottle. That little shot that was still left in there would have us buzzing. That's how it all started! Everybody else in the house would be drinking on some Night Train, Thunderbird, or a beer.

One night they were drinking and smoking, and dancing to the music. Nobody was paying attention so I grabbed a beer off of the coffee table. I hurried and finished the last of the can. My Aunt Pat looked at me and saw the can as I put it down. I looked at her, my eyes were bugged out and red and I was turning blue. All she saw was that beer can. She got pissed. My Uncle Charles and my Uncle Keith thought it was cool; they were laughing their butts off. I was stuck frozen and scared. Then all I remember was seeing my mother flying in the air from out of the corner of my eye. She slapped me on my back so hard. All I remember after that was seeing a cigarette butt fly across the room, and that I could finally breathe again.

See while my aunt was mad and my uncles were laughing, they didn't realize that I was choking to death on a cigarette butt from in that damn beer can about to die. Needless to say, I never did that shit again!

I'll never forget when I was thirteen; I went into the garage where my Uncle Keith was shooting pool with two of his homies from the block. The garage door was open and I could see that it was a nice day out but of course my little bad ass wanted to stir up some mess with my uncle because he's always messing with me. So I walked up to their pool game and I grabbed two of the pool balls and I rolled them across the table messing up their intense pool game. There was money on the table so I knew they were betting but I didn't care. I grabbed their money and I tried to run out to the street. My uncle's homies grabbed me and my uncle starting socking me up. When one of his homies said, "Sup lil man you think you tuff Cuzz?"

"Hell yeah Cuzz, that don't hurt!"

They let go of me and my uncle blasted me in my chest and took their money back. That's what my uncle always did. I was his little punching bag. It was to toughen me up. My Uncle Keith is ten years older than me. He was always like the big brother I never had. He taught me about the hood and how things should be and how I'm supposed to carry myself and how not to be a punk and never back down from nothing or nobody, especially on this particular day. After I was done harassing my uncle and his homies, I went across the street to play with my friends. There was a foster home over there. The kids from that home were bad as hell but so was I, so I gravitated to them. When I went over there to play I met the new fat kids from the foster home. There was five of us playing, two girls that lived next door to the foster home and two of my boys that I played with every day that lived in the home. We would always try to kiss the girls or grab their booties. We would grab their butts and they would chase us all through the yard until they were out of breath. I had just grabbed one of the girls' booty and I started running. I ran through the yard and all of a sudden I tripped and fell on my face. I jumped up after I realized that this kid tripped me on purpose.

The kid that tripped me was a new kid that I had never seen before. He looked like he could've been Faizon Love at thirteen years old. He was a big fat black greasy little kid. He was standing over me laughing when

I fell. When I jumped up I asked him what the hell his problem was.

"You punk! What you gonna do about it?" he said. I pushed his big ass and he didn't budge. Then he pushed me back. By now all the kids were gathering around. Contrary to what you may be thinking because I'm a big dude, when I was a kid I was a skinny little twerp until I was about seventeen. So when I punched him in his belly it didn't even faze him. Next thing I knew he pushed me again this time into some hedge bushes. He tried to jump on me while I was on the ground entangled in the bushes with dust flying everywhere. He was trying to get a swing in but I had my guards up. I was out weighed, and I could barely see from all the dirt flying. Then I peeked through one of my eyes and I could see sunlight right between his legs so I kicked him in his chubby balls. He grabbed his nuts so I took that opportunity to roll out of the hedges and I ran home. My uncle and his two homies saw what happened. When I ran across the street my uncle snatched me up and he said, "Hell naw nephew, you never run from a fight. You gotta go back

over there and finish that. You never ever run from a fight."
I told my uncle that I tied.

"I hit him but it didn't hurt him."

"You gotta hit him in his soft spot," my uncle said. He told
me dudes that are big like that you hit them in their nose.
"Now get over there, make a fist and go bust him in his nose
as hard as you can." I looked across the street and little fat
Faizon was standing there pacing like a mad bull in an
arena, all my friends were standing there too. My uncle was
still holding my arm as he stood up and pushed me in the
direction of the mad bull. I ran across the street.

"Why'd you run home to mommy?" The fat kid teased.

"Shut up punk!"

"Yeah who's gonna make me? You?"

"Yep."

The fat kid pushed me and I fell back onto my neighbor's
driveway. I got up and I looked across the street. My uncle
and his two homies were looking. My uncle balled his fist to
remind me of what he just told me. The fat kid went to push
me again but this time he wasn't so lucky. I squeezed my fist
really tight and closed my eyes and I swung as hard as I
could. When I opened my eyes, the little fat bastard was on
the ground holding his nose. He jumped up and looked into

his hand, saw blood, and started crying as he ran into the foster home. Next thing I know the girl that was chasing me for grabbing her booty walked up and kissed me on the cheek. My boys came over and slapped me five. They told me that he just came into their foster home and they did not like him. They said he was a bully. I ran back across the street to my uncle and his homies and they slapped me five too!

One of my uncles homies said, "you down little Cuzz. We see you got heart. You might be ready to be from the hood."

"Hell yeah!" I said. "Oh yeah?" All three of them took me on the side of my grandparents' house and they beat the shit out of me. My shoulders, chest, even my legs were sore. After they were done whooping on me for what seemed like forever my uncle said, "now you down with the hood Cuzz."

CHAPTER 2

Birthday Suit

It was spring of 1986 and I had just turned 14 years old. I was barely passing the 8thgrade at Curtis Junior High School in Carson, California. This year was when I had some of my best memories. I was still living with my grandparents which mean I had a lot of freedom.

I remember the last couple of months of 8th grade at Curtis like they were yesterday. Break dancing and

Hip Hop was in full affect. The dancers wore shoes called Creepers and their hair was cut in a high top fades with Sun-in sprayed in it to dye parts of their hair or their duck tails.

Girls were wearing Levi skirts, their hair all done up with fake braids in basket weaves or crimped with bamboo earrings. But not me and my homies we were the gangsters of the streets of Carson and you knew it when you saw us coming.

While the dancers were at home practicing their moves in the mirror or in their drive-way on a card board box, I would be at home all night on my ironing board and a full can of Niagara spray starch creasing the hell out of my corduroy pants that my grandparents bought me from the Gap inside the Carson Mall.

They came in almost every color that you can think of. I had Hood colors like the black ones, charcoal grey, light grey, navy blue, royal blue, neighborhood blue, and of course I had a white pair that I had just wore on my C-Day. I was clean as a whistle that day as I snuck out of my grandparents' room wearing my all white cords that were starched so much they stood up next to my bed all night waiting for me to wake up and put them on and when I did I could hear the starch cracking as I slid my foot in each leg. But that's what creasing your pants properly will do. You iron and iron until that whole can of starch is empty. There was an art to ironing and creasing your pants perfectly. If you used that cheap starch then you would have white flakes all over your pants, especially at the bottom where your cuffs were. You had to get the lemon scent so you would smell so fresh and so clean-clean. To go with my all white cords I had on some fresh out the box all white K-Swiss shoes. That's all I wore besides Nike Cortez, my boulevards, or my black or blue house shoes. All gangster attire, I never was a Jordan shoe type of nigga. With my all white cords, and my all white K-Swiss I had on a White Tee and to top it all off I just borrowed my grandmother's Los Angeles Raiders Starter. My grandparents had matching jackets. My grandfather bought the jackets months ago but I would never see them wearing them. So I knew that they wouldn't miss it this one time if I wore it to school to get my floss on for my birthday.

I checked myself out in the mirror and walked out the door for the world to see me. Everybody walked to school in my neighborhood. As soon as I got to the end of my block, I loosened my blue snakeskin belt and got my hellava sag-on. It took me extra-long to get to school that morning. I had to walk very slow, being careful not to dirty up the bottom of the cuffs of my white pants. Plus I had starched them so much that the crease would pinch the back of my legs behind my knees if I walked too fast, and that would not have looked good while getting my gangsta stroll on and trying to look cool. I also had to watch my back because people were getting robbed and sometimes shot for these Starter jackets.

When I finally met up with my homies, we were deep. We used to all meet up and bail up to the school together. They praised me for my all white C-Day attire. Each of my homies greeted me with our "Hood High Five" and wished me a happy C-Day. We approached Curtis in our everyday gang bang uniform of our blue C-rags hanging out of our back left pockets for all to see. We all had on our brownies, which were brown gardening gloves we bought from our neighborhood liquor store and of course we always brought Uncle Paul to school with us in our right pocket. But today was my special day, so as we got to the corner of the school where we stopped every day and took swig of our breakfast of champions, while they cracked open their short dogs of Paul Masson I pulled out my half pint of Hennessy from the inside pocket of my Raiders Starters jacket. I cracked that golden seal and we all bowed our heads and poured out a little liquor for our dead homies. Then we threw our bottles up in the air to my birthday and threw our heads back and emptied every drop into our systems, warming our insides and started the day off right.

The day was going great. All the girls were on me and the fellas was jockin my Raiders jacket. I never took it off. I was getting all kinds of love and hugs from the home girls and as I walked across the campus, I would get birthday shout outs; I was the man. Boy you couldn't tell me nothing.

At lunch I was surrounded by my female best friend Felicia and a couple of her girls. They were admiring my new jacket when I heard my name being called over the school P.A. system for me to report to the principal's office. The girls told me that a secret admirer must have had some balloons delivered to me for my birthday. I couldn't think of who would have done that, but they were smiling and looking as if they might have had something to do with it. As I walked across campus and down the hallways to the front of my school, all I could do was think of how embarrassing and non-gangster it would be to walk around the rest of the day carrying some damn birthday balloons. It was a big surprise when I walked into that office and I saw my grandmother standing there with my principal, my heart stopped. My grandmother embarrassed the shit out of me. She was always good at that, but this time took the cake.

"Boy I knew it! I knew you had on my jacket!" She said. "Are you crazy? Don't you know that those gang banging thugs out here will kill you for this jacket? Why do you think me and your grandfather don't wear them. I told him to take those deadly things back to where he got them from!"

I took the jacket off feeling totally embarrassed. I handed over the Starter jacket to my loving grandmother and I thought to myself, if she only knew that the grandson she was trying to protect from those gang banging thugs was one of them himself.

My grandmother thanked the principal, snatched her jacket out of my hands, and as she stormed out of the school office while she still had the door wide open, she looked back at me and yelled, "And pull your damn pants up little boy! You look like one of those damn no good thugs!" It echoed all through the school hallways. Then as she turned to walk out she yelled, "You better not be late for your next class! Oh yeah, happy birthday!"

Needless to say that was one of the most embarrassing moments of my life. When I got to my locker to get my books for my next class, I didn't realize how loud my grandmother was and how much of a scene she had made until I was walking into my next period class and everybody started giggling. When I got to my desk, about to sit down, somebody on the other side of the class yelled, "Lil boy pull your damn pants up."

That's when the whole classroom fell out laughing; even my damn history teacher cracked a smile. Hell I couldn't do anything but laugh my damn self. That's when my female best friend Felicia came over to my desk and gave me a big hug and said, "Happy Birthday Shawn," and kissed me on the cheek. Then, of course, all the kids started in about that too. "Ooohhhhhhhh!" they teased.

That's when my normally prude history teacher went back to his old self and called the class to order by saying, "OK, that's enough! Now open your history books to page 190." I looked over at my beautiful best friend and we smiled at each other as we opened our books to page. One-Nine-O.

When I got home from school that day, it wasn't over. I was walking up the block to my grandmother's house I could see my mother's car. I knew it was all bad once I seen her car. Before I walked in the house I made sure that my damn pants were pulled up. When I opened the door, my mother and my grandmother were in the kitchen. I smelled a cake baking, but the looks on their faces was not a "Happy Birthday" greeting. My mother told me to come to her, but she was at the stove and she had one of those hot combs on it. She was pressing her hair so I really didn't trust her, and the evil look on my grandmother's face said, 'go ahead and burn him, I won't say a word.

See, back then there was no such thing as C.P.S. or 911.Sure, there was a child abuse hotline, and I had that number memorized. But my mother would beat the life out of us with the phone cord, plug the phone back up, and hand us the phone receiver and stand there smoking a cigarette saying, "Go ahead and call the child abuse hotline, I dare you. I bet you'll be dead by the time they get here, and then you can't tell shit. I'll just make up something and tell them that your clumsy ass fell down some stairs, like it was a tragic accident."

So I just stared at them as they both stared at me.

Then my mother startled me and said, "Boy! Get your ass over here before I throw this damn Hennessy bottle that your grandmother found inside her Raiders jacket pocket that you stole from her. After she's been letting your dumb ass stay here, and been feeding you, and put clothes on your back, that's how you repay her?"

"I only borrowed it for today because it was my birthday and that I was gonna return it once I got home from school today, hopefully before she got home from work."

"Well, she surprised you didn't she because she didn't go to work today. She only left to go to "Boys Market" to get the ingredients to bake you a birthday cake. She took a sick day off just for you. But when she came back to get her jacket because it was a little chilly outside, she thought it had been stolen! She tore up the house looking for it and blaming everybody in here for stealing it, but you! Your grandmother said 'There's no way my Shawn would take my jacket without asking.' Not her favorite grandbaby. My mother might as well have said. But to her surprise after hours of searching and accusing your Uncle Keith and your Uncle Charles, I told her to go up to the school to see if you had it, and you did. You're lucky she didn't tell me you had it before you got here and started pressing my hair because I would've come up there and really embarrassed your lil high yella ass!"

Lord knows if my mother would've come up to my school that day it would have been the end of my gang banging career right then. My grandmother had tears in her eyes and said she had never felt so betrayed in her life. Then she pointed to the Hennessy bottle. "Where did you get that?"

I just shrugged my shoulders as if to say I don't know then she made me swear on her giant red Bible that she kept in her "off limits" living room that I was not using drugs. I swore it because at the time I wasn't.

Later on in life I asked the Lord for forgiveness because at the mere age of fourteen I didn't know that alcohol was a drug. My grandmother, with tears in her eyes, said, "Thank You," and gave me a big hug and birthday kiss and told me to go give my mother a hug too. But as I turned to my mother she had just finished parting her hair. She had that hot comb in one hand and a towel with a bunch of burn marks on it in her other hand. She had that blue hair grease everywhere so I told my grandmother that I'd wait until she was done. My mother looked at me while she was pressing her hair and smoke was rising from her head.

"And by the way, since you don't know how to act over here, and you wanna be drinking and gang banging, then as soon as summer is here you're moving back in with me and your brothers and sister.

You're lucky it's so close to the end of the year or I would snatch you out of that damn school tomorrow, but your grandmother begged me not to."

I just stood there tearing up. "But mom this is my home. What about my friends?"

"You mean your homies? You better bang while you can because you're moving to Lakewood in two months, like it or not! Now get out my damn face before I give your ass something to cry for.

CHAPTER 3

Taken From the Streets Of Carson That Raised Me

The last days of school came and summer was here. I was happy it was summer but also sad because I was being ripped from all my childhood friends, Homies, and my beautiful neighborhood of Carson, California. Luckily for me, Lakewood was only a nineteen minute drive away. Trust me, I timed it. My grandmother promised me that I could come spend the weekend with her and my grandfather if my mother didn't mind.

My mother was at Curtis to pick me up and get my school records to check me into my new school in Lakewood. It was a little different in Lakewood because there the ninth grade started high school, which meant I was now a scrub here at Mayfair High School. We went straight there from Curtis.

I told my mother that I needed to go home to pack my clothes and she said, "I'm taking you home, to your new home, those gang-bangin clothes are not coming with me to Lakewood!" Then she told me that she would take me to K-Mart Friday when she got paid to buy me some decent clothes, but right now we were headed to my new school to get me registered and ready to go for September.

"K-Mart clothes mom! What are you trying to do to me mom?"

"I'd rather dress you in jeans and buttons down shirt than you get shot in some drive-by for wearing saggy pants and a white T-shirt."

We pulled up to Mayfair High and we walked into the office to register. This campus was way bigger than Curtis' campus. It was a high school so the students were even bigger. So were the girls, especially their breasts. There were a lot more Mexicans and whites and even a few Asians.

The people in the office were even nice, until they saw what school I was coming from. The lady behind the desk snarled her nose up. "Curtis Junior High School! Isn't that in Compton?"

My mother quickly checked her and said "No! Can't you see right here, it's in Carson, it's an upper middle class black neighborhood."

The lady quickly straightened her face and handed my mother a bunch of forms to fill out.

They wanted to make sure that my mother's address was in their school district, and they needed her work phone number, our home number, and an emergency phone number in case something were to happen to me during school hours.

My mother filled everything out and we got up to walk over to the counter to hand the lady all the information she could ever need about me and whatever else she wanted to know, when big swole white man with sweat pants and a grey t-shirt, that said "coach" on the front and "Mayfair

Monsoons Football" on the back, walked in. He beat us to the lady at the desk "Hi Coach," the lady said.

He started to ask her something when my mother was walking to the counter still going over the paper work to make sure she didn't miss anything accidentally and she bumped into the giant coach. She said excuse me and he turned around to do the same, and one look at my mother he was all GA-Ga.

"Excuse me miss that was rude of me to just jump in your way like that. I had no idea that you were headed to this counter."

That's when the lady behind the desk quickly introduced my mother to the coach and me as her son and now a new student here at Mayfair.

"Welcome to Mayfair we're glad to have you son. Do you play football?" He said shaking my hand.

"I never had the chance to play. I've always played baseball."

"Well now is your chance. I happen to coach the team here and we would love to have you.

You just in time, practice starts in two weeks. Wanna try out?"

"Why not," my mom said.

"Sure! I'll give it a shot!" The coach was delighted and he encouraged my mother to come and cheer us on if she wasn't busy. But I knew what he really wanted.

"Sure, my mom agreed only if she wasn't working then she would be at the games.

"Great I'll see you then." Then he excused himself and left the office.

That's when the lady behind the desk handed my mother another stack of forms.

"I thought I was done?" My mom said.

"You were but now these are for the football sign-ups." My mother looked at me with that look. So I just hurried over to the chairs that we just got up from while my mother started on the new stack of forms.

"The only reason why I'm doing this is so you can stay busy with football instead of getting into to trouble or messing with one of these fast ass little girls and end up getting some girl pregnant. I'm sure you're probably having sex by now," my mom fussed.

The truth was, I was still a virgin. But I didn't respond, I just let my mother think what she wanted. I knew deep down inside she dreaded the thought of her first born having sex. To her, no girl was good enough for her son. But all of that was soon about to change.

Football practice started so I was officially a jock now. Coach had us lifting weights and running drills so much that my little freshman body had no choice but to start developing. By the time school started I was a whole new man. I loved being at school with all those girls running around campus, they were all trying to figure out who the new guy was, especially since I played on the football team. I didn't know about all the attention that came with being on the football team. We even had our own cheerleaders. They were supposed to be off limits so that we could focus on the games but there was one that I had my eye on. She was a junior and she was head of the cheerleading squad. She had that Jada Fire beauty with the body to match. She was a beautiful chocolate complexion, with nice thick legs, and big perfect titties. I didn't want to get kicked off the team so I just admired her from across the campus, plus she was a junior, and I was only a freshman, so she was out of my league.

Practice used to end too quickly for me. I would stay late after practice and lift weights with one of my teammates for as long as I could just to keep from having to go home. See at home it was a madhouse because not only was my mom, my little sister, and my three little brothers at mom's house. It was also my mother's twin Aunt Joan and her three kids were living there too. Oh and there was Charity she was my little teenage crush.

Charity was a friend of the family from back in Cleveland, TN where my mother's side of the family is from. She was only five years older than me but she wanted to try life outside of that little town she was raised in, so she asked my mother if she could stay with us while she gave California a shot. Of course my mother said yes. She really liked Charity, she was a sweet girl; plus my mother could use the help around the house with all the damn kids. Not only was Charity beautiful, she could cook too and she kept the house clean. At least as much as she could considering eight bad ass little kids ran amuck through the house at any given time.

We all slept in one big bedroom. My mother and my baby brother slept in her room and my aunt and my baby cousin Ne-Ne slept on the couch in the living room. But the twins did what they had to do as a family and that meant helping each other out when the other one needed it. As a matter of fact, the twins often shared places and we all lived together on a few occasions. I am exactly eleven months and two weeks older than her and now we were at the same school, which was cool because she always had some cute ass friends, especially at Mayfair. I really liked her new friend named Jenny she was Hispanic and Cuban, and boy was she fine she would always catch up to me and Ki-Ki as we would walk to school. She would meet us at the AM/PM. She would give me a hug every morning and damn did she smell good. She had a beautiful complexion with hair down to her butt that always smelled like she just washed it. She favors the very beautiful and sexy Havana Ginger, same cute little face, same body especially her titties!

She had a beautiful face, nice lips, and thick eyebrows, with a little petit body. I really liked her but I never spoke on it. Especially not to my big mouth cousin. She would have put me on blast! Besides I could already tell that Jenny liked me, so I just left it at that. Who knows what could happen, besides at the moment I was still an amateur. As for making new friends, they came easy because just like me hanging with my cousin because she had some cute friends, dudes wanted to be my friends because I had a pretty cousin, with very cute friends.

One of my buddies lived right across the street from us. He used to come over to my house and we would go to the

Laundromat and play Ms. Pac man and Galiga all day. But I liked to go to his house because he had an older sister she was gorgeous with the prettiest smile and beautiful smooth brown skin and nice round firm breasts. She and IndiaXXX could pass for twins. Every time I would go over to his house I would wanna go inside to see if she was around. She wasn't that much older than us, we were fourteen, and she was sixteen. Ever since my crush with Charity I'd always liked older women.

***

Our first football game came quick. I was nervous as hell. I played receiver, cornerback and also special team kickoff return. Those plays were a lot to learn but I did my best. My stardom came the night of our first game. We were down by six points, the other team had just scored, there was one minute left in the game and they kicked the ball off to us. I caught the ball at the ten yard line and I looked for my blockers. Two of my biggest blockers ran in front of me, I pointed across the field and they followed my lead. I ran across the field and I hit the sideline as I jumped over a defender as he tried to make a diving tackle. Then I ran all the way into the end zone. Now the score was tied 29-29. We lined up for a routine field goal to take the lead. The ball snapped, the kicker ran up, and kicked the ball, hooked it to the left, and missed the easy field goal. We were all devastated but Coach said that we had to shake it off. With nineteen seconds left on the clock I watched our kick off team line up. As I looked into the receiving team's back field I noticed that they had the smallest guy on their team waiting to return the ball, he was wearing the #24 on his jersey. As I yelled, 'let's go defense' from the sideline, I noticed that I had started a chat. That's when I heard everyone from the bleachers backing me up. "Let's go defense, let's go! Let's go defense!" I turned and looked into the stands and I saw my biggest fan and by far the loudest person out there, my beautiful mother. She blew me a kiss when she saw me looking; I waved then turned backed to the field just as we were kicking the ball off to the opposing team. It was a long deep kick. Number 24 caught the ball in the end zone, but instead of downing it he broke out of the end zone with lightning speed and this little dude was fast. I watched from the sideline yelling for my team to, "Get'um!"

He was using his blockers well as he was cutting across the field with speed and grace. Just as he had only one man between him and the end zone, our kicker came and blindsided him, tackling him at the fifty yard line. Coach sent me in the game to play corner back. With only nine seconds left on the clock I knew they would try to throw a quick pass and run out of bounds to stop the clock with only time to kick a field goal for the win. The ball snapped and I back paddled, staying close to my man. I was watching the quarterbacks' eyes as my receiver ran an "Out Pass" I read the play perfectly, I cut the ball off, intercepted it, and ran it back to the end zone for a Pick-6 as the clock ran out of time. We won! Mayfair Monsoon 35 Visitors 29.

CHAPTER 4

Bump and Grind

Monday morning when I got to school I went to my locker, dialed in my combination and removed my lock. When I opened it up, a note fell out and landed at my feet. I reached down to pick it up. I noticed the hearts that were drawn on it and a nice set of lips that had been "kissed" on the note. As I opened it, I could smell a nice scent of perfume that I didn't recognize, but it smelled very sweet. I instantly wanted to know the owner of the scent. If it smelled that good on a piece of paper then I could only imagine what it must smell like on the girl that left this little note with the nice lips print on it. As I read the letter it left me no clue as to who it could be from. It just stated that she wanted to congratulate me on my victory in the game on Friday night. She said she was watching every move that I made that night. She also said that she watched me all day every day but she was shy and didn't know how to approach me. She said she dreamed that I was all hers and when she finally got the courage to step to me that she was going to eat me alive. That she was all mine to do as I pleased, but for me to not even bother trying to figure out who she was. When the time was right I would have no doubt about who she was and that it would be satisfaction guaranteed. It was signed "You're Secret Admirer." I stood at my locker looking dumbfounded then I took a looked around me to see if anyone was watching me to see if maybe this was some sort of joke but there were no signs of it being a prank. So I read it again, inhaling that sweet scent. It was possibly the only real clue to trying to find my secret admirer. Good thing the bell rang or I would have been standing at my locker all day smelling the note and reading its contents. So I hurried off to my class before I was even more late then I already was. I guess I just had to be patient and wait for her to reveal herself so she could do all the things to me that she wrote about in the letter. God knows I sure as hell wouldn't know what to do, but I was willing to let this girl show me the ropes. It was obvious that she wasn't new to this, not from the description in that letter. Now all I had to do was find her. God knows that I have no patience.

Lunch time came around so I met up with my little cousin and her friends so that we could go to our usual spot across the street from the school to grab a slice of pizza at Pa-Pa Johns. Two of my boys met me over there as me and my cousin Ki-Ki walked up with a couple of her friends, then I remembered my little love note. So I figured now would be a good time to start my little investigation as to who this note came from. I went over to her and as I did I leaned in really close and I took a big sniff right below her ear, right next to her neck.

"What's up girl, how you been?" Once I inhaled her salty fumes, I immediately knew that she was not the girl. But that was a relief because she was the "token girl" of the crew. You know every crew has one "Ugmo" girl or guy in their crew to make everybody else look better Although Ki-Ki and her righteous girls didn't need one, I guess they felt sorry for this girl and let her hang with them. This girl shivered when I got close to her neck as my nose gently grazed her ear. She turned quickly and touched her ear and I could see the hairs rising on her hairy ass arms as she smiled.

"Oh hey Shawn! Good game last Friday."

"Thank you," I said as I squinted from the glare the sun made shining off her metal braces. Then I quickly hurried over to the very girl that I was praying that had left that sexy ass love note. She had just caught up to us while we were all in line.

"Hey Jenny! Where's my hug?" I held my arms out, waiting for her fine ass to get to me. I could not wait because whether it was Jenny's note or not, she always smelled good, and after ole Brace Face, I needed a whiff of good ole Jenny. Jenny was all smiles as she walked up to me and she wrapped her arms around my neck. She stood up on her tippy toes and squeezed me tight as I hugged her back. I bent down a little and she put her face deep into my neck, when she did that I shivered and got the same goose bumps as Brace Face did, only I'm not a hairy sea creature. Jenny's long hair flew up and wrapped around me from my head down to the middle of my back. It was like I was in a cocoon of heavenly freshness. As she let go of my neck and came down off her tippy toes, I still had my fingers interlocked at the small of her back,

"Damn what's up with that special hug?" I asked her.

"That's for winning the game for us on Friday."

"Well damn I didn't even know that you were there."

"Yes I was there. I was the one trying to out scream your mother, but that wasn't happening. I see she was proud of her son that night."

"Yeah, Yeah, it was a good game for us on Friday, but if it's gonna get me hugs like that then I'm gonna win us every game this year." She looked at me smiling as I was still taking in her scent.

"I'll have a hug for you just like that for every win we get."

"OK, that's a deal, and I going to hold you to that."

"No need, I'm a lady of my word." Then she smiled.

After lunch I was drinking my root beer as we were walking back onto campus, still stumped because I had no idea who this girl was, I walked over to my locker popped it open and another love note fell out. Now I was convinced that whoever she was knew my routine enough to know that she could slip this note in my locker because I was at Pa-Pa Johns for lunch. But who the hell could this be? I checked

Ki-Ki's friends but I didn't know who else to check. So I opened the letter and read it, hoping that maybe this time there'd be a better clue. The note still had the same lip print on it and same sweet smelling scent, but the words were much more graphic and in full detail. This girl knew exactly how to treat a man. Only problem was that I wasn't a man yet, but I knew by the time she was done with me I was gonna be as much of a man that a fourteen year old man could be.

***

Practice ended early that day and I decided to head home early too for a change. I walked in the house and no one was there. That was a first. I checked every room then I went to the fridge to get some Kool-Aid. On the refrigerator was a note from my mom saying, if you get home before we get back, we all went shopping at K-mart. Sorry I couldn't wait for you but I knew you had practice. I don't know how long we will be, but if you get hungry just make some Cup of Noodles soup till I get home and make us some Hamburger Helper." Hamburger Helper was my favorite so I'd just hold out till they got back. Besides, I was still having bad dreams about when I was six years old and spilled that scolding hot cup of noodles in my lap. I had third degree burns on my right thigh. So no thanks I'd just wait for the Hamburger Helper instead. I checked the fridge and as usual, the white Tupperware container for the Kool-Aid was in there but the damn thing was empty. So I decided to go across the street to my boy's house, they always had Kool-Aid and if his mother was there she would always make me a sandwich. They had the real Oscar Meyer bologna, not the kind my mother used to buy with the red plastic strip of the outside of it. We had to fry it just to get some flavor out of it, but we had to cut it in a couple of place on the outside or it would bubble up in the frying pan and then it will shrivel up so small we have to fry two pieces to get a decent sandwich.

I would top it off with a big thick slice of that government cheese that my grandmother would give us by the brick. Then I throw it on top of the bologna as it was frying. I would leave it frying for another ten minutes because I liked my bologna a little burnt, and that cheese still wouldn't be melted.

I walked over to my boy's house and I knocked on the door. His sister answered. I asked her where her brother was, and she said he had just left to go to the grocery store with their mother.

"Thanks, tell him to come over when he gets back. I'm home alone and bored as hell." Her face lit up when I said I was home alone. That's when she whispered in my ear and asked if I wanted to "do it."

I didn't know exactly what "it" was, but I sure liked how it sounded in my ear. I nodded my head.

"OK, let's go to your house!" She closed her door and grabbed my hand, running off the porch with me in tow. We almost got hit by cars crossing the busy boulevard that separated our homes.

We got to my front door, I put the key in, unlocked the door, and she pushed it open and snatched me inside and closed it.

"Where's your bed?" We were both panting from our near death experience of bolting across the street like a game of Frogger.

I pointed to my room and we walked in. I walked over to my bed and she said, "Pull down your pants." I couldn't believe my ears, but I could clearly see that I heard her correctly because she was pulling down her pants. I pulled my pants down to my ankles just as she did hers. Then she pushed me down on the bed. As I laid there, flat on my back with my underwear and my pants around my ankles, she pulled my shirt up to my chin and stood over me smiling. Then my little IndiaXXX asked if I was ready.

"Yeah I've been ready since you left me that first note in my locker."

"What note silly? Just lay there and be quiet, I'll do all the work!" With her little panties and pants still around her ankles, she pulled her shirt up to her chin exposing her perfectly round breasts and then she laid flat on top of me. At the point of contact I felt a feeling that I'd never felt before. When she lay on top of me, the warmth of her body on top of mine and her warm, round, perky little titties on my chest felt amazing. She was lying flat on my penis and it was fully erect, pointing towards my belly button as she laid on it. She started to grind on it. The heat coming off her vagina and the friction of her pubic hairs gave me a feeling that I had never felt before. Then as she got faster and faster, I felt a sensation building up that was new and shocking. All of a sudden, I made that same sound and I tensed up the same way when I was in the first grade and the prettiest girl in my class kicked me in the nuts. I went home and told my dad what the girl did and he said, "That's what girls do when they like you." He told me to get used to it and he said "When you start liking them, you'll have that feeling but in a different way but you will like it." Right now as it was all coming back to me...I was confused, but I think I was liking it. Then a sudden electrifying sensation went through my body and there was a wet area in her pubic hairs and in my belly button. She stopped grinding. I remember her breathing heavy in my ear, and then she jumped up. She pulled her pants up and her shirt down, smiled, kissed me on my forehead, then just as quick as we came she was gone. I jumped up and tried to follow her out the house, tripping over my pants that were still around my ankles and I yelled, "Wait don't leave! What just happened? Let's "do it" again!" I was totally confused as I stood at my front door pulling up my pants as I watched her crossing the major boulevard dodging the busy traffic. I closed the front door and I turned to go into the bathroom with my shirt still under my chin. I didn't want to get any of whatever it was that came electrifyingly out of my penis onto my favorite shirt. I got inside the bathroom and I grabbed the first face towel that I saw and I cleaned out my belly button and the surrounding area. I remember that bleachy smell and the sticky feeling, until I finally got into the shower where I started experimenting with myself, trying to get that electrifying feeling to come surging through my body again. Before I knew it, one night in the shower, I finally figured it out.

Chapter 5

First Porn Movie

The next morning, as I finished up getting ready for school, I heard a knock at the door. My cousin Ki-Ki answered then yelled to me and asked me if I'm ready because Jay and Ashley from across the street are at the door and they are ready to walk to school. As soon as I heard that Ashley was there, my stomach started to have a funny feeling or at least that area that was deep down in my stomach.

"Yeah I'm coming just let me grab my book bag," I said

I walked out the front door closing it behind me. Ki-Ki and one of her friends were standing in our front yard talking and Ashley was on the sidewalk with one of her girls. She looked back and gave me a little smile and a wave as I walked off my porch to my boy Jay. I said what's up to my homie and we started off to school. But of course we had to stop at the AM/PM to catch up with Jenny and my boy David too.

David was the pervert of my crew. He lived with his dad. His mother ran out on them. He was an only child and his dad was always at work so he was a true "latch Key kid." Hell, he practically took care of himself. Once we got to the AM/PM and met up, we all went inside to grab our morning ritual of snacks.

My boy Jay would always grab a box of Boston Baked Beans, my boy David would grab a box of Red Hots, and Brace Face would always get a bag of those Salty-Plums. You know the ones that were in the red salty juice that you drank before eating the actual shriveled up plum with the seed. That explained her salty pheromones. Jenny would grab a watermelon flavored Big Stick. Ashley would get a Blow-Pop and suck on it all the way to school, Ki-Ki would always get a giant Pickle and a pack of Now and Laters. She would bite the top off the pickle and then stuff a Now and Later in it. I would get a bag of BBQ flavored Corn Nuts and a pack of sunflower seeds. I would open the seeds and have Ki-Ki pour her pickle juice in with my seeds and I would eat them on the way to school, leaving a trail of empty Polly-Seed shells all the way to my locker.

I remember one morning Ki-Ki challenged me to race her. She ran for the track team but I knew I could get her. I tied my shoelaces nice and tight. Ki-Ki took her shoes off and chose to run barefoot. We were always in competition growing up. She always wanted to challenge me. I was gonna show her this time. We lined up while brace face was up the block with her hands up and she said, "On your marks, Get set, Go!" Me and Ki-Ki took off running. I pulled off in the lead. As we got closer to the finish line and it was clear that I was gonna win, full metal Brace Face got excited seeing me run towards her and she smiled. That dreadful smile, plus her even more dreadful face and the blinding glare from her braces reflecting off the morning sunlight, and the fact that we were running against the wind. With all that shinning glare and her saltiness in the air I thought I was at the beach. That shit killed my whole stride and at the last minute KiKi beat me. I still say she cheated by using that damn scarecrow at the finish line. If that would have been

Jenny down there, there's no way I would've lost. After we raced each other, I hurried to my locker to see what my secret dreamed last.

It's crazy because as me and Ashley were crossing the street yesterday playing human Frogger; I just knew that she was my secret admirer. But once we started, and what we did, it was no comparison to what this girl wrote in her letters. The time was coming soon and I was in need of some help, so I went to the one guy that I knew would have some insight for me, my perverted friend David.

I hadn't told anyone about my love notes till then, and at lunchtime when I let David read my letters; he got more excited than I did. He was jumping up and down and patting on my back.

"Damn my man! You've got a live one!"

"Yeah, but I need to know all that you know, so I don't look totally stupid."

"No problem! Don't worry, just stop by my house on your way home from football practice, I've got you covered." I had a puzzled look on my face.

"OK man I'll see you then. Thanks, I hope," I said with a puzzled look on my face.

After football practice I went straight to David's house. I knocked on the door and he answered it with a devious smile on his face. I walked in and he directed me to the living room. We walked into the living room; there was some soda and some Jiffy Pop popcorn.

"OK, what's up? Tell me everything that you know."

"I'm not gonna tell you what I know, even though I know more than you. I'm gonna show you the movie that taught me everything that I know."

"What makes you a professional? You think just because you watched some movie that you're a pro now? Last time I checked you were still a virgin!" I said to him.

"I was up until yesterday thanks to you."

"Thanks to me? What do you mean by that?"

"Remember yesterday at Pa-Pa Johns when you were whispering something in Melanie's ear?"

"Brace Face?"

"Yeah! Whatever you whispered to her got her all hot and bothered."

"You did it to Brace Face?"

"Hell yeah! Why not? She was easy. She wanted you but she saw the way Jenny was all over you and she knew that she couldn't compete with her, so me and her ditched school, and came here after lunch and we did it."

"Damn is your father ever home?"

"Yeah all the time!"

"I've been coming to your house since I've known you and I still haven't met your dad." Then I said

"I still can't believe that you did it to the salty, smelling brace face girl!" " I'm a scrub! Do you know how hard it is for a scrub to get laid at a high school? It's next to impossible!" Then he went on to say, "Everybody's not Mr. Suave with the good hair, or a jock on the football team with secret admirers waiting to jump their bones. And what's up with you and Jenny anyway?

Yesterday, with the way I saw her all over you, I just knew that you two were at least humping."

"Nah man, nothing like that. She was just promising me a hug for every win that our football team get this year, that's all."

"Yeah whatever homie, after you're done watching my dad's movie, you're gonna be ready to take it to the next level. Your amateur days will be over."

"I'm not a total amateur; I just humped a woman last night."

"Yeah that woman is your homie's sister. How do you think Jay is gonna feel about that?"

"Well damn! How in the hell did you know that?"

"Hey, big school, thin walls," David smiled and said.

He pressed play and a porn movie started. I saw body parts and things that I didn't even know existed on human beings. After just five minutes of that tape, I realized that I was still very much a virgin and definitely a total amateur. By the time the movie was over, I was damaged goods and possibly scarred for life; the look on my face said it all. You would've thought I'd just watched my mother give birth.

When it was over David stopped it and hit rewind. He explained to me that he always had to rewind the movie back to the exact part his dad left it at or he would get busted. Once he found his dad's spot on the movie he hit the eject button.

He took the tape back to his dad's room and placed it back in the shoebox on the top shelf of his dad's bedroom closet that was labeled training tapes. David's dad was in the military and he told David that those were old training tapes that he had lying around. David came back into the living room with a big grin on his face. "Well how do you feel? Did that help? Do you feel like a pro? Are you ready for the big leagues?"

"I'm more confused now than ever! But at least I know now where to start." Then I made a mental note that from this moment on, never to kiss mother on the lips again.

When I got home that night, my mother greeted me at the door. That's never good because last time she did that I ended up moving to Lakewood. She said she had a surprise for me. She said that Friday my grandfather wanted to come out to watch me play football. The big surprise was after the game I could ride back to Carson to spend the weekend at my grandparents' house. This would be the first time since I left, so I was excited and couldn't wait for Friday to get here.

Friday night, my grandfather got to the field early enough to watch us run drills and warm up for the game. This was my grandfather's first time watching me play football. Up until then, I had always played baseball and he never missed a game. He really liked to watch me pitch, I had some heat. He was my biggest fan and I really made him proud. My grandfather was the closest thing to a father I had. He always supported me in everything that I wanted to do, and he proved that by coming out to watch me play in my first season of football. But deep down inside I really wished my real father was there.

It was game time. We kicked the ball off to the visiting team. It was caught deep in the end zone, so the special team's player downed the ball. They now had the ball on the twenty yard line. On their first play, the quarterback threw a pass for a fifty yard completion. Coach hadn't put me in the game yet, I guess he was playing me on offense that night. Their next play was a reverse; our whole defensive line fell for it, safety's too.

The entire team got faked out and their running back swooped into the end zone for a thirty yard touchdown. It was our turn to receive the ball and Coach put me in for the kickoff return. It was caught by my teammate at the twenty. I came running towards him out of the end zone. My teammate looked back and he pitched to me as I was running full speed. I headed right up the middle, and then I cut to the left. I found my blockers and took full advantage of them, heading up the field. I found a hole and precisely filled it, slipping through it to open field, never looking back as I took it home into the end zone for a eighty yard kickoff return.

I spiked the ball and dropped to one knee, I made the sign of the cross, giving thanks to God. Then I looked up to my grandfather to see his face. It was priceless. I could tell by the excitement in his face that once again I had made my grandfather proud. My teammates met me in the end zone so we could do the "whop." That was my victory dance and everybody loved it. I ran past the cheerleaders and that familiar sweet scent from my love letters hit me.

Could it have been a coincidence, or was my secret admirer one of the cheerleaders? If so which one? We had twenty girls cheerleading for us, jumping, kicking, and being thrown into the air. How was I supposed to find out when we couldn't even be caught looking their way? Maybe it could've been a gust of wind from the night's breeze blowing that sweet scent in from the bleachers. Maybe she was out there watching me right now. I looked out into the stands and saw Ki-Ki and Jenny talking to my grandfather. They saw me looking and started waving. Jenny was a beautiful sight to see, she had a big beautiful smile on her face and she seemed very happy to see me. Then I said a quick prayer. "Lord please let that be Jenny over there smelling like that." I was dying to try out everything I saw on that tape. I was gonna make sure we won that game so I could collect my special hug from Jenny.

After the game, I hurried to the locker room so I could take off my sweaty football gear and hit the shower. Then it would be time to go claim my weekly victory prize from Jenny. After I showered, I sprayed on my "Cool Water" cologne so I smelled fresh, then I got dressed, looking like a million bucks.

I walked out to meet up with Ki-Ki, Jenny, and my proud grandfather. As soon as I walked out the locker room, Jenny came running up to me and jumped into my arms, and for the first time ever she planted a nice soft kiss on my lips. Since her long pretty hair was blocking their view, Ki-Ki and my grandfather didn't see the quick passionate kiss nor did they hear Jenny whisper in my ear that she wanted me. I couldn't believe what I was hearing. Then she whispered to me to come over tonight because she was gonna be home alone because her mother went to Las Vegas for the weekend. You should have seen the devastation on my face. I went into an instant state of depression. I had to bust Jenny's bubble by letting her know that I couldn't make it because I was leaving right then to go spend the weekend in Carson with my grandparents. If it wasn't for that, me and Jenny would have left running straight to her house. I would have left my little cousin standing right there at Mayfair. She would've made it home on her own.

I was looking into her beautiful, dark brown eyes and she closed them because they were starting to water.

Ki-Ki and Jenny wanted to walk home. Jenny was still noticeably upset. We said goodbye to them and I went to talk to Jenny and get my hug before she left. She put her head on my chest and that's when I realized that it wasn't her. That sweet smelling scent had not come from Jenny. Jenny had her own special scent and I loved it. But I just knew after that kiss and the offer to come to her house tonight that I had my secret admirer in my arms. But no, still not her.

After we said our goodbyes, I hopped in the truck and headed off to Carson. Yes, finally going back to Carson. My true "Home Sweet Home." I missed the hood and my homies, but most of all I missed having my own room. I was turning into a man and I needed my own space. I didn't need to be sharing a room with eight other kids. Family or not, that's ludicrous! But truth is, I was getting back used to it again.

Like I said this wasn't the first time we were all living under one roof. Last time we were all crammed into a little two bedroom apartment in Long Beach and it only had one bathroom. Now those were some tight quarters!

CHAPTER 6

* * *ing Cousins

On the ride back to Carson I thanked my grandfather again for coming out. He said he really enjoyed the game. Then he apologized for waiting till the end of the season to come out. I told him that the season wasn't over yet, that we were doing very well and that my team had a good record. I let him know that next week was our last game, but if we win it, then we'd be in the playoffs, and there would be plenty more games for him to come see me play.

We walked in the door as my grandmother was making our plates. I put my book bag down and gave her a great big hug.

"Hi Mom-Mom! I missed you so much," I said

"Welcome home son. I missed you too!"

I noticed that she set the dining room table for four. I took a big whiff of her delicious home cooking and I couldn't wait to dig in. She made pot roast with celery, carrots, potatoes, and onions; some green beans; mashed potatoes and gravy; and my favorite, fried Okra. She also fried me some hot water corn bread. She had some Sun Tea made too, nice and sweet just how I like it. I closed the lid on the crock pot after I was done inhaling its contents.

"Everything looks and smells wonderful Mom-Mom, but why did you set the table for four?" "Oh because your cousin Jasmine is here, she's upstairs putting her son to sleep in your old bedroom. She came over last minute to get away from her abusive baby daddy for a couple days."

I automatically said, "In my old bedroom? Ya'll gave up my room already? Now where am I supposed to sleep tonight?"

"Shawn don't start. You know that will always be your room. For tonight you can sleep in one of the bedrooms downstairs. Besides that's your second cousin up there so be nice."

"OK, but he better not pee in my bed!"

My cousin Jasmine was my Aunt Pat's daughter. She was eight years older than me. When she was younger, I remember the family got her head shots done and took her to a few auditions for her to do modeling or even some commercials. But like everybody else in my family she got pregnant at a young age and started drinking and drugging.

As my grandmother finished making our plates, Jasmine came sneaking down the stairs very carefully. She didn't to wake her son after it took almost an hour to put him to sleep. When she saw me she was happy. "Hey little Cuzz! I heard you're a big football star now! Look at you; you even got a couple muscles on you now, check you out little man!" Jasmine gave me a hug. I missed my big cousin.

We all sat down and bowed our heads as my grandfather blessed the food. The food was so good that I was just shoving it in my mouth and swallowing it. It wasn't long until I was asking my grandmother for seconds. She proudly jumped up and fixed me a second helping of her priceless and very delicious food.

"I hope you saved room for dessert."

"There's no way I can eat another bite of anything."

"That's too bad because I made your favorite, my special banana pudding," she said while opening the refrigerator. I quickly grabbed a bowl and asked her to please fill it up!

"You know I cannot resist your special banana pudding."

After she filled up my bowl, I gave her a hug then a kiss on each cheek. I took my bowl of pudding into the entertainment room to watch TV with my big cousin. Our grandparents came in to say goodnight to us. Me and Jasmine gave them hugs and said goodnight. They said that it was getting late for them and for us to not stay up all night and to make sure we turn off the TV and the lights before we fall asleep. They gave us both blankets and pillows to sleep on the couch or on the floor. Then they retired upstairs to their master suite.

Me and Jasmine watched TV and ate banana pudding till the wee hours of the night. She made a pallet on the floor and I laid on the couch. We both agreed that it was getting late and that maybe we should turn off the TV before we both passed out. But first we wanted to finish up the movie we were watching.

At that time of night, anything was liable to come on the screen. That's when a scene of a beautiful woman taking a shower came on we and we both got quiet. A man walked in and joined her. We were both glued to the TV. I was more so than her because I was still very new to this type of content.

"Boy close your mouth, you act like you never seen two people naked before."

"My mouth is closed, besides I've seen people do it before."

"Oh? Do you think you're a professional now that you're in high school?"

"No! But I tried to do it to a girl the other day, but I don't think I did it right."

"What do you mean you don't think you did it right?"

"I haven't actually did it, did it, to a girl yet. But I've been trying to learn how to because I have a secret admirer at my school and she keep leaving me love notes saying how she wants me to do it to her and I don't wanna look stupid. I could have done it tonight with one of Ki-Ki's friends but Pa-Pa came to get me to spend the weekend over here."

"Well, how was you gonna pull that off if you don't know what the hell you doin?" my cousin asked me.

"I saw a porn movie yesterday after school at my friend's house. So now I have a good idea of what to do, I just haven't had a chance to try it."

Jasmine shook her head and turned the TV off. It was the only light source in the room. Then she said, "sounds like you're in over your head little Cuzz."

"No Cuzz! I got this. I just need some practice," I said.

"Bullshit!" Jasmine said. "You don't know shit little boy! Now come here and let me show you what you are supposed to do and how to do it."

It was pitch black in that room, but as big as my eyes got when she said that I'm sure they probably lit up that whole entire room.

"What? Are you serious? You're gonna let me put it in?"

"Yeah, imma show you what to do so you don't look stupid," she said "Now come on before I change my mind!"

She pulled the covers off her. She was laying on her back with nothing on but an oversized t-shirt. I got up off the couch and slowly walked over to where she was laying. I pulled my pants and my underwear down. I got down on my knees with my penis still fully erect from the shower scene I had just watched.

There I was with my ding a ling out, not knowing what was really happening, or if it should be happening at all. I just knew that this was my opportunity to practice and get this "do it" thing right so I could go back to Lakewood and lose my virginity to my little Havana Ginger girl or my sweet smelling secret admirer.

Jasmine asked me if I wanted to turn the light on so I could see what I was getting into.

"No, I don't wanna see nothing," I said.

"Come a little closer so I can reach it and put it in for you," she said firmly "You better not cum inside me!"

"OK, I won't. I'll pull out, I promise."

I felt her warm hand wrap around my dick as she guided me into her hot, wet opening. I closed my eyes, I could smell her special scent, and I could see her beautiful long hair. I buried my face in her hair and I started pumping away, imitating the missionary style position that I had just watched the night before.

With my eyes closed tight and my little hips moving, I could hear her whisper in my ear that she wanted me. I pumped fast. She kept whispering in my ear and I pumped faster, and heard her say that her mother left to go to Las Vegas for the weekend. I pumped even faster, and felt her plant a nice soft kiss on my lips. As my knees started to burn from the carpet, I started to feel that feeling from deep inside the lower bottom of my stomach; my toes started to curl, my rhythm got thrown off, and my whole body locked up.

That's when I lost her scent. I could no longer feel her soft lips planted on mine, and instead of hearing her sweet voice whispering that she wanted me, I heard Jasmine say, "Boy why did you stop? Are you cumming?" she pushed my little ass off of her as I felt a feeling that I had never before. It was way more intense and electrifying than what I felt with Ashley.

All I remember after that was laying on my back, on the floor next to the couch, trying to catch my breath. Jasmine jumped up and ran to the bathroom cursing under her breath. She came back with a hot soapy towel and she gave me a little bird bath. "I think you're gonna give your little secret admirer a run for her money."

"Do you think so? Do you think I'm ready?" "Hell yeah; your little ass wore me out boy! Thanks to you imma sleep good tonight."

I wasn't sure if I was supposed to thank her for letting me practice. I wasn't sure what any of this meant, but one thing I did know for sure was that I was ready for the big leagues. When Jasmine was done washing me up, she noticed that I was still hard.

"Damn, boy you ready again?"

"Yeah I guess so."

"Yeah you're definitely ready for your secret admirer and Ki-Ki's friend too!"

I confessed that I was hard again because I was just thinking about something I saw yesterday on that porn movie.

"What was that?"

"The guys in the movie were letting the girls suck it," I said.

"Yeah, that's called a blowjob."

"No, they were putting it in their mouths and sucking it. Not blowing on it, and the guys seemed like they loved it."

"You wanna feel it?"

"Hell yes!"

"If you cum in my mouth I'm gonna kill you!"

"OK don't worry, I won't. I'll pull out."

"Did you pull out earlier?"

"I was about to but you pushed me on the floor."

"Yeah good thing I did because you didn't know it but your little ass was cumming." "Hell yeah; I had your nut all in my pussy hairs."

"I was wondering why you was cursing."

"Come here," she said. "This is called a blowjob because I'm about to blow your mind."

I walked over to her with my dick in my hand. First she licked it like a lollipop, next thing I knew; I felt her warm mouth all over my entire dick. It felt incredible. She wrapped her tongue around my dick and started twirling it around. It was a feeling that I couldn't even understand. The sensation was so intense that without even realizing it, I had put both my hands on her head. Then she started to suck it from the head of my now swollen dick back and forth from the tip of my dick till there was no more. I could feel every inch of my dick being massaged by her warm, skillful, and seductive tongue. Just imagine getting head from

Obsession and Carmen Hayes at the same damn time. When it got too intense for me to allow her to continue, I snatched my dick out of her mouth. It sounded like taking a titty out of a baby's mouth. As quickly as I snatched it out, she reached out with both her hands and grabbed my butt cheeks, one in each hand. She squeezed them, pulling me back to her. She opened her mouth while pulling my hips to her, forcing my dick back into her warm slippery mouth. My swollen, veiny, throbbing dick went deep into her throat. She inhaled it, still grabbing my ass, shoving it deeper and deeper into her throat. That bigger feeling of sensation had never stopped, it only got greater. I instinctively put my hands back on the sides of her head and thrust my hips, fucking her throat. The pressure was too much to hold back, and by now she was in a feeding frenzy of my meat. It was obvious that she wanted to make my first experience a truly mind blowing and unforgettable one. I realized then that she wanted me to do it. She wanted me to cum in her mouth. So I did it, I did it! I exploded my hot cum straight down her throat. She never got a chance to taste it. Then as my grapes were being drained into tiny little raisins; I felt her lips back at the tip my dick. I felt her head in my hands making giant circles, slowly, around and around, just like Ashley did with her blow pop every morning as we walked to school. She sucked out every last drop. Then from the sensational aftermath of me climaxing so hard; my body could no longer take it. It was too much for me to handle.

My arms locked out as I jumped up to my tippy toes and I heard that loud smacking sound again as my now lifeless dick was once again snatched out of my cousin's mouth.

The next morning I woke up to my little baby cousin bashing me over my head with his bottle.

I sat up rubbing my head. As my blurry vision cleared up, I saw the Smurfs playing on the TV. I don't like cartoons, I never did. I looked over at the couch and saw Jasmine sitting over there eating a bowl of Cocoa Puffs cereal.

"Sup little Cuzz!"

"Sup," I said back to her. "Anymore cereal left?"

"Yes there's plenty."

"Cool imma go make me a bowl before I step outside to go visit a couple of my homies."

"Come back and eat your cereal in here till you go."

"Hell naw, I don't watch no cartoons Cuzz."

"No I just had those on for my son. I'm about to turn to "Soul Train" it's coming on in five minutes." "Soul Train; Damn is it that late?"

"Yeah you were knocked out! It's almost noon," she said. "Mom-Mom and Pa-Pa tried to wake you up to go to church with them, but you wasn't budging so they gave up, and left without you."

"Thank God! Who goes to church on Saturday anyway? That's the one and only thing I don't miss about living here, mandatory church. Seven day Adventist is so backwards to me. While all my friends were at the park or chilling at the malls on Saturday, I was at church with Mom~Mom and Pa~Pa."

"Trust me I know. They tried to make me go with them this morning then they remembered how embarrassing my son was last time and they left me alone."

"Oh yeah, your friend Sammy called from up the street he said you called him earlier this week and said that you would be here so he was calling to see if you made it. I told him yeah, but you were sleep because you were up late practicing." She looked at me and laughed.

"Shut up Cuzz, don't be playing like that."

"Don't worry, everything is cool, take it easy." Then she said, "Sammy said to come over when you get up. He said don't call just come over. He wouldn't hear the phone because he and his brother would be swimming in the pool so bring your trunks."

"Hell yeah! I'm throwing on my swimming trunks and heading over there right now, thanks cousin!"

"What about your breakfast? What about Soul Train, that's your favorite show."

"It is my favorite show, but swimming is my favorite thing to do, I'll just grab a sandwich on the way out. Bye Cuzz."

CHAPTER 7

She Wants Me to Teach Her How to Work a * * * K

That weekend flew by. After that first night I couldn't wait to get back to my Lakewood ladies. I couldn't wait to catch up with Ashley so I could show her how it was really done. I prayed to God that I got another opportunity to be invited over to Jenny's house again, but Lord only knew if that would ever happen. As far as my secret admirer, it's time for her to come forward because now I knew exactly what to do to her. Now I'm even more eager to know who I'm gonna be doin it too.

Monday morning came and as usual I hurried to my locker hoping for a note closer to finding out who this sweet smelling secret admirer is. I opened my locker and there's my note. This time I got Mr.

Salty balls David all over my back as I'm reading my letter. That's his name ever since he did it to Melanie.

Then we both read my note at the same time. It was my first real clue. In my note she said that "she really enjoyed watching me play last week and that she was cheering me on the whole entire game."

Me and Salty Balls looked at each other and our eyes lit up as we both came to the conclusion that my sweet secret admirer was definitely one of the cheerleaders. Now we had to investigate and find out just which one she was. Since the cheerleaders are off limits to the football players. I had to send my good ole buddy David to go and do my little dirty work.

After reading the mystery girl's note, he wanted to find out who this horny little girl was too. He figured any girl who's writing letters like that could never get enough sex, and she would probably be willing to do the whole football team. So he gladly made it his horny little mission to help me find her.

Even though he wasn't on the football team, he figured knowing me would be good enough to get in on a piece of the action from the horny little mystery girl too, and of course I would make that happen for my boy.

First thing first, let me put David on the right scent. I gave him one of the notes and I told him there are twenty cheerleaders for him to sniff out. I told him to keep this letter on him to keep the scent fresh in his head. Then one by one, casually sniff each cheerleader that he runs into till he find our girl. "Once you've found her, be discreet don't say a word. Just let me know which one she is and we'll go from there.

Then I said, "Got it?"

"Yep, I got it, piece of cake; I'm your man, homie. I'll sniff her out in no time."

With my dog hot on the trail, it was only a matter of time before the mystery girl was revealed. As for my girl Jenny, it was time to get back in her good graces.

It was Wednesday morning; me, Jay, Ashley, and Ki-Ki were waiting at the AM/PM for the rest of our clan to catch up with us. David walked up, so I hit him up for an update on our mystery girl. He said no luck yet but he's hot on her trail. He told me that he sniffed fifteen cheerleaders and he hoped to find the mystery girl soon because he's starting to look like some type of weirdo perv or something, and that he was probably one sniff away from getting expelled from school.

"David, you are a weirdo, perv! You're the most perverted dude I know!"

"Yeah I know Huh?" We both started laughing and I gave my boy dap, then outta nowhere, a blue

Suzuki Jeep came swooping into the AM/PM parking lot driving crazy, almost hitting us as it skidded to a stop and stalled. We all looked inside the Jeep. All I could see was hair. Then I heard Ki-Ki yelling. "That's my girl Jenny!"

We all looked shocked and amazed as we walked up to the brand new truck. Jenny head was resting on the steering wheel and she wasn't moving. Ki-Ki snatched open the passenger side door. Inside the radio was blasting LA's #1

Hip Hop station, 1580 K-Day, on the AM dial! Ki-Ki touched Jenny's arm.

"Hey girl! Is this your ride?" Jenny jumped so high that she scared the shit out of my cousin. She looked over to Ki-Ki and she had tears running down her beautiful face. "Jenny what's wrong? Are you OK? Are you in trouble?" Then Ki-Ki said, "Girl! Your little Mexican ass didn't steal this car did you?"

"No my mother bought it for me with a jackpot she hit in Las Vegas."

"That's a good thing girl! Why you crying?"

"Look," she said and pointed down to the gear shifter of the brand new jeep. "I don't know how to drive a stick shift girl. I've been trying all morning that's why I'm late."

"Yeah that explains why you almost ran us over too!" Ki-Ki said

Jenny said she didn't even see us; she was looking down at the gear shifter trying to get the damn thing into the right gear. Then she stepped on the brake instead of the clutch, that's when the Jeep stalled. She said she was so distraught that she just put her head on the steering wheel and broke down crying. That's when I knocked on Jenny's window. She rolled the window down when she saw that it was me. A tear rolled down her cheek and I gently wiped it away with me thumb.

"Good morning beautiful. Where's my morning hug?" Then I asked her "Are you still upset at me?"

"No, I have bigger fish to fry."

"Oh yeah? Bigger than me?" Then I said. "Nice truck, too bad yo ass don't know how to drive." Jenny looked at me.

"I know how to drive asshole. I just don't know how to drive a damn stick shift. I told my mother that I did because I wanted this jeep so bad. I figured I could learn real quick, no problem, but it's a lot harder than I thought. I don't know what I'm gonna do."

"You can start by getting the hell out the way and letting a pro work those gears." Jenny's head popped up.

"What? You know how to drive a stick?"

"Yeah silly, my grandfather taught me how in that truck you saw us in last Friday." Then I pointed to Ki-Ki and I said. "Ask my cousin."

"Yeah girl he drive my grandfather's truck all the time!"

Then Jenny unbuckled her seat belt and opened the door and jumped into my arms.

"Save me please! Please help me baby! Will you please drive this thing to school and then teach me how to work the gears at lunch, and maybe after school?"

"Oh now I get my morning hug, and now I'm your baby?" I said. "Yeah I'll teach you how to drive a stick. By the end of the day you will be a pro."

Jenny started to clap and jumping up and down. "But, It's gonna cost you," I said.

"OK, OK, I gotchu, just please help me! I'll owe you big time. I promise."

Then I looked at her in those beautiful dark brown eyes and I said, "Bigger then you know," and I smiled.

"OK whatever let's just go! We're gonna be late for first period if we don't hurry!" Then Jenny ran around to the passenger seat and said, "Everybody get ya'll asses in, let's go. We've gotta get to school!"

We packed into that little jeep and I drove us to school. I started my lesson with Jenny as I drove to school but she was looking confused and lost as hell. She was totally abashed. But by the end of the day that would change back to pure confidence. I swung the jeep into the school's parking lot going a little too fast and everybody went sliding to one side.

"Babe be careful, do you know how easy these things roll over?"

"Yeah, yeah, don't worry I got this." Then I pull into the parking stall with the curb that had principal spray painted on it. I locked up the truck and I tossed Jenny her keys. She tossed them back to me, and then gave me one of her special hugs followed by a nice soft kiss on the lips.

"Damn that was nice!"

"You're my hero, there's more where that came from," she said. "You hold onto those keys, besides you're gonna have to come out and move it once they make the announcement on the P.A. System to move out of the principal's parking space crazy man." Jenny smiled and walked off with my little cousin. Jay and

David walked up to me and told me that I was a lucky son-of-a-bitch. Then the bell rang and we hurried off to our classes.

After third period, I hurried to the locker to put my books away. It was lunch time and it's time for Jenny's first lesson in driving a stick shift. I popped open my locker and a note fell out. I picked it up and stuff my books in and slam my locker close. Then I head to the student parking lot as I'm reading my new letter. In the letter she says that she knows that I've at least figured out that she's one of the cheerleaders and that she can be recognized by her perfume. She said she knows that because she's noticed my little perverted friend has been running around sticking his nose into all her cheerleader friends' armpits. Then she writes "Please call off your dog and I promise to meet up with you after our game Friday. This is probably our last one because Friday we play Mountain View. Their team is made of giants and way before

I was captain of the cheerleading squad we've had trouble beating them."

I realized, she just revealed herself! She's my Jada Fire looking girl! She's the captain of the cheerleading squad. She's my favorite little cheerleader, my chocolate crush that I thought was outta my league. She's a junior and definitely in the big leagues. But now I'm ready and I couldn't wait till the season was over. I mean I hope we won Friday, but at the same time I want my little chocolate crush. Either way it goes she already agreed to meet up with me after the game so it was on.

I walked out to the parking lot to a crowd of kids surrounding Jenny's jeep. I had skipped homeroom and I moved her jeep to the back of the lot so it wouldn't attract too much attention but I guess that didn't work so well. Jenny was already one of the prettiest girls at our school plus she was a junior and she was one of the only sixteen year old girls with her drivers permit. Everybody used to wonder why she hung around my younger cousin. But that was because Ki-Ki was on her level. Not only was my little Cuzz book smart but she was also street smart. She had already been though a lot and seen a lot by this time.

That's what growing up in Long Beach, Compton, and Carson will do to you.

At the age of thirteen, my little cousin was already a seasoned vet and she could fight too. So when

Ki-Ki met Jenny she was relieved that a girl as pretty as her, with the similar type of background, that she could relate to, had finally arrived.

I walked up to Jenny and I said, "Hello miss celebrity. I see you found your jeep."

"Yeah it was easy to spot I just looked for the crowd of kids."

"Yeah I peeped that when I got to the lot. Are you ready for your first lesson?"

"Yes." I gave her the keys then I yelled to everybody to backup for their own safety.

Jenny looked at me with her mouth wide open. She was looking all shocked and appalled. Then she said

"Oh? OK! Back up for your own safety huh? I'll get you back for that one!"

I laughed my ass off as we both got into the jeep for Jenny's stick shift 101 lesson. First we buckled up for safety, and then Jenny turned the key. The jeep jerked back and forth and stalled.

"Lesson one, step on the clutch when starting a stick shift car, have the gears in neutral, then press on the brake, then release the parking brake, then with the clutch engaged put it in first gear." I quickly showed her where all the gears were, I also showed her how to find reverse. "Now slowly come off the clutch while giving it a little gas."

She tried it; she came off the clutch too fast, stalling the jeep. I told her not to worry try it again.

Jenny tried it the second time and we started rolling and she got excited and happy. "I'm doing it!"

I told her to calm down. Now it's time to switch to second gear. She engaged the clutch and switched to second and released the clutch and smoothly continued to roll. I looked at her and I said, "Good job! You're a fast learner. Let's pull out the parking lot and head over to Pa-Pa Johns, let you buy me lunch." She looked at me.

"Hey keep your eyes on the road! Besides you owe me "Big Time" remember?"

"You're right, I got you." I laughed as I coached her all the way to Pa-Pa Johns pizza.

Our crew caught up with us at Pa-Pa Johns. My cousin is talking with Jenny. They're already making plans to go hit all the malls to get their shopping on and to go get some boys' numbers. Pm was in line Jay and

David walked up. I said what up to my boys, and then I told David the good news.

"Yo David I know who our mystery girl is!"

"Really, how did you find out before me? I'm the one out here doing all the dirty work!"

"Speaking of your dirty work; I got another note today from my little secret admirer. She let me know exactly who she is, and asked me to call off my armpit sniffing perverted ass homeboy!" That's when

Jay jumped in.

"What the hell are you two talking about?" Then he looked at David. "What's up with you sniffing girls' armpits? My sister told me that you sniffed her pits before, but I defended you and I told my big sister that she was tripping!" Then Jay turned to me. "And you, Mr. Humpty Dance! I don't even want to go into that with you right now!"

I tried to plead my case to my homie by saying his sister is older than me. I tried to explain to Jay that it was all her idea, and that she practically attacked me. He wasn't really feeling the fact that me and his big sister had bumped uglies, but he's my boy, so he forgave me.

I quickly changed the subject by explaining to Jay what me and Mr. Pits were talking about. I got Jay up to speed on everything and I described the mystery girl to both of them. They both knew exactly who she was and begged me for a piece of the action. Then they both told me that I was a lucky son-of-a-bitch and asked me to please hook them up

"From the sound of those letters you just explained to me she'll probably do all three of us!" Jay said

"Yeah hook up a train homie! I'll go last! I don't mind being the caboose," David said.

Me and Jay looked at each other and shook our heads for obvious reasons. We ordered our food and drinks; mine was compliments of Miss Jenny. We all ate our food together. While we praised Jenny for her new whip, and we made her promise to pick us all up at the AM/PM every morning for school. She pinky swore that she would so it was official. Jenny pulled into the school parking lot and parked her jeep.

She put the jeep in neutral and set the parking, and turned off the truck. I told her that she was a very fast learner and that it seemed like she had the basics down, and that she should be fine for now and the rest will come as she drives.

"Now what is this lesson really gonna cost me?"

"I don't know, you agreed to owe me big time, so what's big to you?"

"I don't know either. What were you thinking?"

"I have a question. This was bothering me all weekend. What did I miss by not coming over last Friday? Was that gonna be big?"

"Oh yeah, that was gonna be real big!"

"Dammit! I knew it! I saw it all over your face when I was holding you."

"I've been looking for the right guy to have my first sexual experience with for a while, and that night I decided that you were that right guy and the timing couldn't have been more perfect because I was home alone, and you turned me down."

"Hold on babe! I never turned you down! I asked for a rain check, besides you saw that I already had plans that I couldn't cancel!"

"Yeah I guess, well what are we supposed to do now? I really want you to be my first!"

"I would love to be your first baby and I'm definitely the right guy."

"OK then you need to make it happen."

"Don't trip! I will make it happen! I'll make that happen real soon!"

"Soon? OK when is soon?"

"Now!"

"Not now fool! We've got class in five minutes!"

I laughed even though I was serious as cancer and I said, "Not for real! I know, I know we can't "do it" now." Then I said. "If David's father isn't around this Saturday then we can go to his house!"

"Your little armpit smelling homie?"

"Damn, he got you too?"

"No! But I heard about him, he got too close to me once and I threatened to kick him in the nuts.

Since then he saw that I don't play, so he's been keeping it respectful!"

"As long as you guys are cool then it's all good. He owes me one. I'll work on him don't worry."

"OK, but I still don't trust his nasty ass! Just make sure we can have the place to ourselves. I really want this to be special."

"Of course baby, no worries. I got you."

Jenny looked at me with her beautiful dark brown eyes and she thanked me for being so understanding. I looked into those sexy dark brown eyes, and I went in for a French kiss, I wanted some tongue action, you know, a little tonsil hockey. I turned my head, closed my eyes, and leaned forward. Then that's when I felt a pointy little elbow hit me hard in my chest, and then I heard Jenny yell, "Back up! It's for your own safety!" She gave me that gotchu back look as she hopped out of her jeep and walked off to her fourth period class smiling, leaving me sitting in her jeep looking stupid with my mouth still open and my tongue hanging halfway out my mouth.

CHAPTER 8

It's Finally Goin' Down

It's Friday morning, Ki-Ki and my boy Jay were walking in front of Ashley and me as we headed to our pick up spot at the AM/PM. Today was going to be a big day for me and a very busy one too. Tonight is our biggest game of the season. Not only because it's a win or go home game but because from what I heard, those Mountain View football players are big! I'm not worried about it though because win, lose, or draw, my little chocolate crush agreed to meet up with me after the game. I'm trying to hit and little does she know, I'm trying to make sure my homies get some of that too, especially my boy David. I need him to hit so he'll owe me one. Then hopefully I'll be able to bring Jenny over to use his house since his dad is never at home.

Ashley asked me if I was nervous about tonight. I asked her why she would ask me something like that. Damn does she know about my chocolate crush?

"This game tonight is important because if we win, not only will it be our first time ever beating

Mountain View, but it will be our first time making it into the playoffs," Ashley said.

"Oh yeah; our big game, yeah I'm a little nervous, but that's normal. I'm just gonna play my best!"

"From what I heard you are the best!"

"I don't know who told you that, but thanks. I just play hard and do the best I can do."

"I know the captain of the cheerleading squad. She's in my fifth period class. She's always bragging about your moves on the field. She speaks highly of you."

"Oh really, that's nice of her."

"Hey, I was wondering if I could see you again this weekend if you're going to be around and that is, if you enjoyed yourself last time."

"Oh yeah I definitely did, but this weekend I'm booked, Oops! I mean, I'm gonna be too busy hanging out and grabbing some pizza and Saturday I'm pretty busy too."

Ashley looked disappointed as she turned and walked over to her friends that were patiently waiting for her so they could walk to school.

"What about Sunday? I'm not doin anything on Sunday."

Ashley quickly turned around and said, "Sunday is perfect! I'll walk over around noon, that way my little brother won't be all in my business."

"OK cool! I'll see you Sunday at noon."

Then I put my finger to my lips and I said "Let's keep this on the low, we don't want your brother finding out, OK?"

She agreed then she turned to catch up with her friends and they headed off towards the school. They were talking and giggling and looking back in my direction. I'm sure she was already telling them about our plans for Sunday. Little does she know, I don't really care about her brother finding out. I don't want to mess up my opportunity I have with my chocolate crush before I get a chance to hit that.

I turned and I saw everybody posted up at Jenny's truck. I walked over I said what's up to my little Latin beauty. She wished me a good morning then she asked me if I've talked to David yet. I said no not yet and that I hoping to talk to him this morning but I haven't seen him yet.

"Yeah where he at because if we wait any longer we're gonna be late for class."

"I don't know but if he's not here in the next five minutes then he's probably at home sick or he's not coming."

Five minutes passed and still no David so we headed off to school. Jenny parked in the school parking lot.

We hopped out and headed towards the school. As we were walking up to the curb, we heard a horn honk so we looked back. It's my boy David, he's driving up in a Mustang 5.0.

"Damn look at my boy rolling up in style!" Jay said.

He pulled up to the sidewalk and hopped out with the engine still running. Me and Jay walked up and we gave our boy dap. Ki-Ki and Jenny waved to David and went to their class.

The passenger door opened up and a man walked up to us.

"Hi I'm David's dad!" I couldn't believe it. He really did exist. Me and Jay shook his hand and said hi and that it's finally nice to meet him. Then he handed David a twenty dollar bill. "Bye buddy, I'll see you Sunday night. I'll let you drive some more when I get back, but you did good son. You boys have a good day at school." Then he drove off.

We praised our homie for rolling up on us like a straight G and for having a cool ass dad. He explained to me and Jay that he was running late because at the last minute his dad decided to give him a quick driving lesson. He said that he tried to pull up on us at the AM/PM but we had already left. He said

that his dad really felt bad because he work so much, that he doesn't spend as much time with him as he'd like to.

"Speaking of that, what did he mean when he said; he'll see you Sunday night?"

"He's on his way to San Diego to go on his annual deep sea fishing trip and he'll be gone till

Sunday night!"

"Holy shit! Do you boys know what this means?"

"Say what?" They both looked at me maliciously and said

"This means that tonight after the game we can take our little cheerleader freak to David's house and run that train on her." Then both of their eyes lit up and they got excited.

"That's what I'm talking about homie! You talked to her for us? It's all hooked up?" Jay said.

"No, I haven't got that far yet, but after the game when we meet, imma let her know that ya'll are my boys and if ya'll can't "Hit" then I'm not touching her."

"You really gonna do that for us?" David asked.

"Hell yeah Cuzz! Ya'll already know how I feel. Ain't no fun if my homies can't have none!"

They both dapped me up and praised me for my loyalty. Then I turned to David and said, "Now I'm gonna do something for you two, now I need a big favor from you -on Saturday."

"After tonight anything you want homie. What's up?"

"I need to use your house Saturday."

"Fasho! What time Saturday and what for?"

"All day Saturday homie, I need it for something special!"

"Something special or someone special?"

"Both! So what's up?"

"OK homie, but what the hell am I supposed to do all day Saturday?"

"Is your dad's car a stick shift?"

"Yeah, why?"

"Because if you know how to drive a stick and you promise not to wreck Jenny's truck, then I'll talk her into letting you use her jeep to go pick up Jay and ya'll roll out to the mall for the day while me and her are using your house."

The looks on both of their faces were priceless as they both yelled.

"Jenny?!" Then they both said, "You're a Lucky Son-of-a-bitch!" I started cracking up as I told them both to chill out.

***

It was game time so we ran out onto the field. I looked out into the bleachers. I saw my little cousin

Ki-Ki, then I saw Jenny, then I saw my homie's big sister Ashley, then I saw both my boys. Then as I got to our sideline, I looked up at the cheerleaders and I saw my little chocolate crush. She smiled and waved to me. So I waved back. Then as I looked across the field, I saw those gigantic ass Mountain View football players. Coach saw the look on my face and he said, "Don't worry about them son. They don't have a freshmen team, so every year we have to play their junior varsity team. Just do your best, that's all I expect.

Before kickoff, Ki-Ki and Jenny called me to the fence. I jogged to them to see what was up. Ki-Ki told me that my grandfather said that he was working late and that he couldn't make it tonight and he wished me luck, and said for me to win tonight so he can root for us in the playoffs.

"OK thanks for the message. I was wondering why he wasn't standing with you and Jenny." Then that's when Jenny leaned over the fence and planted a kiss on my lips.

"Is that a good luck kiss for the game?"

"No, that was a good luck kiss for our Saturday plans."

"Where's my good luck kiss for the game?" That's when Jenny leaned in and planted another kiss on my lips.

"There, that one was for the game."

I threw my helmet on, and then I snapped it and put my mouth piece in and jogged over to my team.

It was kick off time and Mountain View got the ball first. These guys were unstoppable. They scored on their first drive almost effortlessly. We had the ball on the forty yard line. I was playing wide receiver. The quarterback called a running play. The running back got the ball and swept around me. I went low and took my man out and made a big hole for my running back. He blew through the hole and ran the ball in for the score.

Our next drive coach called a pass play. The center hikes the ball. I ran out ten yards turned around and boom! The ball was in my chest. I wrapped my arms around it, I turned up the field and I got clobbered by two defenders. I limped back to the huddle and I shook off the brutal tackle I had just received. The quarterback called the play. I had two men on me, so the quarterback searched the field and threw it to the tight end. He caught the ball; I broke away from my two defenders to go block for him. I ran up to the two defenders that were headed his way. My tight end swept beside me, and then I threw my whole body at the legs of the giant defenders taking them out as our tight end ran the ball in for a touchdown. I jumped up and ran to meet him in the end zone to do the whop for the first time that night. We took the lead as the game went into half time. It's half time and we barely managed to keep up with those guys. The score as MONSOON 24 MOUNTAIN VIEW 21.

Coach said if it wasn't for me out there sacrificing my body with those incredible brave blocks then we wouldn't be in the lead right now He encouraged me to keep up the great work. Before we hit the field coach gave us a pep talk. He told us that he was proud of us, and that we've got heart, and that we were playing some big boys. He said he saw that we are playing our hardest and to just keep it up, and don't give up! It was kick-off time. I was in the back field ready to run like hell. The ball was kicked towards me high in the sky. I ran out the end zone to field the ball as it was coming down around the five yard line. I looked up to catch the ball. As soon as I caught it, I looked to see which way to start running. All I saw was a total eclipse of darkness. Then instantly smashed, I got flattened by two of the biggest guys I've ever seen on a football field in my life.

After I was tackled, two of my teammates came to scrape me up off the field.

"You took a vicious hit! Are you alright?"

"Yeah I'm good, just help me up." As I attempted to get up, I felt an electrifying pain shooting up my inner thigh as I limped all the way to the bench. Coach came up to me and noticed that I still had the ball in my hands.

"Well at least you didn't drop the ball."

"Yeah I'm keeping this ball cuz after that hit this is my last football game ever!"

"Well for this season, at least cuz if you hurt then it looks like this game is theirs," Coach said.

"Hell yes! My inner thigh is killing me!" He had me examined and they said that I pulled a groin ligament and I would have to sit out.

I called my boys over to let them know that I was hurt and how painful this shit was. That's when

Jenny came running over to me because she saw me limping and noticeably hurt. I told her that I needed a ride and to pull her jeep over to the locker room.

As I'm explaining to my boys that there's gonna be a slight change of plans, and it looked like their gonna have to take the little freak to David's house while I have Jenny take me home, then imma shake her, and meet them over at David's place, the little freak walked over to check on me.

She asked me if was ok and if we were still on for tonight. I told her that we were just discussing that, and then I introduced her to Jay and David. Then I explained to her that I had to go home and ice my leg for about an hour, but for her to go on and head over to David's house with my boys, and that I'll meet her over there in a little while. She asked me if I was sure I was coming, because she didn't want to go if I wasn't coming. I promised her after I iced my leg I would come thru.

I turned to my boys, popped my collar, and said "Did ya'll hear that?"

"Hell yes!" They both said and they thanked me for making it happen.

***

On the way home I had Jenny stop at the AM/PM. Ki-Ki went inside to grab a bag of ice so I would have enough to ice my injury all night, or at least after I got back home from David's house visiting my little chocolate freak.

While Ki-Ki was in the store I told Jenny the good news. She was excited and thanked me for making it happen.

"There's one little catch."

"What's that?"

"I told David that you would let him take your jeep to the mall, so we could have the house all day."

"As long as he knows what he's doing. He better not wreck shit!"

"I told him if he wrecks your jeep then you're gonna kick him in his nuts."

She started laughing. "I think he might actually like that babe. You should've told him that if he wrecks my shit then I'm gonna cut his nuts off!"

"Hell naw Cuzz! I'm not telling my homie no shit like that! Just the thought of that is making my stomach hurt!"

Jenny was cracking up at the faces I was making from her sadistic punishment, even though David would probably be masochistic about it!

Ki-Ki hopped in the jeep and said, "What are you laughing about Jenny? What the heck did I miss?"

"You don't wanna know trust me!" Jenny said with tears in her eyes.

Then Ki-Ki asked me why my face all was screwed up like I just got kicked in my balls.

"Because Jenny was in here talking about David's balls."

"OK stop! Jenny was right I didn't want to know, so spare me the details please." All three of us started cracking up as Jenny pulled out of the AM/PM.

Jenny pulled up in my driveway. Ki-Ki told her goodbye and took the bag of ice into the house. I finally got some tongue action from Jenny. Then I told her thanks for the ride and that I'll see her around noon tomorrow. I gave her a final kiss good night, and then I limped to my front porch.

My mother greeted me at the front door which was never a good thing. But I just figured that Ki-Ki must have told her about my football injury. But the mean mug face that she was making was not one of concern.

As I walked into the door I looked at my cousin, she was looking scared. She shook her head then she lowered it. I looked at my mother as she was standing at the front door staring out at Jenny's truck. Once I was all the way in the house I said,"Hi mother." She slammed the door.

"Don't hi mother me!" she said. "Who the hell is that driving you around?"

"That's just Jenny mom. Her mother bought her a new truck; she's got her drivers permit. What's the problem?"

"Is that her? Is that your little nasty ass secret admirer?" My heart dropped and I didn't know what to do. So I got on the defense."

What the fuck mom! You've been going through my stuff invading the little bit of privacy that I do have?"

My mother couldn't believe that I just talked to her like that. Before I knew it, It was a cat-like reflex. My mother's hand came up and slapped the shit outta me. I didn't even see it coming. All I remember was a high pitch tone in my left ear like a phone was ringing. Then I felt the skin on my face start to burn like hell.

"Little boy as long as your my son, you have no privacy! I was washing your little shit stained draws and when I went to put them in your dresser drawer, your whole damn drawer was full of them skanky little sex letters sprayed with some cheap ass perfume. Now tell me who she is!"

"I don't know."

"Oh yeah! Well you'll never know, ever! Go in your room and pack your shit I'm taking you back to Carson!"

"But mom what about my friends and football?"

"Boy Ki-Ki said ya'll lost tonight, the season is over! You think I'm stupid? You got your friends in Carson. I'll let your ass go and get shot with your homies in some drive by before I let you make me a grandmother at the age of thirty two, over my dead body! Not gonna happen. Now get in there and pack your shit! You lucky you got fucked up tonight in your game or I'd be beating your ass right now! I told you to stay away from those fast ass little nasty heifers!"

I put my head down and I thought to myself. Is my mother some kind of dick detective when it comes to me? I went in my room, packed some of my clothes. Half of that shit was some K-mart specials and there was no way I could wear that shit in Carson, so I gave it all to my little brothers. I still had a closet full of clothes in Carson waiting for me anyway.

I said goodbye to my little brothers and my little sister, and to all my little cousins. I gave Charity a big hug and kissed her on the cheek. I hugged my aunt Joan and I walked slowly over to my mother's car. I really didn't want to go. I had the weekend that I would have never forgotten planned and now the "Dick Detective" foiled my plans. It was total silence the whole nineteen minute ride back to Carson. My true home sweet home. All I could do was sit in the passenger seat, and just imagine what my boys were doing to my little chocolate crush.

CHAPTER 9

Back in Carson: The City that Made Me

Once I was back in Carson, I picked up where I left off, back chillin with my homies hanging and banging. One Friday night, somebody threw a house party on the east side of Del Amo. Everything was cool the music was bumping, so the girls were live and freaking dudes on the dance floor. But not me I was posted up watching, holding up the walls and pointing at the freaks that were breaking it down on the floor. They'd be freaking so hard that the guys would be sweating as if they were fucking. The girls would be freaking it back so hard they would be sweating out the crimps in their hair. The homies was deep. Then some off brand niggas got wind of the party, and they started showing up. Then one of the homies brand new Fila's got stepped on, and it was on! That dude got the brakes beat off his ass and tossed out the party. Then everything went back to normal. The girls went back to freaking dudes while me and a few of the homies was posted up out front shooting dice and sippin on our drinks.

Then outta nowhere a truck pulled up with that same off brand dude in it with his homies. He had his gun waving it all out the window. We all saw the gun and scattered.

We all stuck together except one of the twins. Twin ran up the driveway between the cars. The guy with the gun saw him and hopped out the truck and chased my homie down and shot him. When the rest of us heard the gunshot, we thought we were all together, so we thought we were all good. We heard the truck speed off and a girl scream. We ran over there and that's when we realized we had one man down. He was quickly put in the car and raced to the hospital where he was placed on life support. Two days later he was taken off life support and placed in ICU in critical but stable condition. We all went up to the hospital to see him, to support our homie and to let him know how lucky he was to still be living through those gunshots.

But he wasn't so lucky because the next morning while we were all at school the announcement came over the P.A. System that he had passed away. The whole school did a moment of silence. Our remaining twin had lost his other half. It was devastating to us all, but especially to him. Needless to say, things got worse around the hood, that meant more hanging at night, protecting my hood.

***

Carson high school was my favorite school. I'm in the tenth grade and a sophomore. The girls here in Carson were incredibly fine. Now that I had a couple of muscles on me, I had to keep them up, and I was trying to build more. One day, me and my best friend, Troy, was at our second period gym class lifting weights in the weight room. Troy was a little guy and I was always protective of my best friend because he was a little dude. That's why when this big ass

Samoan kid punked little ass Troy for his spot in the weight room I told his big ass to pick on somebody his own size. The oversized tenth grader turned to me and said "like you?"

I looked at that big ass dude and I thought to myself, hell no, you gigantic ass mutant high school freak of nature, but I couldn't say that. That would be punking out and where I'm from, there ain't no punks, you can't be no punk, and you never down a fade!

"Yeah Cuzz like me!" I said and I got all up in his face. By now a crowd was building, everybody had stopped lifting weights and all eyes were on us. The giant looked around then he looked down at me.

"OK, me and you after school, by the Taco Bell!"

"By the Taco Bell? What's up with right here right now? Take off where you fall off Loc!" I figured right there with my boy Troy there we could pick up a couple of dumb bells and we could both whoop his big ass because there ain't no fair fights where I'm from either.

"No, not during school. After school, and you better be there!" the giant said.

"I'll be there as soon as school is out!"

As soon as the final school bell rang, I was at my locker where me Troy met to go catch the Carson Circuit home from school every day. I was waiting there because he was standing right there when he heard the giant tell me to meet him at the Taco Bell after school. Troy didn't show up so I thought maybe he must have walked straight over to the Taco Bell and he was waiting for me there. I hurried over to the Taco Bell to look for Troy hoping that he wasn't over there with the giant by himself. When I got over there-there was no Troy and no giant. As I'm waiting for the giant all by myself, one of my homies from my hood walked up to me.

He saw me standing there with my brownies on. "What's up Cuzz! You straight?"

"Yeah Cuzz I'm straight, I'm just waiting for this fool to get here so we can get down real quick.

"Where this fool at Cuzz. I got yo back!" My homie Marcus said.

"I don't know. He's supposed to meet me right here after school."

"That fool scared Cuzz! He ain't even here."

Thirty minutes passed so me and my nigga Marcus started walking towards the Carson Circuit.

As the bus pulled up, a big Scooby Doo van pulled up and stopped. The two back doors opened and the big shirtless giant hopped out the back.

"What's up homie you ready?"

"Damn Cuzz that's him?" Marcus said.

"Yep, I guess he ain't scared after all!"

Marcus was a swole ass nigga, he saw the look on my face as the giant came walking up fast.

"What's up Cuzz, you want me to take this fade for you Loc?"

"Hell naw Cuzz! This is my fight!"

"OK Cuzz, imma stay right here and make sure his boys don't jump in."

The giant came up with three of his boys behind him looking pissed with his shirt off and his long bushy hair looking all wild.

"Don't worry about my homies, they just here to watch my back, they won't jump in. It's just me and you." Then he said, "Where's your homie that you took up for? He don't have your back?"

I was thinking the same thing. But reality was that there was no way Troy little ass could have helped me with this big ass Samoan giant. He looked even bigger than he did at school this morning. Only if that bus would have pulled up one minute sooner. I'd be halfway home right now. Then he would look like a scary ass punk, and I would be gangsta because I showed up. But then I would have to deal with it again tomorrow.

"I don't need him to have my back, it's just me and you right?"

"That's right, you ready to do this?"

"Yeah fool, let's go!" I said.

We squared off, I heard Marcus yell, "Swing Cuzz! Get um!" So I started swinging. I connected with two good hits. But the giant just shook them off. Then I saw the giant as he tried to get low and rush in on me, but his big ass was too slow so I spun around him and punched him in his ribs.

"Cuzz watch him he's trying to get you on the ground! Don't' let him Cuzz! Stay on your feet and don't wrestle him!" Marcus yelled again. I heard what Marcus said but I had already noticed that. But for some reason I wasn't able to avoid it and the next thing I knew I was tired as hell from all the swinging.

The next time I swung, I put all my might into it but I missed. Next thing I knew the giant grabbed me. He had his tree like arms wrapped around me then he flipped me upside down. He went to pile drive me like one of those Hulk Hogan moves but luckily I found enough strength to twist at the last minute. We both were falling over to the side; his feet flew up causing all the weight to come down on me while he still had me upside down.

We landed on the asphalt. My head hit first then we fell to the side. He let go and was holding his shoulder then I hurried to my feet, keeping my eyes on him as he struggled to get up. Then we both stood there huffing and puffing looking at each. Then I felt an itching feeling at the top of my forehead, when I scratched it, it was wet. I looked at my fingers and they were bloody. That's when the giant looked at me still huffing and he said, "You had enough?"

I'm still huffing and my face was all screwed up. I looked down at my bloody fingers, and then I looked at him.

"Yeah! Have you?"

"Yeah," the giant said.

The giant walked up all in my face and he stuck his hand out. "You got heart homie, at least you didn't run."

"I ain't no punk."

"You alright with me homie, see you in gym class tomorrow." Then he went back and hopped in the Scooby Doo van, closed the two back doors, and it drove off.

I turned around to my homie Marcus, he was shaking his head. "Cuzz I told you his big ass was trying to wrestle you."

"Cuzz that was a big mutha fucka!"

Marcus started laughing and he said, "I know, but you didn't run Cuzz, you got heart!"

I asked Marcus how bad was my head. He said "It's a small hole right by your hair line but it's not noticeable besides the blood." We got on the Carson Circuit; I got a napkin and stopped the bleeding.

The next day at school I saw the giant at gym class. I went up to him.

"What's up? How's your head?"

"It's got a hole in it, other than that it's fine," I said. "Where the hell did you learn those wrestling moves?"

The giant smiled at me and he said "My uncle is Jimmy Superfly Snookum."

"What the fuck! No wonder!"

"I've been waiting to practice those moves."

"That's some fucked up shit! You were supposed to let me know that homie, that's cheating."

The giant put his fist out to give me "Dap" and he said, "We're friends now so you don't have to worry about it." The giant that I was just fighting the day before became my new friend.

CHAPTER 10

Oral Escapade

By the time summer came, my mother was tired of me getting into trouble from hanging out with my homies, gang banging. I would get picked up a lot for being out past curfew. My mother would have to come pick me up from the Carson Sheriff Police station.

She had remarried and moved way out to the San Fernando Valley. They lived in a run-down apartment building in the city of Van Nuys. It was about an hour and a half drive to Van Nuys to Carson.

My mother came to the Carson Sheriff Police station all the way from Van Nuys after letting me sit in there for what seemed like forever. She didn't pick me up until 8 the next morning too, call herself teaching me a lesson. She had all my clothes in the trunk of her car. We left the police station and she got right back on the 405 freeway heading north bound all the way to the raggedy ass apartment building in Van Nuys. It was a two bedroom, one bathroom, closet sized apartment. It was a major difference from what I had going for me in Carson. One bedroom was my mother's and her loser ass husband. I hadn't even had a chance to meet this dude before I was dragged off to their seven person wedding.

I remember one night I heard a loud thump. I rushed into the bedroom that the sound came from. I saw my little brother Mikey lying face down on the bedroom floor. Poor guy was sleeping on the top bunk but he slept so wild that he fell off. I picked up my poor little brothers lifeless body as my mother came running into the room with her robe on. She grabbed my little brother and she asked what happened. I told her that he just fell off his bed and he was still sound asleep. She kissed my little brother as he opened his eyes. She asked him if he was alright. He was blinking his eyes as he nodded his head so I my mother tucked him back in his bed and we all went back to sleep.

The next morning when we came out for breakfast, my mother damn near fainted. Mikey looked like the elephant man after he had a fight with Mike Tyson. Both of his eyes were literally black. His whole forehead was swollen and purple. I had tears in my eyes just looking at my poor little brother as he just stood there blinking his eyes. Poor Mikey had already been hit by a car twice, two separate times and had loss his memory. He was also hit in the head with a two by four with nails in it by my little brother Joey. So this was the last thing he needed. Luckily he was a fast healer and in a week he was back to normal. At least his face was. He was still doing that blinking thing though.

As I got settled in over there in Van Nuys I didn't like not having any money so while it was still summer break I got a job at Cads Jr. I liked working because I liked money in my pocket and I didn't like being home around my mother's sorry ass husband. I was fifteen now and I didn't like little things that I Noticed around my mom's apartment.

One day I found out what the late night activity was about. I had just got paid from my job at Carl's Jr. my mother noticed how much money I was carrying around. She told me that I didn't need to be having that much money on me. She told me to let her start holding my money for me. So for my next few checks I would only keep fifty dollars of my three hundred dollar checks, the rest I gave to her.

School was about to start. I was starting at a whole new high school, AGAIN. My mother figured

that I was so far away from Carson that I wouldn't get into trouble at my new school out there in Van Nuys at Birmingham High School. I wanted to take my money that my mother was saving up for me to go shopping in downtown L.A. That's where they had all the deals on all the latest gear. I knew I could get more for my money in the downtown Los Angeles fashion district. So I hit my mother up for my money and I told her that I wanted to go downtown to do some school shopping. She yelled and told me that she would take me school shopping when she took my brothers and sister shopping. That we would all go to Kmart together at the same time to get everything that we all needed.

"Hell no! I don't wear that shit anymore! That's why I worked hard all summer so I could buy my own clothes, so I can wear what I like to wear. So just give me my money that you've been saving for me and I'll go get my own stuff."

"What money! Boy you ain't got no money! What about this roof over your head and the food on your plate? That shit ain't free! Now get the hell out my face!"

I was so mad and hurt that I had tears in my eyes. I couldn't believe my mother had betrayed me like that. Luckily for me, I had my last two checks hidden in my little Velcro wallet. One was from my checks that I didn't give to my mother, and the other was from my final check because I got fired from Carl's Jr. for using my fifty percent discount on my day off. That was some petty shit on their behalf but I definitely learned my lesson.

***

When school started I was clean. I stepped on campus the first day of school with all fresh gear on.

A couple of gold ropes and my gold nugget rings with my white with blue snake skin Georgio Brutini's tennis shoes on. You couldn't tell me nothing. I got a job at the McDonald's that was right across the street from Birmingham High. I got the job so I could keep up with my fly wardrobe, to keep money in my pocket, and to stay out of trouble. That didn't last long because what my mother failed to realize was that while she moved me way out there to the San Fernando Valley to get me away from my homies in Carson and to keep me away from the Los Angeles, bullshit trouble came to Birmingham High because it was a magnet school. They bussed in bad ass little boys like me every morning for school from all over the Los Angeles area. I had a little girlfriend for a minute but I found out that the girl that I was messing with out there was a rat. I found out from a couple of my boys that was messing with her. So she had to go.

Eventually trouble found me again. Gang banging was everywhere. I ended up getting into it with from some fool from Compton, and the rest was history. I got into trouble at school and when I got home my mother was waiting for me at the front door. That's never a good thing. She told me that she knew that I was suspended for five days from school for a gang fight. During the five days that I was suspended I could not leave the apartment building. I told her that I had to work but she didn't care. I called up to my job. I told my supervisor that I was not able to make it to work for the next five days. My mom grabbed the phone out of my hand and told my supervisor that I got suspended from school for a gang fight and that she probably would not want to have any gang bangers working for her. She agreed with my mother and fired me right over the phone.

Now I'm at home alone for the next five days and jobless. While I'm in my building standing outside my apartment door, my mom's neighbor walked by on her way to the laundry room. She was a pretty, tall and thin white lady with curly red hair. She was about twenty five years old. She looked a lot like Triple X Star, Joselyn James. She had the pretty curly hair, big breasts and those luscious long legs.

"Hi."

"What's up?" I said.

"Aren't you supposed to be at school?"

"No! Not few the next few days. I got suspended for fighting," I said.

"Oh, you like to fight? You should be a lover not a fighter," she said.

"Are you a gangbanger?" She said.

"Hell yeah!" I said.

She was all up on me. "Oh I like gangstas."

"Then you'll love me." She smiled.

We ended up talking most of the morning. She was a lonely horny ass white-woman. She told me that her boyfriend was in the LA County Jail and that she was all alone in her apartment and she missed sucking his dick all day every day. She told me that's her favorite thing to do. Then she asked me if

I've ever been with a white girl before.

"No."

"You don't know what you're missing," she said.

"Why don't you show me?"

"You really wanna know?"

"Hell yeah! What's up?" I asked her.

Then my little Joselyn James told me that she would really enjoy sucking the life out of me for hours and hours. She said that we couldn't do it there because we might get caught. She said it wouldn't be good if somebody saw me walking out of her apartment. So she said since it's gonna be my first time with a white girl then she wanted to make it special. She wanted to have me all to herself with no interruptions and she wanted to make sure that I never ever forgot her. She told me to be ready at nine the next morning after my mom was long gone to work. "I'll see you in the morning baby boy as she walked over to her apartment. She switched her nice little ass all the way into her apartment door.

I went inside and closed the door so I could celebrate and jump around like a fifteen year old fool without anybody seeing me. I was so excited and in full anticipation. I immediately started to get ready. I knew I had until tomorrow morning but I wanted to make sure that I was prepared. I made sure I had some clean undies, some clean socks, and a fresh pair of pants and a fresh tee.

Then I checked my pockets. "Oh shit! No Jimmies!" I needed some condoms; I tore up the house hoping that my mother wasn't silly enough to be trying to have another baby, especially not with this clown. So I went through all the kitchen drawers and I finally found one. I held it up like a catholic priest did at communion. I kept looking because the way she sounded I'm gonna need at least three jimmies. So I searched on top of the refrigerator. When I reached up there, I accidently knocked down a yellow envelope.

When the envelope landed on the kitchen floor and its contents fell out, I just froze. I didn't want to believe what I was seeing, but being from Carson and doing what we did for money to keep the hood popping with dough, I knew exactly what I was looking at. I was so mad as I picked it all up. I opened our apartment door, went down stairs to the dumpster, and I threw away all the drugs and its paraphernalia. All my hard earned summer money flashed before my eyes. It was all making sense now; my money gone, she and her q husband and their late night activities. It all made sense. This also confirmed the rumor I heard about a neighbor in our building accusing my mother of stealing their dope stash, and that dude wasn't too happy about it either. I also remember one late night I was woken up by a loud scream. I heard the noise come from my mother and her husband's room. I go bust in their room and they were naked. He was standing over her while her back was against her bed with her arm up as if she was defending herself from him. My mother yelled for me to get out but I didn't budge until she told me that she was alright and he took his ass to the other side of the bed. There was a metal smell in the air but I was worried about my mother. She assured me that she was fine and she screamed for me to get out and to never come busting in her room again.

As I was walking back into the apartment, I was trying to figure out what I was going say. I knew I was gonna be confronted by my mom's or her crack head ass husband when they realized that their stash was missing. But I didn't care. I was gonna stand my ground on this shit. I was just hoping that it would go unnoticed until after my little sexcapade tomorrow. That night after my mother got home from work I was watching TV sitting on my couch that I slept on. There was a knock at the door. My mother's neighbor asked her to come over because she wanted to talk to her. Next thing I know, I heard my mother screaming and hollering. I ran to our door. When I opened it I saw my mother kicking and banging on the horny little red heads door calling her all kinds of nasty ass bitches and sluts. My mother told that bitch to bring her white ass out of her house so she could beat her white redheaded ass. When my mother realized that the scary white bitch was not about to come out of her house, my mother yelled, "you nasty little white bitch! You keep your nasty ass away from him! He's only fifteen years old!" That's when my mother ran over to the front door where I was standing rooting for my mother to whoop that white bitch's ass that was until I realized that it was all because of me. Then all the anger that I had about my mother's little drug stash went back to fear as she met me at the front door, and you know that's never a good thing. I had never seen my mother that mad before in my life. She snatched me by my arm, pushed me inside, and slammed the door.

My mother told me that my little oral escapade on the beach tomorrow morning had been canceled. She said that her next door neighbor heard the whole nasty ass conversation that me and that little red head white bitch had this morning. I started shaking my flicking head and thinking to myself, the Dick Detective strikes again. My mother picked up the house phone and she called my dad. She told him to be there in the morning to pick up me and my two little brothers. She told my dad that she was sick and tired of our little bad asses. That night my mother packed all of our shit while my dad drove from Apache Junction, Arizona.

Our dad picked our asses up and drove us straight back to Arizona cussing us out the whole way there.

Chapter 11

Blow Job Betty

By this time my dad had been remarried about eight years now to a Filipino woman, who was damn near twice his age. Once I was enrolled in school it was then that it hit me. My mother sent me out here where it was almost impossible to get into trouble. We lived in a small town in the middle of nowhere called Apache Junction.

On the first day of school I realized that I was the only black person in the whole damn city. Being a black thug from Los Angeles made me an outcast almost instantly. Walking through the halls I would get a couple of looks but no stares. No one spoke to me because they were scared I was gonna pull out a gun and start shooting up the place. I didn't blame them because I fit that description. I was still wearing my LA attire of Brownies. They were those brown garden gloves we bought at a 7-11 stores. I had on my blue flannel shirt and my blue corduroy house shoes that I wore every day and of course a pair of creased up khaki's. I had on all of that while it was one hundred and five degrees in the shade. It took me a few weeks to start socializing so I could try to make a friend or two.

Once the cool kids saw that I was cool and I saw that they were cool, and I didn't have to kick their asses then everything was cool. I became very popular and finally accepted. I started getting invited to hangout; they would throw big keg parties in the desert out in the middle of nowhere. We would drive down a little dirt road for miles, and then all of a sudden you make a right turn into a ditch and drive through bushes and shrubs. Then you would see a big bonfire with cars and trucks parked around it. There would be about four trucks backed up to the bonfire with kegs in the back. We'd pay five dollars, they'd put an "X" on the back of our hand then we could drink all we wanted. It was wild, crazy, and hella fun! Those white boys sure knew how to party. That night I tried weed for the first time but I didn't get high. I'm more of a drinker anyway, so no loss.

In my spare time I would put all my energy into lifting weights. I quickly saw results. Everybody noticed even the football coach. He was so impressed that he asked me to join the football team. I thought about what happened last time but I still accepted and joined the team. We had a couple months before we started practicing. So the coach started us out on the weights. I was a skinny little twig. The coach had me drinking weight gain protein shakes and drinking raw eggs. I was also taking amino acid pills. He picked me and a few of the other guys up from the Circle K at the end of my block. We would lift weights with two of the coaches before school. With my new and improved body I was turning heads and finally getting the attention I was waiting for from the girls.

One day I stayed after to workout with one of the guys from the team. We were in the gym and a sexy little platinum blonde with an ass like Alexis Texas and just as beautiful, walked up to me. She was captain of the cheerleading squad.

"Hi do you remember me?" she said.

"No have we met?"

"Yes my name is Betty we met at the bonfire party a few weeks ago." I apologized and told her that I didn't recall. But I told her that it was possible but I don't remember much about that night because I was wasted as hell.

"That would explain why I didn't hear from you."

"My bad," I said.

She said she's had her eye on me but she didn't know how to approach me. Then she said for me to give her my number this time and that she'd be calling me soon. I gave Betty my house number, and she said, "Perfect! I got you now." She said she was going to call me Saturday and that she guarantees that I won't forget her this time.

"Sounds good! Talk to you then."

"Oh and bring your friend he's cute; I'll bring one of my girls from my squad," she said. Saturday came and all four of us went to the Salt River. When we got there she kicked her friend out of the car and my boy followed her so we could have a little privacy. Betty looked at me with a big ass smile of anticipation and she told me to climb in the backseat and sit in the middle. I hurried and climbed into the back seat thinking, my mother can't cock block on this shit today. Blowjob Betty is about to put it down and the Dick Detective is not around to cancel this Oral Escapade.

She lay between the two front seats and she tore into my pants like it was a happy meal. She pulled my dick out and she slapped it on her tongue and she licked around it like it was a melting ice cream cone.

She squeezed really hard at the base of my dick with her tiny little sixteen year old hands. Then she used her teeth and she grazed the sides of my dick like she was eating corn on the cob. When she got my dick nice and wet, she stroked it with her little fingers. She was all hyper and smiles and for a minute, I even think she forgot it was attached to me.

She was in her own world as she played with my dick like it was the Christmas present she always wanted Santa to leave for her in her Christmas stocking. So I gave her instructions, "suck this dick!" The bitch went crazy. After going ham on my dick for fifteen minutes straight, nonstop like I needed her to do, she reached down with her hand and she showed me how I just made her cum by telling her to suck my dick.

She continued sucking and coming up for air then taking a deep breath then sucking it like crazy.

Then I told her, "Swallow this dick! She went down as far as she could and choked. I could feel her swollen tonsils constrict at the head of my dick and I exploded.

When she felt that I was cumming she loved it. She started sucking nice and slow using her tongue on my dick as she played with my hot cum in her mouth. Then she pulled my dick out of her mouth and smiled as she swallowed her mouth full of my nut. Then she closed her lips and used my dick like it was a fifty dollar tube of that super shiny lip gloss as she smeared the last of my cum on her thin little lips. She looked at me as those deep throat tears were flowing down her cheeks as she was swallowing the last drops of my hot thick cum. I remember her smiling and saying, "I can feel your babies swimming in my throat."

***

Everything was looking real good for me in Arizona. I was the man on and off campus. I was doing well at work, and everything seemed to be good at home too. We had a pool in our backyard. It was my job to keep it clean. It was quite a chore with all that dirt getting blown around all day living in that desert city. It was well worth it because it would get up to one hundred and ten degrees in the summer and the humidity was not joke. I would have my best friend and a couple girls over during those hot summer days playing water polo and splashing around and throwing the girls in the pool, and diving off my diving board all day until the sun went down. At night time it would still be hot. It would stay in the upper nineties. So we stayed in the pool after it got dark. Then I would turn the lights off in the pool and we would play Marco Polo.

After things got quiet and it looked like my dad and my step mom were winding down, I would sneak in the house and steal a few of my dad's beers. Then we would pair off in the pool and have fun with the girls, making out and doing what teenagers do when alcohol is in the equation. Then after a while me and my boy would switch girls. Like Snoop Dogg says, "Ain't no fun if my homies can't have none."

My dad was starting to get jealous of me. One hot summer day me and my best friend were chilling by the pool. My drunken ass dad came outside. He was working on his second twelve pack of Budweiser. He was talking shit and slurring his words and tried to pick a fight with me in front of my friends. I was only sixteen. He embarrassed the hell out of me. Out of respect for my dad I was not going to fight him but I was so mad that I had tears in my eyes. I was ready to hurt someone but at the same time I was hurting inside. That night I called my grandmother and I told her that she better send for me before something happens and she may never see me again. Since I was her favorite grandson, she sent for me. I left the next day. From that day on me and my dad have never been the same.

CHAPTER 12

Squaring Up

When I arrived at my grandparents' house this time it was a whole lot better. My mother was still married to her loser ass husband that she up and married after only knowing him a few months. Her twin, my aunt Joan, was living with her fiancé' David, he's a pastor at a church. My aunt Pat and her daughter Jasmine was living in the Jungles with her boyfriend. The Jungles is an area in Los Angeles that the police were even afraid to patrol. My Uncle Charles had his own place somewhere in South Central. It was all bad back in those days because this was when the crack epidemic was in full swing. Everyone I just named except my aunt Joan was on it bad.

The city of Carson is where I truly call my home. My grandparents practically raised me there. That was where I would always end up while my parents were busy trying to rebuild their new lives with their new marriages. I didn't mind because my grandparents were the best. I could get away with almost anything while in that house. Carson was known for having the finest girls in L.A. Just ask my friend, former Los Angeles Laker Derrick Fisher. Now I'm seventeen years old and I'm still hanging and banging with D.A. homies and getting into trouble until I met Doris. She was twenty-two and I was seventeen. She already had two little boys. Andre was four, and Poche' was about to have his first birthday. She was beautiful and a lot of guys wanted her. Pulling her made me the man in my hood. At seventeen I was still very sexually inexperienced. The first time we had sex we were in the same room that I had lost my virginity to my big cousin in. We were on the floor spooning and in my head I was having anal sex. I still remember when Doris came to me and told me that she was pregnant. She walked with Andre while pushing Poche' in his stroller. I was standing in the front of my house when she told me. I asked her if she was sure the baby was mine. In my head I thought there was no way she could be pregnant by me because we only have had anal sex.

"Who else baby could it be? You're the only person I've been with! "She said crying. I was standing in front of my house looking confused as hell as Doris started crying as she walked all the way back to her house. It seemed like overnight that I was seventeen years old, with a pregnant woman and two kids and one of them still in diapers. She let everybody know it too. I remember the first day of my senior year at Carson High School. I was chilling with my boys and a bunch of the girls by the lunch tables between classes.

Out of nowhere Doris walked through the girls and up to me, "I'm pregnant! Let's go! School is over you need to get a job and take care of your responsibilities." I was shocked as hell and once again embarrassed in front of my friends. I couldn't ever show my face at that school again even if I wanted to. She grabbed my hand and as she was pulling me to her car I was thinking, what the hell am I going to do? I'm only seventeen how am I gonna take care of this woman and three kids? I accepted my responsibilities and I stepped up and made it happen. I quickly found a job. I applied to Harbor UCLA Medical Center in Torrance. I heard they had a student worker program for high school students that wanted to work as security. They were under the impression that I was still in school so I got the job. I loved that job. I worked there until I turned eighteen and then one of my best friend's father found out that I had a baby on the way and that I needed a better job. He offered me a position at his company. I didn't know what to expect but I gladly accepted. He told me if I did a good then he would help me move up in the company and that I could one day retire from there. I had no idea that he was putting me in a life changing position.

He gave me the address to go apply. I walked in the office and I gave them my name and I told them who sent me. They rolled out the red carpet and gave me the royal treatment. Next thing I knew, I was working at LAX for China Airlines. I was off loading big freight cargo planes, driving tugs and forklifts on the runway. This was the best job an eighteen year old could have.

We lived with my Uncle Keith in his little one bedroom apartment in South Central L.A. It was two blocks away from the Slauson swap meet. Me and my uncle had to be careful over there because we were from a different neighborhood and in 1990 gang banging was in full effect, especially on that block. We lived on 62nd and Western. I was good on 62nd. One day I was walking out to my car to go to work and my neighbor across the street was up to no good. They were in the middle of some illegal activities in front of their apartment. I could see that things were getting intense as they were wrapping up what looked like a big drug transaction. I looked up the street and I saw a police car coming up the block towards us, so I yelled "One-Time!" One of them looked at me and I signaled towards the police car as it was coming closer. My neighbor signaled to his crew and they were able to hurry everything inside and out of sight by the time the police car got up to us.

As the police car rolled by staring and driving real slow, I just played it off by putting on my work jacket. The policemen saw the LAX Airport patch on it and kept on going. After the cop car was gone. Four guys came out of the apartment and walked up to me at my car. I was nervous as hell. They were dressed in all red. The first dude stuck his hand out and said, "Thank you my nigga."

"Fasho!" He told me his name and he hit me up. He asked me my name and where I was from. "I'm from Del Amo in Carson!

"190?"

"East Coast!"

"Do you realize what you just did?" He said. "You just saved our asses young G!" Then he said,

"You straight over here my G. Imma let all the homies know you got a pass over here all day everyday my nigga!"

I told him my uncle lived there too, and that this was his spot. I told them that we were from the same hood and to make sure he was straight too. They all said no problem and told me if I needed anything then to just holler at them. I told them thanks and that I had to get to work. It was all good. I told my uncle what happened and he thanked me. He said he was tired of sneaking in and out of his damn car every day and night before one of them niggas hit him up.

***

One night, about 2 a.m., I was about to leave to go to work. Doris who had been having labor pains all day.

Her water decided to break and she went into labor. As I'm trying to gather everything to head out to the hospital, Doris reached down to pick her pants up and it happened. She screamed my name and when I got to her she was standing there looking scared. I asked her what was wrong.

"The baby is coming!"

"I know let's get to the car!"

"No! Look! The baby's head, it's coming out!" I looked between her legs and I saw the baby's head. I told her to lie on the floor.

"I'm not having my baby on the floor," she yelled and found her way to the couch. "I have to push!"

"No don't push!" I yelled.

"Don't tell me not to push!" She said and looked at me crazy. I told her to hold on because I had to call 911. I started to reach for the house phone that was next to the couch where Doris was now laying with her legs open.

"No it's too late the baby is here!" I got on my knees at the couch. She asked me if I was ready because she's about to push.

"I guess?" and in one hard push I was holding my beautiful little baby girl in my arms. She wasn't even crying nor was she all icky and bloody. Doris was looking down at us.

"What is it?" she asked me.

I was so shocked and amazed at the miracle that just happened.

"Doris you just had a baby on the couch!"

"What is it?"

"I can't believe you just had the baby on the couch," I kept saying to her.

"Is it a boy or a girl?"

"We have a daughter!" She started crying tears of joy as my newborn daughter laid in my arms quiet and content. I reached down for the house phone and finally dialed 911. The lady on the other end of the line asked me a million questions and then gave me instructions. She told me to grab a shoe string and tie it very tight about six inches from the baby's stomach around the umbilical cord. Then she said to lay the baby on the mother's chest and cover them up to keep the baby warm. As soon as I was done tying the shoe string and covering them up, there was a knock at the door. I opened the door and I saw those familiar flashing lights and I could hear the sirens from the ambulance. Only this time they were there to take my naked newborn baby girl to the hospital, not my mother.

After my daughter was born, we needed to move. It was getting real tight in that little apartment. Luckily,

Doris' grandmother had a house on 41st and Vermont that she rented to us. It was one of those big houses.

It was old and needed a lot of work but we loved it. We really appreciated having our own space. It had a big backyard and a nice size front yard. We were two block from the Coliseum. At that time it was the home of the Los Angeles Raiders.

Everything was going good at work until Doris wrecked our car. I started riding my bike to work. I used to cycle with Troy before I had my driver's license. It was just a fitness hobby but it kept me in-shape. I kept my nice 14 speed Nashiki bike from when I was fifteen years old. That ride to LAX airport from our house in LA was a long one. I would be too tired to work once I got there. That would interfere with my job performance. I would be sluggish and it showed. I got a couple of warnings about my job performance but nothing major. They were obviously getting tired of my work ethics and I knew they were waiting for me to slip up so they could get rid of my young ass. Their opportunity came one day, I was riding my bike to work and I caught a flat tire. By the time I got to work they had my final check waiting for me. I couldn't believe it. I was crushed. My life changing position was terminated.

After I lost what was probably the best job I could have ever had, I called my best friend since the third grade and my partner in crime Troy. We've been breaking into cars since we were kids. We'd steal speaker box, bass tubes, pull out

Kenwood, Sony, or Alpine radios, especially cell phones. We would even take Ray-ban sunglasses that would be hanging from the sun visors. We were pretty good at it too. We went on a rampage breaking into cars taking everything we saw. It was good while it lasted. Until one night we left an underground parking structure for some high rises in Beverly Hills. We had a trunk full of radios, amplifiers, speakers. We even had a couple leather jackets. Two black males in a black car out at the blackest hour of night in Beverly Hills wasn't the problem. The problem was Troy had made a rookie mistake. When we pulled out of the parking structure Troy had forgotten to turn his headlights back on.

So here we were driving, doing the speed limit with our seat belts on, on our best behavior thinking we were getting away with our trunk full of goods and the damn headlights were not on. It was a rookie mistake that landed our asses in the dreadful and deadly Los Angeles County Jail. Since it was our first time in the County after a month of that shit hole ass place, they offered both of us community service. We both jumped on that shit. As soon as I was done with my community service Doris wanted to get me out of L.A. So we decided to move our little family to Tennessee.

My grandparents had just sold our family home in my hood and moved back to Tennessee where they were raised. That's where all my family on my mother's side is from. My grandparents bought a much bigger house in Cleveland, Tennessee for a lot less money. It was on five acres of land. It was sitting on a lake for only half the money they sold the house for in Carson. Of course all my aunts and uncles and cousins followed them out there so we did too. I figured it would be a much better place to raise my family.

I took my last check and I put it down on a used Ford Thunderbird Elan. It had a V-8 5.0 liter engine in it. It was all black with grey interior. I had a trailer hitch put on the back of the car. We packed up a U-Haul trailer and I drove us to Tennessee pulling that trailer across America, it seemed like it took forever. We had fun and enjoyed the sights. Except in Oklahoma we had a scare. We had to run from a tornado. We could've been killed. It was close but we made it out of there in one piece. I didn't know that you're NOT supposed to run from a tornado. You're supposed to find shelter, but I guess it's too late now.

We had God on our side so we were good anyway, there's power in prayer!

When we got to my mom's house in Tennessee, she had tears in her eyes as I walked in her house and handed her-her first grandchild. When she laid eyes on my daughter the look on my mother's face was priceless and something I will never forget. Needless to say, my mother would not let her first grandbaby out of her sight. My mother insisted that we stay with her until I got a job and we were able to get our own place. She lived in a three bedroom apartment with my little sister Michelle and my baby brother Denver, whom we call Tiny Suave. My other little brothers Mikey and Joey were in Arizona living with our dad. It was a little crowded but we were happy to be together. I applied at a temp agency. They would call me a few nights a week to work.

They were back breaking jobs at factories at odd hours of the night but it was work. Then one day my mother's neighbor came over to visit she moved to Tennessee from New York. She told me about a carpet mill that was hiring and she said that the pay was good. She gave me the phone number. I called the next day to make an appointment to go apply. I followed the address up the highway and across the state line to a big carpet mill in Dalton, Georgia. I only drove for forty five minutes but now I was in the middle of the carpet capitol of the world. There were carpet mills everywhere. A week later I got a call to come in for my orientation. The interview went real well. They liked my previous job and how I was young and ambitious so they hired me. They started off at the same amount of money I was making at LAX. The work was much harder. I really had to earn this money and I worked twelve hour shifts, but I loved it. The cost of living was so cheap in Tennessee that we were able to move the first month we got there. We went to a realtor to find a rental property, we wanted another house. One day I came home from work tired as hell. When I walked in the door, Doris jumped in my arms.

"Baby I found it! I found our new home!" Before I could sit down and kick off my steel toe boots, I was being dragged out of my mother's apartment and back to the car. Doris insisted that I go see the house that she so badly wanted to be our new home.

It was 8:30 at night. I got up at 5 a.m. five days a week to work my twelve hour shifts. This was my sixth day in a row because I told my plant manager that I was always down for overtime so he made me his main go to guy for overtime. My checks were fat. I was too tired to resist Doris eagerness so I at least asked her to drive. I was just dozing off to take a quick nap when Doris pulled into the driveway

As I opened my red blood shot eyes and my blurry vision started to clear I could see a beautiful-house with a big front yard. I looked to the left of the house then I looked to the right. Our neighbors were at least fifty yards away on either side of us. I got out of the car and Doris gave me a tour from the outside of the house.

I walked around looking in every window sizing up the house imagining my family all moved in living happily ever after. She dragged me to the back of the house to look in the window to the master bedroom. It was nice and spacious with a bathroom inside it and it looked like there was plenty of closet space, for Doris of course.

I turned around to look at what was possibly my new backyard. It was pitch black dark but I could tell that it was a nice flat grassy big yard I couldn't see where it ended.

"The property line goes back two hundred feet," Doris said.

"Who in the hell is going to cut all this grass?"

"I will if I have to! I really want this house can we get it?"

"I don't know Doris. I haven't seen inside the house yet." Then I asked "How much is it anyway?"

"It's a four bedroom, three bathroom and the rent is only four hundred and twenty five dollars a month!"

"No way!" I said.

"Yes way! The house is only five years old. We'll have an option to buy if we ever decided to own it!"

"Wow that sounds good, but I have to see the inside first before I make my decision."

As we drove back to my mom's apartment I told Doris that I was off tomorrow so she could the real estate lady and make an appointment for noon so I was able sleep in a little. I needed to catch up on some much needed sleep.

"I already have an appointment to pick up the key from the realtor's office at eleven." Then she said, "I'll come back for you at noon so we can take a look inside our new home, OK?" As we parked she asked, "One more thing?"

"Sure baby what is it?"

"Can we celebrate tonight if you're not too tired?"

I smiled and said, "I'm never too tired for that baby."

It seemed like as soon as I closed my eyes I was awakened by Doris straddling me while I was on my back in a dead sleep, snoring with my mouth wide open. I opened my eyes to see that Doris was wide awake, fully dressed and she was dangling a set of house keys.

"It's noon baby! Rise and shine! Let's go see our new house!" She realized that my "Buddy" was fully awake. Doris looked down and pulled back the covers. "Oh wow! Glad to see something is awake. Is it celebration time again?" Without saying a word, I just smiled and nodded my head.

***

We pulled up to the house. It looked even better during the day. The yard looked much bigger too. I did a full walk through of the house. This would be my first time renting something on my own, but I made it look like I knew what I was doing. I checked all the appliances to make sure they worked including the microwave, and the dishwasher. I even made sure the garbage disposer worked. I hit the switch and it scared the shit out of Doris. It was loud, but it definitely worked. The house even came with a refrigerator.

All we would need to get is a washer and dryer and of course some furniture. The carpet was new and the paint was fresh. The best thing was that there were no signs of roaches.

"Well?" Doris hugged me and said.

"I like it."

"I love it! Can we get it please?"

"Yeah fuck it. Let's go for it." Doris reached in her purse and pulled out an application. She already had it filled out completely. She was such a manipulator.

"Here baby all we need is your signature, we can drop off the application and leave a deposit. The realtor said if we submit the app. today then she will have an answer by tomorrow." Doris gave me her special look and said, "Did you say, do it?"

I picked Doris up and I sat her on the kitchen counter. I started kissing my wife. She was so beautiful and spontaneous. I loved that about her. It's baffling to me that we didn't end up with eight kids, one for every year that we were together. I called Doris my wife because that's how we lived our life from day one when we met. Not to mention the full wedding we had. Her family was so religious. We had a wedding out of respect for her mother who is a Minister and her father that is a Pastor. So we had him marry us at their church in Los Angeles on Broadway and 52nd. We didn't have a marriage license, so after the wedding Doris' father was confused when he asked us for the paperwork so he could sign it to make the whole ceremony official. We told him that we just wanted to be married in the eyes of the Lord. Neither of her parents were too thrilled about that, but it was what it was. It must have worked because they finally left us alone about being fornicators.

After we christened the house we rushed over to the realtor's office to drop off the application and a check for the deposit. The next day after work when I got to my mom's house, Doris was at the door to greet me with a big beautiful smile as always. I could tell that she was very happy in Tennessee. Tonight she was extra happy and she could not wait to give me the good news. She ran down to the car when she saw me pull up and park.

"Hi baby! Did somebody miss me?" I said.

"Always baby!" she said. "Guess what?"

"Chicken Butt!"

"No silly, not chicken butt, we got the house! We have our own place!"

She explained to me that she's been at the new house all day on her hands and knees cleaning and disinfecting every inch of our new place.

"I hope you paid special attention to the kitchen counter top." She smiled.

"Of course daddy."

"Good! I don't want my kids catching your cooties!"

"If I have any cooties then I got them from you Mister!"

"So you've been working hard today?"

"Yes and I love it! I was so excited I couldn't wait. Your mother took me to the house and I gave her a tour! She loves the house! She's happy for us!"

"OK hope you really love it because it's gonna take a lot of work to keep that big house clean, especially with two babies there full time. At least Andre will be in school during the day."

"I got this daddy; this is what I want to do for you and our family. You work so hard all day, you deserve to come home to a clean house with dinner waiting and me and the kids to greet you at the door with lots of love."

"A man could get used to that! I can't wait."

Doris told me that while she was at the house she had the phone line connected and the gas and the lights turned on and she informed me that the cable would be on in three days. Doris said that my mother had just the place for us to fill up our whole house for a good price. She said that we could Rent-to-Own everything that we needed.

"Rent-to-Own? Who does that?" I said.

"Everybody does that out here. She said that everything in her house was rent-to-own."

"Aight let's check it out."

My next day off came so we went to the rental place. They had everything in there that we needed, even our washer and dryer. We picked out everything for our new home.

Everything was falling into place perfectly. My little family was good. We were loving our new environment, especially me. On my off days I would take the wife and kids to my grandparents. Me and the boys would go down to their lake and fish all day. All my aunts and my uncles and my cousins would come by too. My beautiful grandmother would cook a big meal for all of us. My mother would be there with my little sister and my baby brother. Once it got dark we would go back into the house. Doris would put the kids in the TV room in the basement and they would play games and doze off to sleep while the adults would break out the liquor. We would drink and play cards and dominoes, and tell stories while listening to music. Those were precious moments that I wish I had bottled up to revisit every day. Everybody was happy healthy and still alive.

November came and it was freezing cold. A buddy of mine asked me if I wanted to go deer hunting with him.

"Hell yeah! Where do we go?" He said he knew some property that some people owned about fifteen miles away. "When are we going?"

"In a couple of weeks." Then he asked me what kind of bow I had.

"What's a bow?" I told him that I have a 357 magnum, a .22 rifle with a scope, and a 12 gauge Moss berg shot gun.

"We're not about to go do a drive-by in the hood in Los Angeles! We're going to sit and wait for a big buck to walk by and shoot it with an arrow."

"How in the hell are we gonna get that close? Besides, I've never even seen a bow and arrow."

We left my house to go buy some hunting supplies. I bought a Bear 50 lb. compound bow and a 3-D Deer target for practicing and a full camouflage jump suit with a mosquito mask and gloves. I spent over five hundred dollars for everything I needed including my hunting license and deer tags. When I took all that stuff home I kept the receipt in my wallet and I hid all the supplies in the car so Doris wouldn't find out and start asking me a million and one questions.

I practiced every day when I could for two weeks then I called my buddy and we went out deer hunting. He said that we needed to get to the property before sunrise. I was excited so I was up and ready by four am.

He also told me that we might run into wild pigs or maybe even a bear but not to worry because they very seldom attack you unless they're provoked. I wasn't taking no chances so just in case I brought my .357 magnum and I wore it on my hip in its holster. Shit you never know! Just like back home in the hood, the same principles applied, I'd rather get caught with it, then without it. Plus my buddy was an older country ass white boy from the woods. So you know I had to watch his ass too.

We went out on my first of many deer hunting trips. We didn't even see a deer but we had a blast because after a while I got bored and we broke out my guns and started shooting up the country side. I had to show that country boy that this city slicker had some experience with guns, and an excellent aim too.

CHAPTER 13

Suicidal Suave

Thanksgiving was coming up so Doris sister flew out to spend the holidays with us. She was a very pretty girl with a nice thick body and some big ole titties. We went to junior high school together. We actually used to mess around with each other back then. That's how I met Doris. Dana liked our house she said it was nice and she was very happy for us. Tennessee was very different for us three because we were definitely city folks. But we were all loving the scenery. It was nice slow and peaceful. Sometimes too slow so we'd have to pick up the pace a little.

One night I invited my co-worker over to meet Dana so she wouldn't feel like a third wheel. I figured him and Dana would hit it off, he was a cool brother. Me and him became friends because we were both from big cities and had moved to the country for a better life. He was from New York so we had a little in common.

Jason arrived just in time for dinner, Doris and Dana cooked a nice meal for us. The food was great.

Dana and Jason hit it off good so after dinner I broke out the cards so we could play some spades. As I'm shuffling the cards I asked Jason what he brought to sip on.

"I put it in the freezer to stay cold," Doris said.

"Grab it out of the freezer before the bottle bust babe!" I told her.

"No need to worry this stuff doesn't freeze," Jason said.

"Oh shit what you bring homie?"

"You ready for some?"

"Hell yeah! Let's drank!"

Doris jumped up, grabbed the bag out of the freezer, then she got four glasses and came back to the table.

She pulled out two medium sized bottles that were all black. They looked like Remy bottles and another bottle.

"Oh shit! I've been waiting to try this shit! Good call Jason," I said.

"Hold up Fam! You've never tried Sisco before?"

"Not yet, but I am tonight!" Then I said. "Why you only bring these two little ass bottles?"

"Because it don't take much of this stuff." He told Doris to pour just a little in each glass.

"I'll pour my own. I'm a drinker; it's in my blood homie!" I said.

Then while Doris was pouring their glasses with a little of the orange flavor, I grabbed the grape bottle and broke the seal and poured myself a full glass. I smelled it. It smelled like grape gasoline and it tasted as bad as it smelled. After a couple of swigs, the taste wasn't that bad. By the second hand of spades I poured myself another glass. I guess they were big glasses because that second shot emptied that grape bottle. By the third hand they were still sipping on their first glass of that orange flavor. By then I had finished the grape bottle all by myself. I wanted to try the orange kind, so I poured what was left into my glass. I took a sip and it tasted like Kool-Aid so I downed the whole glass. By our fourth hand, Jason looked at me and asked me if I was alright.

"Yeah I'm alright, are you alright? This is my house Cuzz! Don't be asking me if I'm alright my nigga!" Doris and Dana looked at me, then they looked at each other and they got scared. I started tripping.

I stood up at the table and I threw my cards towards Jason. I was cursing and yelling. Then I stormed out of the kitchen and into our bedroom. When Doris came in five minutes later to check on me, I was sitting at the foot of the bed crying with my shotgun on the floor standing upward with the barrel under my chin. All I remember was that Doris screamed.

"Baby what are you doing!" Then she started crying and started begging me. "Please stop! Don't do this to me and the kids!"

I looked at her as waterfalls of tears ran down her beautiful face. In a split second, the thought of what this would do to her and the kids stopped me and I laid the shotgun on the bedroom floor. Doris grabbed me and hugged me tight as hell. She thanked God for not letting the worst happen. In a matter of a few minutes that Sisco had me happy, mad, paranoid, and then depressed. Now I see why they used to call Sisco "Liquid Sherm." Needless to say I never drank that shit ever again.

I slept all day the next day. That Sisco had me gone! When I finally came to, Doris was walking into the room with a food tray with soup and some oyster crackers on it. She just started shaking her head as she came over to my side of the bed.

"Sit up!" I sat up with one of my eyes still closed. She sat the tray on my lap and she kissed me on my forehead. "Good afternoon."

"Afternoon!"

"Yes, it's almost four PM." Then she asked me. "Do you know what you did last night?"

"Yeah, I whooped some ass in spades, and I drank three glasses of that nasty ass Sisco."

"No! You drank that whole bottle of grape by yourself and half of the orange bottle too!"

"Yeah, but those bottles was small. It wasn't even enough for all of us!"

"Yeah because you drank it all!"

"Yeah and it was some weak ass cheap shit, it only made me pass out!"

"No baby! You blacked out! The way you were acting last night was so embarrassing I don't even know what to say. You don't remember anything at all?" Doris said

"No babe I don't."

"So you don't remember putting a loaded shotgun to your head and almost pulling the trigger?"

"Hell naw! I would never do a dumb ass thing like that!"

"Oh yeah? Well you did last night!" That's when I looked on the wall and I noticed that the only thing hanging on my gun rack was my compound bow.

"Where's my .22 rifle and my 12 gauge shotgun at?"

"I had Jason take them with him when he left. After that stunt you pulled last night, the only weapon you can have in this house is that bow and arrow!" She said. "You need to call Jason and apologize for the way you talked to him last night, and for throwing your cards at him. All he was trying to do was make sure you were ok and you blew a gasket and went the hell off on him."

"He's a big boy he'll get over it! That's my nigga. He knows how I be trippin' and shit. What about

Dana is she ok?"

"Yeah you know her crazy ass is fine. But she said if you would've came near her while you were yelling and cursing then she said that she was gonna crack you in the head with one of those Sisco bottles!

You know Dana don't play!" She said. "Shit as crazy as you were looking last night I was about to grab a bottle too! Remember there was two of them."

"The way my head is pounding right now, I'm starting to wonder if ya'll did hit me with one of those bottles last night, or maybe even both of them!"

I was rubbing my temples with one eye still closed as I was listening to my heart beat. My head felt as if was about to explode when Doris stood up looked at me with a little smirk. "Eat your soup, Imma start dinner," then she giggled as she left the room.

I went to work the next day. Jason was in the break room when I got there. As soon as I saw him, I walked over to him and he started laughing.

"Nigga you was tripping the other night. I thought you was a big alcoholic from Carson,

California?"

"Fuck you nigga! I am! Yo ass bought that liquid crack into my house!" Then I said. "My bad about how a nigga was acting. Doris said I was a little disrespectful."

"You my nigga fam! No need to apologize."

"That's right homie. Now where my damn guns at Cuzz?" We both started laughing our asses off.

"Speaking of that I need to holla at you about something I've been thinking about. I need to know if you're down."

"What's up? Whatever it is you know I'm down, especially if it's about some money."

"That's exactly what it's about son." Jason told me that he needed to make some extra cash and that he's been scoping out a couple spots that would be a quick and easy come up.

"I see that you have the artillery we need. What spots do you have in mind?" He explained to me in detail what he had been doing his homework on. Then we agreed to drive by the spot after work so I could get a better idea of what I'm getting myself into.

After our shift was over we both hopped in his car and went over to the location. He pointed it out and I asked him how long has he been watching this spot and to tell me everything he knew about it. He explained to me that he's been checking this place out for the last three months. He said he's got all the bases covered and that it is only one guy in there and the best day to do it would be on a Thursday.

Thursday came and we were ready. Once we got to the location, we both looked around, and then he popped the trunk. We made a quick plan then hopped out the car. We put the little lick down with no hiccups. We were in and out of there in less than two minutes. Everything went smooth and easy. We got back to my car. I left the rifles with him and I took the money in my car. Then I followed Jason to his apartment so we could split our loot that we just made hella quick. We counted the money and we got ten thousand. That was good for a two minute job. We split the money up and we were hooked! That day Jason became more than just my coworker because when you put your life, freedom, and trust in somebody else hands, and they prove themselves to you in that way, then there's a special bond with that person that's thicker than blood. Jason went from coworker to lifelong friend. Pulling off licks like that was something that was not new to me. The money was cool but that money went fast. You spend it how you get it, fast!

The problem was the high that I got from putting in work like that. Money is the worst drug out there, and I had just relapsed. That was the main reason I moved to Tennessee to get away from my boys that I was getting money with like that. I had a family, so I was trying to stay out of jail. The last time I went to jail was right after my daughter was born. To me it's because of the fact that I have a family now is why I needed to get money. But Doris shut that down as soon as I was released from that raggedy ass Los Angeles county jail. So I kept me and Jason's little part time job away from Doris as any real nigga should. Never pillow talk with your girl! That's a No No!

About a week later I asked Jason to show me the other spot he had ready for us. We met up in the area of the second location. We drove separate cars. He said this place had two guys in there but he said it should have twice the money.

We walked in the spot and I drew down. Jason took the two guys in the back while I gathered the loot. It was too easy. As soon as I put that big ass shotgun in their faces, they screamed like some bitches. They ran in the back on Jason's command. He locked them in the bathroom and we walked out laughing our asses off as we got in our separate cars.

Jason took both guns and I took the loot. We met at Jason's apartment to find out that we passed for twenty thousand this time, each! We were geeked up. I was high off my addiction.

"This calls for a celebration." Jason said.

"Hell yeah! What you got to drink homie?"

"Let's go get a bottle of Sisco!"

I stopped playing with my money, and I looked at Jason with my Ice Cube mean mug face. "Somebody got jokes!"

Even though I had a cool amount of money stacked up all I could think about was getting more.

Christmas was only a few weeks away; I wanted to give my kids the best Christmas ever so as soon as I saw Jason again I hit him up. I arrived at work early. I was chilling in the break room eating a bacon, egg and cheese biscuit that I grabbed on the way to work. Jason walked in as I was making a fresh pot of extra strong coffee.

"My New York gangsta! Top of the morning to ya!"

"Top of the morning to you sir!"

"You're just in time for a fresh pot of some Suaves Special Brew!" He looked at the pot as the final drips dropped.

"That's you that's been in here making that lethal ass coffee?"

"You better know it!"

"Look at it! It looks like motor oil!"

"That's right it's 20/50 weight to be exact. You drinking with me right? I poured you a cup but you gotta come dress it up yourself because I don't know how you take it. I like mine with creamer only, nice and light just how I like my women!"

"What women? Yo ass is married, B! Doris got yo ass on lock down status son! That's my word!"

He started laughing as he finished adding a ton of sugar to his lethal cup of Joe.

"I see you got a dose of the early morning funnies. Just come and sit yo ass down, we need to chop it up before the rest of the shift starts coming in."

"What's good fam?"

"You tell me? This is gonna be my family's first white Christmas so I want it to be real special!"

"Damn Suave, we up, Let's chill for a second yo!"

"Fuck that my nigga! Chillin is for suckas!" I was feigning and I needed a fix. "It looks like Imma have to buy a new car."

"What happen did you wreck your Thunderbird?"

"No nothing like that. I've been coming to work early all week because that old ass Thunderbird is falling apart. It's making some fucked up noises that coming from underneath the hood!"

"Well go get yourself another car! You have enough money to go get whatever car you want!"

"I can't just go out and buy a new car, Doris will be on my ass wondering where I got the money from! She's already trippin because I paid off the Thunderbird."

"How'd she find that out?"

"I sent a cashier's check to the dealership in Cali and they mailed me the title and of course Doris nosey ass opens my mail!"

"Well that's your wifey boo."

"Shut up Loc! I need to figure something out quick! That car is not gonna last too much longer."

"How's your credit?"

"I have a few cars paid off already. I have white peoples credit."

"Well use your good credit to get the loan and trade that damn T-bird in towards the down before it dies on you. Then pay your payments with your lick money. Then Doris won't suspect a thing."

"Yeah that sounds like a plan. Good looking out my New York genius!

CHAPTER 14

The Bank Heist

That Saturday morning I woke up, I told Doris to get ready because we were going car shopping.

"Why? The car we have is still running," she asked

I told her that it was only a matter of time before the Thunderbird quit on us, then I could be late for work or worse, I could miss a day or two and possibly get fired. She suggested that we put the Thunderbird in the shop. I told her that pulling that heavy trailer all the way from California wore out the transmission and that

I had an estimate done and they wanted twenty five hundred to rebuild it.

"Wow that's a lot!"

"I know babe, it wouldn't be worth it!" I said

"How are you gonna be able to afford a new car?" I explained to her that if we hurry before the

Thunderbird breaks all the way down then we could use it as a trade in for the down payment, plus my A-1 credit!

"Are you sure were not getting in over our heads?"

"No baby, I got this, don't you have faith in your man?"

"Of course!"

"OK then. Let me take care of this like I take care of everything else."

"OK daddy! I'm sorry for second guessing you. You are a great provider!" Then she said. "Imma get the kids ready so we can go car shopping!"

We drove from dealership to dealership looking at a bunch of cars until we found the car we wanted. It was a nice four door pearl white Lexus. I test drove the car and fell in love. The salesman said he would work out a good deal for me. I asked him if they take trade-ins. He said of course and he asked me if I owed anything on the Thunderbird.

"Great! Let me check out the car and let you know what I can give you towards the Lexus."

"Sounds good here are the keys."

"The car looks good but the transmission is slipping."

"That's part of the reason I'm car shopping. I live here in Cleveland but I work in Dalton, Georgia."

"Wow that's a bit of a drive. You must work at one of those big carpet mills?"

"Are you a member of their credit union?"

"Yes of course."

He told me that if I go through my credit union then I would get a much better interest rate.

He also said that it would be a lot easier, and that he could print everything out for me and I could take to my credit union and then we could go from there.

I was at my credit union as soon as they opened Monday morning. The loan officer called me into her office and we went over the papers. I filled out the application as she went over the details about the Lexus.

She said "This is a very nice car for such a young man. It's kind of pricey too."

"Yes and I deserve it! You have no idea of the work I've put in, in order to afford this car."

"Yes I do!"

"You do?"

"Yes, you have direct deposit with us, I'm looking at your earnings on my computer screen right now, and the hours that you work are quite extensive! I'm noticing here that you hardly spend your money or make withdrawals. The way you're able to save money is pretty impressive. Don't you have a wife and three kids?"

"Yes but we get by with bare necessities. My wife is very frugal."

She ran my credit and as she did her phone rang. She answered her phone and she asked the person on the phone how she can help them.

"Oh you're trying to make a withdrawal so you can buy a car? OK."

She got on her computer and asked the person their name. She repeated the name as she keyed it into her computer. It's a woman's name. Then she asked the lady on the phone for her account number. She says the number as she keys it into her computer. It's an easy number. So I remembered it and the lady's name. As the information was coming up on her screen, the printer stopped printing my credit report.

I heard the loan officer say "OK here we go Mrs. Smith; I see that you have fourteen thousand available in this account." Then she says "I will note your account that you will be coming in today to make a large withdrawal so that you will have no problems when you get here." She hung up the phone and apologized for the interruption. She turned to the printer and she looked at my report.

Her eyes got very big. "Oh my, you have excellent credit!" She asked, "How are you so young and you already have so many cars paid off?"

I didn't want to tell her that I totaled my first car by falling asleep at the wheel almost killing my wife and our unborn baby girl, and that my wife totaled a couple of cars. So between us both we've had our insurance pay off three wrecked cars, plus I had just paid off the Thunderbird. So my credit is crystal clear and squeaky clean.

"I don't see us having a problem loaning you the money for this car Mr. Dugais. It's gonna take us a couple of hours to cut your check. Can you come back around 2 PM? We'll have the check ready then we'll just need your signature."

"That's perfect! I'll leave you to it so I can go and call the dealership and tell them the great news!"

I stepped out of her office and over to where the bank tellers were. I walked to the area where the withdrawal slips were kept. I grabbed one and I quickly filled it out with the information I just heard in the office. First I put the account number, then Mrs. Smith's full name. I made it out for thirteen thousand, nine hundred and ninety nine dollars. As I'm driving I called home.

"Hi baby, how did it go at the credit union?"

"Better than I thought."

"You got the loan?"

"Yep! I have to pick up the check in two hours." Then I asked Doris if her sister was around.

"Yes baby she's right here."

"Good! Put her on the phone please, it's important." Dana got on the phone.

"Hey Sisco!"

"Ha! Ha! Very funny sis."

"I'm just messing with you, what's up bro.?"

"It's all good. I'm calling because I got something up for us, are you wit it?"

"Hell yeah! Whatchu got up bro?"

"I just need you to be ready in fifteen minutes. I'm on my way to pick you up." I told her dress up a little, like she's going on a job interview.

"Bro I don't want no job."

"It's nothing like that! You trust me right?"

"Of course I do!"

I went and got Dana and went back up to the credit union. I explained everything to her and why I needed her help. I told her everything was good to go and that all she had to do was give the teller the withdrawal slip and collect the money, no questions will be asked. We just needed to hurry up before the real Mrs. Smith gets there.

We pulled up to the credit union. Dana walked in looking the part. It was a little crowded because it's lunch time. She walked up to the teller and handed the man on the other side the withdrawal slip.

"Good afternoon Mrs. Smith! I see you're making a large withdrawal, can I see some identification please?"

"I called in advance to notify the bank that I'd be coming in so the money would be ready."

"Yes Mrs. Smith we've been waiting for you. But it's policy that you show us some form of identification."

"I'm in the middle of buying a car, I was rushing and I've seemed to have left my license at the dealership. Besides when I spoke to your manager she assured me that I would not have any problems."

The teller looks at the computer screen. "Yes I do see that you are making the withdrawal for the large amount to purchase a car."

Then he looked at Dana's triple D cup cleavage that was peeking out just enough from her blouse and her sexy smile. "How would you like your bills Mrs. Smith?"

"Large please." While the teller counted out the money Dana placed her purse on the counter. Then the teller slid her three big envelopes full of large bills. She stuffed them into her purse and grabbed a few lollipops. "Thank you very much, have a nice day."

Dana walked towards the door she saw security headed her way. They walked right passed her. Dana made a sigh of relief then she heard the lady at the teller a couple windows down.

"What do you mean I only have one dollar in my account? I called less than an hour ago and I had fourteen thousand dollars available!"

"I'm sorry Mrs. Smith but I'm showing that you already made that withdrawal today."

"That's impossible!" As Dana walked out smiling, I saw the security guards headed towards the commotion. Then I saw the teller waving them down and pointing to the now very hostile and irate Mrs. Smith.

The next morning, I pulled up at work and I saw Jason getting out of his car. I pulled up next to him and I laid on the horn. Jason jumped out of his work boots. He was pissed as he looked into the window of the pearl white car that he didn't recognize until he saw his partner in crime behind the wheel. I was laughing so hard that I had tears in my eyes. I parked my new baby and hopped out.

"Top of the morning scary Cuzz."

"Yo, B! You play too much, son!"

"Shut your scary ass up Loc!"Jason walked up and we both started laughing. "What's up my real nigga! You alright?"

"Yeah Son. I'm wide awake now thanks to that stunt you just pulled." He finally looked at the car. "Damn Son! You doin' it like this now? Nice wheels, kid!"

"Yeah my nigga! I took your advice and I picked this up yesterday."

"I didn't know you was gonna get a Lex-bubble, is your credit that good or did you rob a bank?"

"Both."

Jason stopped in his tracks and he looked at me. "Yo Son! You went out and knocked off a bank and you didn't cut me in?"

"Look my nigga you was preaching to me about wanting to chill and you wanted to fall back for a minute so.... Besides it was a last minute spur of the moment situation."

Jason was pissed but he got over it quick. That's what real niggas do! Bitch niggas act like hoes and hold grudges!

At lunch time I grabbed Jason and I said, "Come on homie lunch is on me. We taking my car. Let me show you the leather interior in my new baby."

"Hell yeah! Let me check out your new wheel, God." We walked back into the break room with our

BBQ plates that we ordered from up the road.

As we started grubbing on our food the secretary from the front office came in.

"Hey boys, how my city slickers doing?"

"Fine and you?" We both said.

"I'm fine; I just have a new memo to post on the bulletin board."

"A new memo? We're not doing layoffs are we?" I said.

"No nothing like that. It seems some little lady robbed our credit union yesterday so they faxed us over this wanted poster of her picture and a description."

My eyes got big as the rims on my Lexus. "What? How did that happen?"

She said "I don't know all the details but they say she just walked in and the teller gave her the money. She didn't even have a gun."

"Wow is it that easy?"

The country ass secretary with the strong backwoods drawl she said, "I know. I wish I would have thought of it myself; I could use some extra Christmas cash right now! I need to get some presents for my youngins!

Only three days left till Santa's coming to town, hope ya'll boys are ready. But if not, I reckon all you have to do is find this girl. There's a number to CRIME STOPPERS right here. They're offering a twenty five hundred dollar reward for any information leading to her arrest."

The secretary pinned up the poster and walked out the break room. As soon as she was gone me and

Jason jumped up and rushed over to the bulletin board. Jason's jaw hit the floor as he stared at the picture of the girl that he's been dating for the last six weeks.

"Damn Son! You really did do a bank lick! I thought you were bullshittin."

"Nigga I told you I wanted my wife and kids to have the best Christmas ever! This is our first white

Christmas, plus I'm not trying to be broke because I bought a car. My next step is to buy us a house."

"Yeah but you've got your sister involved now, and possibly some prison time!"

"Nigga shut yo bitch ass up! Only people that know about this is me, you, and the girl that's on that poster. I know she ain't tellin on herself! I damn sure ain't talkin!" Then I looked at Jason. "I know you not about to say shit, right nigga?"

"C'mon Son! You know your ace nigga is solid, B!"

"Alright then there's nothing to worry about then is it!" Then I said. "Besides look at that picture.

It's all blurry and shit. It doesn't even look like Dana! Right? These crackers think all us niggas look alike anyway."

CHAPTER 15

Christmas

Tragedy

A couple hours after lunch I heard my name over the P.A. System, I was being paged to the break room. I had an emergency phone call waiting on the payphone. I stopped my machines and I hurried to take the call. Jason was there, he had been getting some coffee when the phone rang.

He was standing there holding the phone. "It's Doris and she's crying." My heart dropped. Jason handed me the receiver.

"Doris?"

"Baby you have to come home right now. We have to leave town!"

"Baby I know! I know! Let's not panic!"

"You know? How could you know?"

"Because I set the whole thing up, it was my idea."

"What? So you're telling me that you set it up?"

"Yes baby, I did it for us, so you and the kids can have a nice Christmas."

"So you had my brother shot?"

My jaw dropped and I was in total shock. "What? What are you talking about Doris?"

"What are you talking about?"

"Wait a minute babe, back up, start over. What happened?"

"My mother just called. My brother has been shot and they don't know if he's gonna make it!"

I said "Oh my god, baby. I had no idea. I'm so sorry boo. I'm leaving work right now! I'm on my way baby!"

I hung up the phone and Jason said, "Is it Dana? Is everything OK?"

"No it's not Dana, and no everything is not OK. It's Tony, Doris and Dana's brother, he's been shot, and they don't know if he's gonna make it. I gotta let the plant manager know that I have to leave."

"Just go let him know that you had to leave, we'll see you in the morning son."

"No we're leaving first thing in the morning."

"What? Are you serious yo?"

"Yeah man I'm driving us to Cali. We have to before there for Doris' brother. Tony and Doris are very tight so I know she'll take it hard if he doesn't pull through. This shit is crazy my nigga, but what's crazier is that Tony's birthday is in two days."

Jason said, "That is crazy."

"Yeah and there goes our first white Christmas."

I got home in record time. When I walked in the house Doris was balled up on the couch in fetal position crying uncontrollably. Dana was rubbing her back as tears ran down her cheeks. The kids were staring and looking confused. Kristin waddled up to me, I picked her up and I kissed her on the cheek. Kristin looked at her mommy and pointed and said, "Mommy crying, daddy look, mommy cry." I looked at Dana.

"How is he?"

Dana shook her head. "Mommy just called, Tony didn't make it."

I put my daughter down and I went over to the couch to hold my wife. I knew my wife was in tremendous pain, I knew how much she loved her little brother and how he loved her. The little time that I knew Tony I witnessed a true brother and sister bond. We all used to kick it back in LA. They laughed and smiled every time they were together and they had each other's back, Doris didn't just lose her brother that day, she had just lost her best friend.

I barely got any sleep that night. Doris was up packing while I took little cat naps. I would wake up every hour on the hour checking for my beautiful wife to be snuggled up under me like we always slept, but she wouldn't be there.

Then I woke up and I found her on her knees hunched over a suitcase weeping softly quietly trying not to wake me. I walked over to her and got on the floor to hold her tight, and as soon as I had her in my arms she broke down. I never have seen anyone cry so hard in my nineteen years of living till that day. I just held her and rocked her till she cried herself to sleep. We slept right there on the floor that night. I was sitting up with my back to the foot of the bed. I was holding Doris while she was sleeping at the very spot that not too long ago I had my 12 gauge shotgun to my head. It seemed like it took forever for morning to come. Once it did, I woke up and the house was quieter than ever. It was 8 a.m., by this time I'm usually at work. I pictured the house being loud and over ran by my three screaming and very demanding little kids. As I was thinking, my daughter banged on our bedroom door screaming. "Mommy eat, eat!" Doris instinctively opened her eyes, sat up, and hurried to the door. As she swung it open, all three of the kids were standing there and they said, "Mommy can we have some pannycakes?" Doris bent down and gave all three of them a hug.

"Good morning to you too!"

"Good morning mommy! We love you!"

"I love you too." Then she said, "Now go give your daddy a hug and tell him good morning too while I go make us some pancakes!" As soon as Doris said that Andre and Poche' jumped on the bed. I grabbed the comforter and covered up. Both of them attacked me by jumping on my head yelling, "Good morning dad get up mommy making us pannycakes!"

Kristin couldn't get on the bed with all that commotion going on so she just slapped the side of the bed and yelled "Daddy, get up! Daddy eat pannycakes!"

Then as the boys got tired from all the jumping on the bed, I jumped up quick and I threw the comforter off me.

I grabbed one of my pillows and started swinging away hitting Poche' on his legs so hard he did a cartwheel. Kristin waddled fast out the door screaming and giggling. As Andre tried to follow her, I threw the pillow at his head. The pillow hit him so hard he fell into the hallway then he crawled fast into the living room and Poche' ran behind him laughing and screaming.

I got up and washed my face and brushed my teeth, and then I joined my family in the kitchen to eat breakfast. Dana came out of the guest bedroom. "Did ya'll look outside yet?"

As I stood up to look out of the window towards the backyard, I could see snowflakes coming down. They were the size of Frisbees. As I got to the window my mouth dropped, it was beautiful. It was all white everything. It was as if the clouds from the heavens were lying on the ground outside my window as far as the eye could see. Doris and the kids rushed over. They were in awe. I picked up my baby girl.

Then she started pointing, making little finger prints all on the glass saying, "Look daddy Cot Canny!"

"No baby that's not Cotton Candy, that's snow baby, do you wanna go see?" My daughter nodded her head. I told the boys to come on and I opened the back door and I took my kids out into the backyard so we could all go play in the snow for the very first time.

"Get my babies in here before they get sick!" Dana and I laughed at her as we continued playing with the kids in the snow. Next thing I know I felt a "POW!" in the back of my head. I looked back and it was Doris and the kids throwing snowballs at me. I recruited Dana and next thing I know it was war.

Snowballs were flying everywhere. We were all yelling and screaming, running, sliding, and falling while we were having the time of our lives. I'm sure our neighbors were looking through their windows thinking that we city folks were strange for being out at eight thirty in the morning playing in the snow. They could clearly tell that this was our first time ever in the snow.

As our wet bodies went back into the house, Doris rushed the kids into their rooms to change them into some dry clothes. After we were all changed we were finished up breakfast, I sat there reflecting on how nice of a time we just had in the snow, and how for that short period of time we were able to have a little fun in the midst of the tragic loss. It was good to see my wife smiling for that short brief moment.

Even though I knew her heart was still aching with pain. My wife was strong so I knew she did it for the kids while I loaded our car with our luggage, Doris made us some snacks for our two day drive to California. The roads were starting to clear up once the sun began shining through the clouds. I checked the forecast for the 1-40 westbound. It was not looking good but we had to get going. It snowed the whole drive till we got to the interstate 10 in Arizona; it was zero visibility till then. The only thing that I could see was the two tire tracks from an eighteen wheeler that was in front of me. I could barely see its tail lights as I tried to keep up with it. If I were to go any slower the tracks would disappear and we would have gone off the road and crashed, or maybe even gone off a cliff. We prayed the whole way there. It was an act of God that we made it through all of that snow. Here we were driving 30 miles per hour on interstate 40 in a blizzard on Christmas day. Dana, Doris, me and our three kids packed in a Lexus like Mexicans. It was the worst Christmas of our lives.

Once we got to Doris parents' house back home in Carson, they were already preparing for the funeral. Doris hugged her mother as she greeted us at the door. Poor Doris broke down in her mother's arms. Her mother was being strong, and she didn't shed a tear. She was a very religious woman and she knew that Tony was in a much better place. Doris father was a printer so he was busy preparing the obituaries. Once they were printed out, they looked like GQ magazines with a very good celebration of

Tony's life with beautiful pictures of him with his kids, him with Doris and pictures with Tony with their mother and grandmother, and even pictures of Tony and Doris uncle that we all used to live with, the one and only Johnny "Guitar" Watson. Uncle John took Tony's death real bad, those two were inseparable. Tony did music and used to tour with Uncle John. He would open for uncle John, Tony was coming up in his footsteps. The funeral was beautiful. I'm sure Tony was looking down smiling from ear to ear. There were so many fine ass women there on Tony's behalf; I thought a cat fight was going to break out at any minute.

But it was very respectful. The re-pass was nice too. Doris' mother cooked some very good food. That's where Doris got her good cooking from. My mother in law had buried herself in the cooking to keep her mind off of the reality. She stayed too busy to even think of what was going on. I found it very odd and unhealthy that I didn't see her cry not once. She's a very strong black woman, plus she was being strong for her family. I only had a week off of work to make it to the funeral so the morning after the service we packed up and said goodbye to Doris' mother, father, and her baby brother and of course Dana. Dana was glad to be back home. She thanked us for our hospitality and for her great experience with the country life.

She even said that one day she may even want to come back to stay. We told her no problem and that she was always welcome.

I looked at my wife as we drove away with her family waving goodbye as she cried looking out the window holding her brother's obituary in her arms, feeling hollow inside. I reached for her hand and she squeezed mine very tight as we turned off their street to head for interstate 10. We took the southern route home this time. I stayed on the 10 to 1-75 then headed north. I thought I'd never get through Texas. That was the longest state I'd ever driven through.

There was no better feeling then being at home. The kids could not wait to get inside to finally be able to have a Christmas. We left the presents and stockings in place so we could open them once we returned to try and make the best of our Christmas fiasco road trip from hell. We went from a snowball fight and being so happy to be seeing snow. To driving in a blizzard for a day and a half straight, and never ever wanting to see snow ever again.

When we walked in the house there was a terrible smell. As I did a walk-through of our house that we haven't been in the last six days. I noticed that the toilets in all three bathrooms were backed up with brown water. The bath tubs and showers had brown water in them too. As the kids were tearing into their presents I grabbed the phone and I called my grandfather. My grandfather told me that after the snow fell it rained for the last few days.

"What does that have to do with my entire house being flooded with sewage?" He told me to go look in my back yard. I went to the window. "What am I looking for?"

"Is it flooded?"

"Yeah! How did you know?"

"How bad?"

"It looks like damn lake! What the hell does that mean Pa-Pa?"

"You live in the country now son, this is not the Carson City life with sewer drainages. You have a septic tank in your backyard and that's where all your sewage goes. It seems like it's full because of your flooding situation you've got in your backyard."

"What am I supposed to do?" He said it's not an easy fix and that I should call that realtor's office and have them get somebody out there to have it checked out. I explained to him that tomorrow was my last day off, and then I had to get back to work so I was going to call them first thing in the morning.

We hung up and I hurried over to my wife and kids. We were happy again for the moment as we handed out our gifts and opened them to see what Santa brought us this year.

The next morning I called the realtors office about our plumbing problem. They apologized for the inconvenience and they promised to have someone out to look at it the very next day. I explained to them that I would be at work but my wife and kids would be there waiting for the plumber. I told them that I have 3 small kids here at the house and it's not healthy for us to be in this house in its current condition.

When I arrived at work, Jason was in the break room attempting to make a pot of coffee.

"Watch out nephew! Let a real "G" make some coffee!"

"Yo "B" I've been missing you, Son! No homo!"

"Yeah Cuzz! It better be no homo!"

We both started laughing our asses off as we gave each other dap. Jason stepped aside so I could make my famous and powerful "Motor Oil Rocket Fuel Coffee."

I caught my boy up on my very wild and emotional week that my little family had just been through. I even told him about the new problem at the house.

"Damn kid! When it rains it pours right?"

"Hell yeah, enough is enough!" Then I said, "First the car, then Tony, now the house. They say they come in threes."

"Speaking of the car, how did it drive?"

"Like a dream. Almost too comfortable! I loved it!"

On my lunch break I hurried to the lunch room to use the payphone to call home to see how the plumbing situation was coming along.

"I knew you were gonna call on your lunch break, I've been waiting here with the plumber."

"Why didn't you just call my job babe?"

"No it wasn't an emergency so I didn't want to get you in trouble. You just got back to work today baby."

"Well put the plumber on the phone I'm curious to see what he has to say."

"Oh yeah? It's a shocker! Wait till you hear this."

"Hear what?" The plumber got on the phone and he explained to me that he's been out to that house numerous times and that we are the third family that he's seen here in the last 2 years. He said that every time it rains heavy and floods, he's called out to that house and that it's been an ongoing problem since the house was built five years ago. He said that the way they built the house and installed the septic tank is all wrong and that it's been a problem since day one. I could not believe my ears. Our little dream home was going down the drain, literally! He said that he could work on it and that we would have a temporary fix but we should start looking for another place to live unless somebody was willing to redo that septic tank all over again.

I thanked the man for his honesty and I spoke back to Doris. I told her to let him finish up there at the house and when he's done to pack up the kids and go to my mom's house and get them bathed and cleaned and that we were going to stay with her till we get our house situation cleared up. Then I told her to call the realtor and tell them we know about that "Money Pit" house that they moved us into and that they needed to make it right, immediately!

I hung up the phone shaking my head in disbelief. When I turned around my ace nigga was standing there with two orders of fish and chips from Captain D's.

"Here you go, son."

"Thanks but I just lost my appetite."

"What? You? This must be serious!" Then he said. "Sit down fam and tell me what happen now."

"It's that damn house! They built it wrong! That plumbing problem has been an ongoing thing since it's been built. There's no way of fixing it unless we damn near rebuild the house! I have Doris packing some clothes and going to my mom's house. We're gonna stay over there till they do something about that house or imma sue that damn company!" Our dream home was all of a sudden A Nightmare on Elm Street.

CHAPTER 16

HIV Positive

Two days later, the realtor's office called us to say that they fixed the house and that they even had a cleaning service go over and they scrubbed, cleaned, and disinfected every inch of our home. She said that the house has never smelled better. I thanked her and I explained to her that we cannot ever have that problem again. If so then we would have to break our lease. She understood fully and she assured me that if we had any problems at all then she would not have a problem refunding our money back if necessary.

We hurried home to our house. Being at my mom's apartment for those two days made us really appreciate our own space even more. Plus it was New Year's Eve. We wanted to bring in our new year in our home. It was mandatory that we bring it in "LA Style."

In Carson, California and in Los Angeles period, New Year's Eve was the night that you broke out all your new guns, and artillery to test them out and or to just shoot off your automatic weapons to let everybody on your block know, don't ever try to come rob their house. Plus it was a good excuse to let off some steam. The big difference with where we lived now was that going into your front yard and letting off a few hundred rounds was totally legal. I called my little brothers and my cousins to come over so we could do our thang, and when midnight hit, we set it off like Queen Latifah!

We were in my front yard shooting off rounds for about thirty minutes straight. Then we went out to the street and we lit about two hundred dollars' worth of fireworks. We were drinking laughing and having a blast. That was a crazy and wild night.

The next morning I woke up with a hangover out of this world. As I opened my eyes my beautiful wife was sitting up looking down at me and she was crying. She had been up staring at me all night.

"Hey you, what are you doing?"

"Just looking at you."

"Do you always watch me while I'm sleeping?"

"Yep every night."

"And why is that?"

"To make sure you're OK." Then she said. "Do you know I worry about you when you sleep because a lot of times you stop breathing in your sleep? I can't sleep unless you're snoring."

"Why is that, shouldn't it be the other way around?"

"No, because if your snoring then I know you're alive."

"Wow, is it that bad?"

"Yes baby, you stop breathing and you start choking on your tongue, then I shake you and you start to breathe again."

I took my thumb and gently wiped the tears from her eyes.

"Hey boo, there's no need to worry about me. I'm not dying anytime soon."

"I know because I'm your guardian angel and as long as we're together you will make it through the night." I thanked my wife for her beautiful and very sweet gesture.

"Now go brush your teeth before you kill me with that morning breath."

Doris jaw dropped open, she was shocked and appalled. She covered her mouth, jumped out the bed, and ran into the bathroom and she yelled, "Just for that you're getting cold cereal for breakfast mister!" I started laughing my ass off as I walked to the kitchen and I yelled, "That's cool I love cereal!"

I walked into the kitchen and my three little gremlins were at the table. They had beaten me to the cereal. I grabbed a bowl and poured me some Cinnamon Toast Crunch. I haven't had any in a while. I couldn't wait!

I went to the fridge and I grabbed the carton of milk and I poured the container over my bowl and about two spoonful's of milk came out. Andre and Poche' started laughing thinking that it was funny. "Oh yeah?" Ya'll think that this is funny?"

I threw the empty milk carton away and I went over to the sink and I filled my bowl of cereal with water and I sat at the table with my kids. They were staring at me like as if I was crazy or something.

I told my kids that daddy might look strange eating this cereal with water in it, but we should always appreciate what we have and that we should never waste food. I explained to them that there are a lot of people out there in the world that don't have anything to eat and that we always need to thank God for what we have.

"What's all the commotion about?" Doris walked in and said. I told her that the kids used all the milk and that I was eating my cereal with water to teach the kids that we shouldn't waste food. "That's good!" Then I offered her a bowl so she could join me. "No thanks, I'll just make myself an omelet with cheese, and lots of onions, since my breath is so smelly anyway, right Edsel?"

I said "What about my omelet?"

She said "No that wouldn't be setting a good example for the kids. So just go ahead and eat your cereal before it gets soggy."

I just shook my head and took a spoon full of my already soggy cereal and I said "This year is not getting off to a good start."

Doris started laughing as she started on her little gourmet omelet and whatever else she was whipping up.

Whatever it was it was smelling so good. Then moments later Doris walked over to me and placed a plate on the table with a freshly made omelet, some turkey bacon, and two biscuits with some peach jam on the side. She kissed me on the cheek.

"Here baby, let's start this year off the proper way for my King."

I smiled and I said thank you my queen as she slid the plate and a tall glass of orange juice in front of me.

We were all dressed nice as we hopped into our still new all white Lexus. I love that new car smell.

I can still smell that new leather smell as we buckled the kids in their car seats and seat belts. We stopped at the gas station on the way to my grandparents' house to pick up a case of beer.

That's all we can buy in Cleveland, TN. It's a dry county. It's right in the middle of the Bible belt. The closet place to get a bottle of liquor was thirty miles away, in the opposite direction in Chattanooga. But knowing my alcoholic ass family somebody was making that trip right now. I was sure my grandparents was going to have a bottle of Hennessey stashed somewhere in their house and I was sure my little cousins was going to have some vodka and orange juice and probably some Southern Comfort and Coca-Cola.

We pulled up to my grandparents' house around 1 p.m. We thought we were early but as we got closer to the house and I started driving up the hill towards the driveway it looked like a car show. It must have been ten cars parked in the driveway. We pulled around to the back of the house and all we saw was my little cousin's jaws drop when they saw our new car.

My aunt and uncles were on the back patio playing dominoes and ping pong. Some of my cousins were playing basketball by the garage and everybody stopped and came to check out my new whip. I hopped out and unbuckled Andre and Poche' while Doris grabbed Kristin. I popped the trunk and grabbed the case of beers and everybody cheered. I wasn't sure if it was for my new car or because I had just pulled out a whole case of beers.

I couldn't wait to see my grandparents. They were so special to me. I placed the case of beers on the kitchen counter and I snuck over to my grandmother, who was putting some dinner rolls in the oven, a big hug from behind and kissed her on her cheek.

"Guess who?"

"Shawn! Hi baby! I'm so happy your here!" She said quickly.

"Thank you Mom-Mom! But you know I wouldn't miss this for the world!"

I went over to the sink where the twins were busy washing the greens. First I hugged my beautiful mother and I kissed her on the cheek, then I hugged and kissed my mother's twin, my aunt Joan is my favorite aunt of course because she is my mother's other half. My aunt Pat was my mother's oldest sister.

My poor aunt Patricia had the dirty job of the day; she was outside by the water hose with two red buckets.

She was cleaning the chitterlings. I looked out at my aunt Pat, she didn't look to happy. I called her name and blew her a kiss because I was not going anywhere near those red buckets!

I walked into my grandparents' bedroom to say hi to my grandfather. He was always in his bed watching sports.

"Hey Shawny Shawn! How you doing?"

"HeyPa-Pa! Whatchu up to?"

"Nothing much just relaxing, watching this Lakers game. How's your family doing?"

"Everything is good, and everybody's fine."

My grandfather peeked out his window towards the backyard and he said, "I see that everything must be very fine, that's a nice ride out there. How are you able to afford that Shawn?"

"Come on Pa-Pa you know I work eighty hour weeks as often as I can."

My grandfather looked at me over his glasses and he said "Boy don't forget I raised you, I know you better than you know yourself." Then he said. "Whatever it is you're doing I pray that you do not mess up your beautiful family over it!" The only thing that I could do was look him in his eyes.

There was no fooling my grandfather. He was a very smart and hip man, and yes he did know me better than I knew myself and he still loved me. Both my grandparents loved me even though I was always into trouble. They had a special unconditional love for me, and I loved them for that. They never judged me or turned their backs on me, or sent me away no matter how bad I'd messed up. That love is priceless and unheard of nowadays.

My grandfather sat up and gave me a big hug and said, "Thanks Son. Now go get us a couple of those cold beers I saw you carrying in earlier."

"Yes sir! Coming right up, I'll be right back!"

As I walked back into the kitchen to grab the beers I noticed my Uncle David was all alone sitting at the dining room table. My Uncle David was married to my Aunt Joan. They hadn't been married too long.

Uncle David was a Pastor; he was at the dining room table reading his bible. He is a very humble and quiet man. He was also me and Doris marriage counselor.

"Hi Uncle David. How you doing today? Happy New Year."

"Hi Edsel Happy New Year to you too! How are you and Doris doing these days?"

He was one of the very few people that still called me by my first name. "We're blessed uncle David and we're doing pretty good these days, thanks for asking! I'm just grabbing a couple of ice cold beers for me and Pa-Pa. Do you wanna come watch the Laker's game with us?"

"No, I'm doing some studying right now, but thank you." Then he looked out the sliding glass door to the backyard and he said. "I see that you are blessed. Are you being good nephew?"

"Yes of course Uncle David. I've been working very hard these days." I picked up the two cans of beer and I said, "But thank you for asking Unc." My Uncle David closed his bible and he looked at me.

"Edsel, God has changed your life and he's brought you out here to Tennessee to start over fresh and new He's blessed you with a beautiful family, a good job, a nice house and car. But if you're not living

"Christ Like" then as quick as he giveth God will taketh it all away!" Then he said "I haven't seen ya'll at church lately." Then he said. "You know a family that prays together, stays together."

"Yes Uncle David I do know that, and I promise you we'll be at church this Sunday." I hurried back to my grandparent's room.

"Damn Son the game is almost over! What happened to you?"

"I ran into Uncle David while getting the beers, they were ice cold but not so much now." I passed one of the beers to my grandfather. He looked at me and opened his beer.

"That definitely explains that." Then he picked up the glass that was on his night stand and he passed it to me and he said, "Here, I'm sure you need this shot more than me right now."

I took the glass and I gently swirled the Hennessey around and around then I took the shot of the smooth Cognac. It burned a little going down my throat and it instantly warmed my insides. I quickly chased it with my not so ice cold brew. Instantly, I caught a buzz, and then everything was lovely as the Lakers won the game. By the time we finished our second beer my grandmother came and told us that the food was ready, and that Uncle David was ready to bless the table. Me and my grandfather went into the dining room to join everyone at the table. All the food was laid out looking good and smelling great. There was so many of us that we had to all spread out to eat. Doris took all the little ones down to the basement and put them in front of the TV and let them eat down there. The bigger kids ate out back on the patio.

Most of the adults ate at the dining room table, and the rest of us ate in the living room sitting on the couch eating off the coffee table. Doris and my big cousin Jasmine were eating on the other side of the living room, chit chatting about whatever girls talk about. All I knew was after I took my first bite of those delicious chitterlings Doris wouldn't come near me. Doris fixed me a ginormous plate of everything. The food was delicious as always. I tried to get

Doris to try the chitterlings and she refused. We were all laughing at her. She would NOT try them. After my third plate of all that goodness I'd had enough. But I made sure that I left room for some of my grandmother's delicious special banana pudding. She made the best banana pudding in the world! I was careful not to drink anymore because I knew that there would be DUI checkpoints out that night. Before we left, my grandmother fixed us all plates to take with us. The kids were spread out all through the house sleeping everywhere. We finally rounded up the kids so we could leave. My aunts and uncles were leaving too so I said my goodbyes to them as I was going back and forth to the car buckling in the little ones. My poor little daughter snored just as loud as me! I was a little sleepy so to be on the safe side, I let Doris drive home.

Before Doris could get out of the driveway I was passed out. I woke up to Doris kissing me on the cheek after she had parked the car in our driveway. We got the kids tucked away in their beds and Doris put all the plates in the fridge. I asked her to please pack mine up for my lunch tomorrow. I had to be at work at 7a.m. so I took a quick shower while Doris packed my lunch. By the time I got out the shower, Doris was knocked out in the bed. So I quietly crawled in and snuggled up with her being careful not to wake her. We were all tired. We had a long beautiful New Year's Day with my family. I would give anything to relive that very day.

The next day at work was a rough one. I was a little sluggish until I got some of my famous and extremely strong Motor Oil Rocket Fuel Coffee in my system. By lunch I was wide awake. I walked into the break room as my boy Jason was carrying in some delicious BBQ for lunch, he told me to come grab some. He said he had brought plenty to share. I asked Jason why he brought so much food. He said he wanted to have enough to share with his California Fam.

"Thanks, tomorrow is on me."

"There wouldn't be a tomorrow!"

"What the hell are you talking about? Are you off tomorrow or something because as long as we've been working here we have had the same exact shifts."

"Naw fam I'm not off, I'm switching to nights, shift B."

"Night shift what's up with that?" He told me that it pays more and that he could use the extra cash.

I told him that if he needed some extra cash then he knows exactly how we can go get some.

"Naw I'm good on that for a minute, son! Yo ass acting like you on a suicide mission; you need to chill for a minute too! But to be truthful I met this little chick. This shift is conflicting with hers. So imma switch it up to spend a little more time with my new shorty."

"Oh OK, I feel that homie, that's what's up. Congratulations! Who I she? When do I get to meet her? "Soon, don't trip, son."

The pay phone in the break room rung and I answered it, it was Doris.

"Hey baby, how's your day going?"

"It started off a little sluggish but I'm good now, I was just wrapping up lunch with Jason."

"That's good."

"What's wrong baby is everything alright?"

Then she asked me if I noticed anything strange about Jasmine yesterday. I told her not really but I did see that you two were in deep conversation most of the day. I've noticed since Jasmine left her boyfriend in California and moved to Tennessee she's been a little depressed but that's normal.

"Yeah, about her boyfriend."

"What about him? What's going on?"

"The family knows how close you and your big cousin are so they didn't know how to tell you."

Doris explained to me that while we were driving through a blizzard on Christmas day, Jasmine got a call from her boyfriend's mother. She told Jasmine that she was sorry to have to tell her this news on Christmas day but Robert had just died.

"Aw damn, that's fucked up! I see why she's depressed."

"Wait there's more. Roberts's mother told Jasmine that she may wanted to go and get tested as soon as possible because Robert died from Acquired Immunodeficiency Syndrome.

"AIDS!?"

"Yes baby, Jasmine went to her doctor the next day to get tested and her doctor told her that it was gonna take a week for the results to come in. Jasmine has been worried sick ever since she got the news."

I asked Doris when exactly she was supposed to find out. Doris said that my mother just called because

Jasmine told her to make sure she knew so Doris could be sure to let me know. Instantly I thought why Jasmine would want to make sure that I knew. I frantically asked Doris what the results were. All that was running through my mind was that this is the woman who I lost my virginity to. But of course I couldn't tell

Doris that. I could never tell anybody about that night. I'm still not even sure about how I feel about it. I've been confused about sex ever since that experience.

Doris said that Jasmine's results came back "HIV POSITIVE!" I instantly felt weak in the knees. I told Doris that I gotta go and I hung up the phone. Then my mind went crazy! "Do I have it too? Did my own cousin give me the HIV Virus?" All of a sudden I didn't feel so good. I sat down at the break table that I was just eating lunch at. I was so nervous that I was ready to throw up that whole meal. I started calculating and doing the math. I finally added it all up and I realized that Robert came along after Jasmine took my virginity. I stopped shaking and I swallowed my lunch back down my throat. I could finally breathe again. I put my head down and I thanked God. I just sat there the rest of my break with my head on the table praying for my cousin that I loved so much and thinking how that was a hell of a scare and too damn close to home, literally!

When I got home, it was obvious that the news Doris had given me earlier was still very heavy on my mind. I asked Doris how Jasmine was doing. She said that she didn't know, nobody knows because after Jasmine got the tragic news, she disappeared. My grandmother and everybody was afraid that she might have started back using drugs after she got the results.

All I could think was my poor big cousin. Then I wondered what could possibly be going through her mind. Doris saw the look on my face so she hugged me and we said a prayer for Jasmine right there where we stood.

My cousin Jasmine lived for ten more years until she later succumbed to the virus in a Tennessee State Penitentiary. R.I.P. to my big cousin Jasmine I Love You and Miss You Always Cuzz.

CHAPTER 17

On Fleek

One afternoon, Doris was on the phone talking to her mother. Doris told her that she shouldn't have rushed back to work so soon after Tony's death and that she should be at home taking it easy. Her mother assured her that she was fine and that she needed to be at work to take her mind off of everything that she's been dealing with lately. But she did finally admit that all this had her under tremendous pressure. Doris said

"OK" to her mother and told her to call her if she needed her and to maybe even think about coming out to visit us in Tennessee. Her mother thanked her and told her that she'll call her when she got home later on that day.

An hour later, Dana called Doris crying telling her that their mother was on the way to the hospital because she was found at her job on the floor under her desk. They later found out that their mother had suffered a massive stroke.

Doris decided that she needed to be back in California because she knew that a stroke was very serious and that her mother would definitely need her help around the house. So Doris packed some suitcases for her and the kids so they could fly out to California. I didn't like that my family was leaving me but I knew that she needed to be there for her mother. It was a long and quiet drive to the airport but they had to go. I kissed my kids and my wife goodbye. I told Doris to hurry back home to me. She guaranteed me that she'd be back as soon as her mother was able to fend for herself. Then Doris gave me one last kiss before her and the kids disappeared to the terminal to catch their flight.

A couple days after Doris and the kids had left; I was walking into the break room to make some of my famous and powerful Motor Oil Rocket Fuel Coffee and my boy Jason walked in.

"Damn yo! What the deal! You here early fam!"

"Yeah I'm home alone these days. It's nice and quiet so I've been getting my sleep in."

"What? You home alone? Why is that? What happen to the fam?"

I explained to my New York partner that Doris' mother had a stroke and that Doris went to Cali to help her mom's at home and she took the kids with her.

"Yo! My bad homie, sorry to hear that. I hope Ma Duke gets better, fam."

"Thanks homie! It's kinda good they're not at the house right now because the day after they left we had a bad rainstorm and now the whole damn house is backed up again. I talked to the realtors and I told them to run me my money back because I'm moving! I can't deal with that shitty ass house anymore, it's a wrap Cuzz I'm outta there!"

"Damn son, sorry to hear that."

"It's all good. I don't need to be in that big ass house by myself anyway. I'll prolly go stay at my grandparents' house till Doris and the kids decide to come back."

"Damn isn't your grandparents house further away?"

"Yeah but it's just a temporary situation."

"If it's only temporary then why don't you crash at my crib? It's small but since we work opposite shifts it'll work out, because when I'm home you're at work and when you're home I'm at work. Plus my apartment is right here in Dalton only ten minutes away from work! I'm always with my shorty anyway so I'm hardly ever there. We'll split the rent; it'll be nothing, fam!" Then he said, "I'm outta here my shift is over just call me and let me know what's good my dude, peace."

The next weekend I got my little cousins to help me out. I packed up my whole house, I got a U-Haul truck and I put everything into storage in Dalton, GA. I moved a few things into Jason's little studio apartment I gave him half the rent and he gave me a key.

"Here you go homie, only thing I ask is, don't eat up all my food or drink my last beer and we good

fam. Oh yeah, if you bring a little shorty over then make sure ya'll don't mess up my sheets."

"Now homie, I'm married, I ain't even tripping like that."

"You saying that because you haven't been to the park yet."

"The park? What's cracking at the park?"

"That's where everything is cracking! Go check it out, them shorty's at the park be chilling with those small ass shorts on looking sexy as hell. With your new ride, and because you from Cali, they gonna be all on you, God.

No shit? Where's this park at my nigga?"

"Over there off Central on the Eastside."

"The Eastside is the best side!"

"It's poppin from Thursday to Sunday, but it's live up there every night because it's the dope spot too. Fools be over there getting their serve on."

"Now you talkin' my language! Imma need to go check that spot out ASAP."

That next Friday was my birthday; I was trying to figure out what I was going to do, to bring my special day in right! I was off work; Jason was at the apartment with his new little chick. I finally got to meet her, she was nothing like I expected. She was a white girl.

I couldn't believe this street; hood nigga from New York is out here in Klan Land laid up with a white girl. Don't he know that these crackers out here will lynch his New York black ass! I guess he'll soon find out! I wasn't tripping, that was his business as long as the lynch mob don't come fucking with me, then it was all good.

I rode out to the mall in Chattanooga to grab me a fresh all white Birthday Suit to rock for my B-Day.

While I was at the mall, my pager went off. It was Doris. I called her right back because I knew her and the kids wanted to wish me a happy birthday.

After I was done grabbing my all white fit, I headed back to Dalton. I grabbed me a bottle of Seagram 7&7up. I sipped on my way back to Dalton. As my buzz started to kick in, I started to think more and more about the park. It was just starting to get dark. Jason's ass was probably still cup caking at the apartment with his white girl. His shift didn't start for few more hours. I was not about to go home and chill with him and his little white girl especially as clean as I was looking. So I decided to go on and head over to this park and check it out.

I was clean in all white, and my car was clean and all white. I had my 357magnum for the suckers and haters and I had my 7&7 to sip on. I pulled into the park not knowing what to expect. Once I parked and looked around I thought I was back home on Crenshaw Blvd. I reached in my glove box and grabbed my homies, Smith and Wesson. I tuck them into my waistband, grabbed my 7&7, and I stepped out and of course all eyes was on me. I posted up and stayed close to my car in case something popped off. Plus so I could show off my ride. I was aware that I was out of bounds but I was buzzing so tuff that I didn't even give a damn! Besides I always stayed on point! I was just killing time until Jason cleared the apartment then I'm going to take my buzzing ass home and go to sleep anyway.

I was halfway finished with my second cup of drank when this tall skinny nigga walked up to me like he knew me.

"Cali?"

"Yeah cuzz what's up?"

It was my mother's friend's nephew. She's the one that got me my job out here in Dalton. They were all from Brooklyn, New York.

"I thought that was you over here looking clean as a new crispy one hunnit dollar bill."

"Thanks homie, today's my birthday!"

"Oh shit! Happy birthday, son! I've never seen you up here before. You must be here for the freaks?"

"I'm just peeping out-the scene. Whatchu doin here?"

"Shit Son I'm here for the money! This park be poppin like the Marcy's Son!"

"Oh yeah is that right? So you got it poppin over here homie?"

"All you gotta say is you here with New York and you can get your shit poppin too!"

"Now, New York, I ain't tryin to get my hands dirty. That's why I'm talking to you. If I bring you a "zip" at a time, can you flip that for me? You know I can't be trusting these Bama ass niggas round here.

Me and you Fam because your aunt and my mother are tight, plus we both from the big city. I'm from Los Angeles and you're from Brooklyn. Let's sew this shit up! I'll move you up in weight as you show me that you can handle it."

New York said. We set up a meeting for the next afternoon so we could start our operation.

I already knew where I could pick up my work so New York could handle his business. I hope he knew better than to try and play me because I don't play when it comes to my money. Now that I've squared away what I was really went there to do, it was time to scope out some these hoes. It was still my birthday. I still needed a birthday present.

After everybody saw that I was cool with New York, I stopped getting the mean mugs and stares.

Niggas started to chill, and the ladies started to get friendly. But I knew that could be some set up shit, so I stayed on point.

There was one little lady that I had my eye on. She was a stallion. She had a Halle Berry haircut, with some long chocolate legs that were shining off the light from the full moon that night. She had some perfectly round perky ass B-cup breast with the top three buttons open on her shirt showing her creamy chocolate cleavage. She had on some all-white daisy duke shorts. It was as if she was mine already the way we matched.

Her voluptuous Georgia peach ass was rising out the top of her shorts revealing her ass cleavage and exposing her bright red thong straps. She had a booty like Cherokee D'Ass. The side view of it as she was walking my way was incredible!

Damn I really wasn't tripping off taking anything home but I was buzzing and I had just got some good news about making some money and it is my fucking birthday, so I caught her checking a nigga out, so I figured that was my que. I took my finger and called her over to me. The way she was working those long ass legs and with the long sexy crisscrossing strides she was making as she followed my command to come over to me, I just knew she had to have some good pussy marinating between those luscious thick healthy firm thighs. When she finally stopped in front of me, I just looked at her for a second making sure I had the finest girl in the park. That's when looked down at her waist and I realized, damn I could see her ass from the front! Yes, this girl is fine! Happy birthday to me! This girl is the one. My birthday present has arrived.

"What's up beautiful, what is your name?"

"Hi my name is Amber, what's yours?"

"You can call me Carson," and I stuck my hand out. She put her soft tiny little fingers into my hand.

"I've never seen you here before, where you from?" I told her that I was from Cali and that I had just moved into the area and that today was my birthday. As I said that my pager went off again, it's Doris and she's been blowing me up since I've been at this damn park. It's like she knows something, damn women's intuition.

I checked my pager then I put it back on my hip. Amber asked me if I had to go.

"Yeah that was my alcohol paging. I need to go get a birthday drink why don't you come join me."

"Sure whatchu drinking?"

"Seagram's seven and Seven Up."

"That's my drink!"

"Hop in let's go somewhere a little more private."

"OK, but do you mind following me to my house so I can drop off my car and take a quick shower?

It was very humid today."

"Of course not."

"OK I'm in the Blue Maxima; just follow me I live right up that hill."

I followed the Blue Maxima up the hill and I parked behind it. Amber got out of the car and she signaled for me to come in. I got out of my car and we walked to the door. As we walked in she explained to me that she lived with her grandmother and if she was going to be leaving with me then her grandmother had to meet me. She went and got her grandmother. Instantly I could see exactly where she got her beauty from. I talked to Amber's grandmother while Amber went upstairs to freshen up.

She came back down looking much better than before. I could tell that this was the real Amber. She looked much more comfortable in her Pink tank top and Blue jeans. Her jeans fit just enough to make her back pockets useless under all that pressure. She threw on a cute little cashmere sweater and we walked out.

We got in my car and pulled off. I checked my pager to see if Jason had hit me with his code to let me know that he was leaving the apartment. But when I checked my pager all I saw was pages from Doris.

I felt bad and I was praying that nothing was wrong with her mother or my kids, but at the very moment I was enjoying my birthday with this stallion that was in my passenger seat, and damn she was looking and smelling edible!

I told Amber that the 7 & 7 was in the bag in the backseat along with some cups. I told her to make us some drinks while I pulled up to this gas station to fill up and grab us some ice. The drinks were right, the mood was right. All I needed now was for Jason's ass to get the hell out of his apartment. Me and Amber sipped on our drinks while I drove a quarter of a tank of gas out of my damn Lexus.

When I looked at my pager I still didn't see Jason's page but I did notice that it was fifteen minutes till his shift started. So I just figured that my boy had went to work and he had forgotten to page me to let me know that he had left and the Coast was clear. I told Amber that we're going to head over to my boy's spot so we can get a little more comfortable while we kill this bottle of Seagram's Seven.

I pulled up at the apartment and I saw Jason's car but I didn't see Sarah's. Amber and I got out of the car. I closed the door, locked my car, and my pager went off. I looked down at it as me and Amber were walking to the apartment and I saw Jason's code. I figured Sarah must have just taken him in her car and

I'm just now getting the page. Then as me and Amber got to the door it opened up, Jason came walking out with Sarah behind him. Even though Sarah and Doris never met, Sarah knows of Doris because Doris was constantly calling for me on Jason's house phone. She clearly knew that Doris is my wife. So I did not want Sarah seeing me with Amber. This was a bad look.

"Happy birthday!" Sarah said as she walked to Jason's car. I asked Jason how in the hell did Sarah know it's my birthday! He whispered to me that Doris had been calling all night and she and Sarah talked for a while and they kind of became friends. I thought to myself, there goes my manipulative ass Aries wife! She was the master manipulator. She used her charisma to buddy up with Sarah to drain her of any and all information that she could. So then I told my New York player partner to make sure his bitch keeps her mouth shut!

He guaranteed me that he got his girl in check and that I don't have anything to worry about. He told me to go inside and take the phone off the hook because it's going to be ringing any second. I knew Doris was going to be calling soon because she knew that I come in once Jason goes to work.

Then he said for me to go inside and enjoy what's left of my birthday with that sexy ass young stallion that he just saw walk into his apartment. I smiled from the visual I instantly got of Amber with that Cherokee D'Ass booty.

As I'm locking the door, my pager was going off and Jason's house phone was ringing at the same damn time. How in the hell did she do that? I carefully unplugged the phone from the wall jack. I looked down as my pager started vibrated again and it read "Lo-Batt" on the display I just shook my head and put it back on my hip.

As I walked into, the kitchen area I asked my sexy little guest if she was ready for another drink.

She asked if my friend was coming back anytime soon. I told her no that he went to work and that he won't be back for at least twelve hours. "Good! Then make my drink a double while I get a little more comfortable."

I generously poured our drinks making them both doubles. I stirred them, and then I took a sip of mine. It was nice and strong! Exactly what I needed after that run in with Sarah. Knowing Doris she could be on her way from California right now so I better start unwrapping my little birthday present that I just brought home. I turned around and almost dropped our drinks. I looked on the bed and I saw the sexiest site I've seen since my wife went to California. It was my birthday present.

Amber was lying on the bed on a bright red sheet. She was wearing a Victoria's Secret all white cup less bra with the matching all white laced panties with that Cherokee booty hanging all out the back of them. I looked at her young nineteen year old perfectly ripe body. Her perfectly complected skin was glistening like as if she had just rubbed it down with baby oil.

I walked up to the bed for a closer look and to make sure what I was seeing was real. As I looked down to take in the lovely vision, I started at her feet. They were small, slender, pretty, and perfectly done. They were looked as if they were fresh out of an Asian woman's hands. Finally, I got a look at her perfectly round perky titties that I've been dying to see since I first laid eyes on her chocolaty creamy skinned cleavage. Then I noticed something in her hand. It was a teddy bear shaped bottle of honey. She popped the top off and Amber began applying the sweet nectar to the most sensitive and erotic points on her body. She stared at her pretty little baby soft feet. She delicately placed one drop of honey on the top of each foot.

Then she worked her way up and she placed a drop on each of her knees. Then she came up and strategically placed one drop of honey on her inner thighs. Then she stopped mid-way up and she let a drop land just above her panty line right on her hip bone. Then she let a drip drop on her cute little belly button.

Then as Amber looked down between her breasts, she let honey drip between them. She cupped one of her titties with one hand as she let three drops drip on her breast around her areola. After that she gently placed a drop directly onto her nipple, she cupped her other titty with her other small petite hand and she repeated the same sensual process. After that she put a drop on each collar bone, and then finally one on the nape of her neck.

Then I looked down and pointed to the sexy white laced panties and I asked her if she had missed a spot. "No! That already tastes like honey." On those white laced panties I noticed a pretty little blue bow; she had placed it right above her clitoris. Then Amber looked into my eyes and she said, "Happy Birthday. You're twenty years old. I put twenty drops of honey on my body and a bow. Now lick me clean. Then open your present, and lick me dry. Then I want you to fuck me till I squirt. Then I'm gonna use the rest of this honey on you and hopefully by the time I'm done you will be ready for round two. Now let's cheer to your birthday, down these drinks and hurry up and get started because we only have about eleven hours and thirty minutes until our little alone time is over."

That night it went down in a major way. Round two was a close tie with round one, but round three was by far the tie breaker. By sunrise I was spent. I still managed to get up with enough time to put my birthday present back into my car and I returned it. Then I got back to the apartment with enough time to straighten up, shower, and be at work with plenty of time to make my famous extremely strong Motor

Oil Rocket Fuel Coffee. I really needed some after that wild and memorable sleepless night I'd just had. I had a cup with my playa partner before he left to go home. I told my boy all about it as I put some honey in my coffee, one drip drop at a time.

CHAPTER 18

All Hell Breaks Loose

The payphone in the break room rang, Jason answered it.

"Hold on, he's fine, he's right here sis calm down." Jason turned to me as I was changing the battery of my pager and he said, "Yo fam! It's Doris, and she's crying my dude."

I knew I had to think fast or I was caught. I slowly walked over to the phone as I was quickly thinking of what the hell I was gonna say.

"Hello baby, what's wrong? Are you and the kids OK?"

"Me and the kids are fine. What happen to you last night? I've been worried sick! You haven't returned any of my pages since we talked yesterday at the mall! What's going on?"

"Nothing Doris." Why would you start thinking the worst just because you didn't hear from me last night." I'm fine baby."

"Well why didn't you return my pages?"

"My battery on my pager went dead last night babe. I was hanging out at the pool hall shooting pool and drinking beer until Jason left for work then I went home. I didn't want to disturb him and his girl."

"Well why didn't you answer the house phone I was calling it all night? I haven't slept all night because I've been up worried that something was wrong!"

Doris, I had a few beers at the pool hall while I was waiting for Jason and his girl to leave the damn apartment. So by the time I got there I was so tired that I must have passed out. You know better than anybody in this world how hard I sleep baby. I'm sorry boo! I just replaced the battery in my pager just now so I'll be sure to check it all day baby in case you try to hit me later. You just calm down everything is fine baby. Listen I have to start my shift. I want you to get some sleep and hit me on my hip as soon as you wake up. Stop whatever I'm doing and call you right back, OK? You try and get some sleep baby, OK?"

"OK," she said as she was still sniffling into the phone, but I could tell that she was calming down. I told Doris that I loved her then I hung up the phone. I turned to Jason.

"Damn that was a close one. She's cool now I got her to calm down some. But I know Doris; she's no dummy so please make sure your girl minds her damn business, Cuzz!

My boy assured me again that everything was cool. I trusted my boy. I gave him Dap and left the break room to take my ass to work.

That day went by slow as hell because I was tired as hell! I had too much liquor and honey, that shit don't mix too well, I had a slight hangover and I was still semi drunk all day.

As I was clocking out to go home my pager went off. I already knew who it was before I checked it. I looked down at my Blue NEC pager, it was a number that I didn't recognize so I checked the code and I remembered it from last night. It was my nigga New York. I rushed into the break room to use the payphone. As I walked up to it, it started ringing.

"Hey! You told me that you were gonna return my pages! What happen?"

"What are you talking about Doris? I ain't got no pages from you babe!" Then as I'm saying that my pager goes off. I picked it up and I put it to the phone and I said "Do you hear that? I'm just now getting your page babe! So chill out it's not me it's this damn country ass service I got!" I said. "Remember I have Tennessee service and I live in Georgia now. It's nationwide but it still takes me a minute for me to get my pages sometimes baby."

I tried to change the subject by asking Doris how she and the kids were doing. Then I asked her how her mother was doing too. She told me that all was well out there in Cali and everybody is fine and she was fine too, other than her being worried sick about me all night. She told that she was finally able to get some sleep but as far as her mom goes it may take her a little more time to recover so she's not sure how much longer her and the kids would be out there. Then she said after last night that she's been having a bad feeling about us being apart like this. She said that she had a bad dream about me being out here. I told her that everything is fine and that she needed to stop overreacting and being paranoid and that everything was all good!

Doris kept pressing the issue. I told Doris that I was at work and that this was not the place for me to be having this discussion. I told Doris that I would call her when I got home and that we could finish this conversation then. I hurried and dialed the number that was on my pager and my boy New York picked up on the first ring. We arranged to meet back up at the park. I hung up the payphone and I drove straight over to the park to meet up with my New York hustler. We went over everything and from what he told me I stand to make a nice little profit. I told him that I'll meet him same time tomorrow to drop off that work. He told me that he already has a major plug at a bomb price and it's some "Butter!" He told me the price and gave me the run down and it all sounded good so I broke my boy off the bread to go buy the butter so we can get baking. I dapped it up with my New York hustler and I hop in my ride so I could bounce. "Yo New York, come correct my nigga. I got a wife and three kids, so I don't play when it comes to my money. I work hard for my shits so don't try to play me, Cuzz!" My nigga looked me in my eyes and he said, "Yo it's all good fam! That's on "Ma Duke!" I looked at my nigga.

"Auight bet, let's do dis!" I rolled my window up as I backed out of the parking spot and chirped out and headed to Jason's apartment.

I got to the crib and I started eating my fried chicken dinner that I picked up on the way. I popped on the TV to relax for a second so I could take everything in. It's been a long week so I just wanted to chill.

My pager went off and it was Doris. I was going to call her as soon as I was done eating my chicken dinner but I guess my little two piece with a Biscuit was going to have to wait, and of course after last night I wanted some honey on the side. I reached for the phone and I started dialing but there wasn't a dial tone.

That's when I realized I hadn't plugged the phone back into the wall jack this morning when I woke up. As soon as I plugged the phone back into the jack it started ringing. Well I knew who the hell that was, so I answered it. Of course it was Doris going off tripping talking about her bad ass dreams she's been having the last few days and terrible feelings about us being apart. Then she started saying how she wanted me to come back to Cali.

I explained to her the she was seriously overreacting and that I am not about to quit my good paying job to come back to Cali to no job and some high ass rent. She started crying and asking me about her and the kids. I told Doris once her mother was back to herself and she was able to get around and help herself then her and the kids will be back out here and we'll be one big happy family again. She didn't like it but she agreed.

I had her put the kids on the phone. I spoke to all three of them and I told them that I missed them and that daddy loves them. I told them to be good and listen to their mommy. After I was done talking to them, Doris got back on the phone and we talked for a while. We were finally able to have a decent conversation and we ended our phone call on a good note.

I went into the kitchen area and I reheated my chicken dinner. I ate it while I watched a little TV then I hopped in the shower. I got out the shower and I threw on some sweats and a tee. Then the house phone rang. It was my boy Jason. He was checking on me and Doris. I told him that everything was cool and that I may stick around a little longer than expected. I told him that I was going to look into getting my own spot.

I explained to him that it had nothing to do with her at all and that the little stallion chick don't even have my number or my name. I told him that she was just a birthday fling, a simple one night stand. I told him that this time apart let me see that I liked being by myself, and being single. I could have little flings if I wanted to and then drop their asses back off to where I found them with no strings attached no twenty questions just "Blip Blam! Thank You Ma'am!"

"Plus I had a meeting today and I made an investment, feel me? Pm trying to flip this money and build something," I told him, finishing up my story.

My boy understood me as a street nigga but he told me that I should really think about my family first before I make my final decision. He said for me to trade the street life for my beautiful family wouldn't be wise. He confessed that it was starting to feel weird not seeing me with my family.

"Hold up homie! You not getting soft on me are you?"

"Never that!" He said he was just saying that he knew that Doris really loved me, and that I really loved her and them kids and that I should really think long and hard about this first! I told Jason thanks for his input but my mind is kinda made up. I told him that the sad part is that I'm going to miss the kids more than anything. Jason told me that his break was over and that he had to get off the phone and get his ass back to work. I told him I was tired and I was about to crash.

A few days had gone by so after work and I decided to pop up at the park to check on some things.

I saw my New York hustla and I asked him how business was doing and he told me that everything was good money. He said it was going slow but it's going. He had his girl with him. He introduced me to his little fat friend. She said she be up there watching his back at night but she's a nurse during the day.

New York told his little fat girlfriend to give me what she had. The little 5"2, Two hundred and forty five pound girl waddled up to me and handed me what she had. I counted it out and it came out to be about half of what New York owed me.

"This is cool but this is only half, Cuzz." New York said that he wanted me to come back in two days for the rest of my bread. I wasn't trippin because at least I had the money that I initially put in, but something didn't seem right about the other half of my shit. But I didn't say anything I decided to be patient and give my nigga the benefit of the doubt.

I left the park still feeling some kind of way. I stopped off and grabbed something to eat on the way back to the apartment. When I walked in the door my pager went off. I checked my hip to see that it was my wife. I put my food down and I grabbed the phone. As I was dialing Doris number I heard a voice. So I looked at the phone and I said, "Hello?"

"What are you doing?"

"I just walked in the house and my pager went off, so I grabbed the phone to call you before you get to tripping for not calling you right back, but I guess you beat me to it." I started laughing but Doris didn't think it was so funny. That's when I knew that something was wrong.

"We need to talk."

"What about Doris? What's up?"

"I want you to tell me the truth about what's going on between me and you?"

"Nothing's going on babe. Whatchu tripping about now?"

"Something's up and I know it. All I want you to do is be honest so we can work this out and everything will be alright." She said.

"I don't know what you're talking about Doris."

"Just tell me the truth Edsel! Are you cheating on me?"

I knew when Doris called me by my government that this was serious and that she probably knew something. By this time I was tired of all the pages, phone calls, questioning and arguing.

"Yes Doris I cheated!"

"What?"

"I cheated, you asked for the truth now there you go!" It was pure silence on the phone, then I continued. "The night of my birthday when you were trying to reach me I was with someone. I'm tired of lying about it and I'm tired of you asking me about it and basically I'm telling you the truth about it now because I think you should just stay in California with your family and I stay out here with mine and we both move on. This married life is not cool no more. I'm tired of all the arguing and questions, it's over!"

There was complete silence on the phone. All I heard was my heart beating loudly. Then all of a sudden I heard Doris crying trying not to let me hear her. She had put the phone down but I could still hear her. I yelled her name into the phone because I didn't know what she was doing or if she was alright. I yelled her name again, and then I heard her pick up the phone.

"Doris are you OK?"

"Yeah, I'm here, I'm fine, or at least I'll be fine. One day!" She whispered

"I'm sorry but I'm just tired of all the arguing and the bullshit that comes along with the marriage. I tried but it's not working out Doris!"

"What about me and the kids you just gonna leave us out here with nothing?"

"I love those kids, I promise to always be in their lives, all three of them. Those boys are my sons and you know I love my daughter. But I don't wanna argue anymore. You have your family out there, you'll be alright. I'll send you money every payday and I'll still check on you and the kids and you are welcome to call me anytime you want and who knows maybe we can try again one day."

"That's it! That's all! It's over like that? You just gonna leave your family in California for some girl you just met in a fucking park!"

"What?"

"Yeah I know all about Amber! You think I'm stupid? I was just waiting to see how long it would take you to tell me! I asked your boy Jason if you was cheating on me! You wanna know what he said? He told me that he don't know and that I should come out there and see for myself. So I told Jason to put Sarah on the phone and I asked her and she knew everything! She told me all about Amber!"

I was in shock. My New York partner and his punk ass white bitch sold me out! I should have known not to trust a brotha that date a white girl. That's a sign of weakness to me. It's like they can't handle a strong black woman so they settle for a weak ass white girl that will just shut up and listen. They know a black woman ain't going for that shit!

I told Doris that Amber had nothing to do with my decision and that I don't even talk to her, nor have I as much as seen her since my birthday. Doris didn't believe me and we argued for a while about that.

"Look Doris I told you the truth because I lied to you, now I know that you've known all this time basically holding back information that you already knew. That's pretty much like lying to me! My supposed to be homeboy and his girl have been ratting me out this whole entire time! This is all too much right now. So Imma think this all through and I'll call you in a few days. Bye!" I hung up the phone before

Doris could start back arguing.

The phone started ringing and my pager started blowing up. I unplugged the phone from the jack and I turned my damn pager off before she burned this battery up too. I sat at the foot of the bed shaking my fucking head in disbelief. My boy from the Marcy's in Brooklyn New York that I've done all these robberies with is a weak ass bitch ass nigga that's stabbing me in the back with his little white bitch. I pray to God he don't ever get caught up on anything because this fool might start snitching!

The next couple of days, I was off work so I went to Tennessee to visit my family and to stay away from Jason and that white bitch before I do something to both of them bitches.

When I got back Dalton I rolled up to the park to collect the rest of my money from New York. I really needed it now because I definitely wasn't gonna stay under the same roof with that snitch ass nigga, New York, and his backstabbing ass girl.

I got to the park and I posted up till I saw my peoples. I brought a bottle to sip on so I could chill for a second because Jason was still at the spot. His shift didn't start for another two hours. I haven't seen him or spoke to him in two days. I wasn't sure of what I might do if I saw him or his girl.

That's why I've been staying away and being non-social, maybe they'll get the hint.

I'm sitting on the hood of my Lexus in the same spot I'm always at waiting for New York. He's usually right here in this area. Two hour passed and still no New York or his fat little nurse bitch.

I stayed a little longer, I finished half my bottle and still no New York so I left to go grab some food. I ate at the restaurant to give Jason and his girl enough time to leave. I got to the apartment and I paged New York. He didn't hit me back. I watched TV and dozed off. I woke up in just enough time to shower and get to work.

***

As I'm making my famous Motor Oil Rocket Fuel Coffee Jason walked into the break room.

"Yo kid what's good! Where you been yo? I haven't seen you in a couple days fam."

"What's up with you and your girl telling Doris all my business homie? I thought you had yo bitch in check Cuzz!? Or is it you that needs to be checked?"

"Whoa, whatchu mean fam? I never told Doris anything my dude."

"Yeah I know. You told her to come out here to see for herself. I don't know about New York but in Cali that's called dry snitching my nigga! What's up with that shit, Cuzz? Didn't I talk to you as my potna that I thought I could trust, and yo ass went home and pillow talked with your little white bitch and repeated everything I said to her then that bitch ran and told Doris! Where they do that at? What type of nigga is you?"

Jason tried to plead his case by saying that he was just trying to help Doris because she sounded so hurt on the phone and he didn't mean no harm by it.

"You know what my nigga; I ain't got no words for you, Cuzz. So when you see me don't even bother speaking! Just do it moving! I'm moving out in a week. Then we ain't gotta speak each other period, except for being professional at work "Hi and Bye" dat's it!"

"Auight if that's how you want it I respect that." Jason put his fist out for a dap.

I turned and walked out the break room with a cup of my special brew leaving Jason hanging, standing there with his fist out waiting for a dap. Yeah right, fuck outta here bitch nigga!

After work Jason was walking in as I was leaving. "Yo fam, you still mad my dude?"

I chunked up the deuces and walked out the plant.

I headed straight to the park. I still had half of my bottle left so I continued to sip on that as I waiting around for my New York hustla. What the hell is going on with me and my New

York niggas? This shit is getting outta hand. As I sat there killing off the last of my bottle, I was thinking about everything that I've been going through lately. I was getting all turnt up.

Then I saw two people that kind of looked familiar but they was looking a little too dirty to be who I thought it was. But as I look harder, I noticed New York's girl. She was not looking as fat as she did when I first met her ass a couple of weeks ago. They didn't see me so I went in my car and popped my glove box and I tucked away my homies Smith and Wesson and I walked up to New York.

"What's up my nigga, I've been looking for you, Cuzzo." New York turned around startled once he heard my voice and realized that it was me. His eyes got as big as pool balls. He was looking all dusty. He and his girl looked like they had lost some weight.

"Cali what's up, yo? You were supposed to meet me here last night kid!"

"I was here last night homie whatchu talkin bout?"

Yeah? I was here too. I didn't even see you fam."

"Look nigga I already told you, don't try to play me my nigga! Fuck all that Cuzz where's my bread?"

"Baby give him whatchu got." His no longer fat bitch handed me a balled up twenty dollar bill.

"What the fuck is this?"

"That's all I have tonight." He said last night he had more but he didn't see me so he took what he had and re-upped because the last quarter piece he had melted when he hid it on top of the wall heater and his girl's grandmother turned it on and it melted all my dope.

"Nigga you think I'm stupid? Bring your ass behind this bathroom, let me holla at chu, Loc!"

I took New York to the back of the building where nobody was at and I pulled out my homies on him.

"Cali! Whatchu doin yo? We fam remember?"

"Nigga I told you not to play me!"

My gun went off hitting him in his leg. "Nigga that's for playing with my money, Cuzz! You better have my shit by this time tomorrow and you better not take yo ass to the hospital nigga!"

"What about my leg? The God is hit!"

"Yo bitch is a nurse nigga have her take care of it!" I went to my car and left before a anybody knew exactly what happened. I went and grabbed some food before heading home to shower and wind down after that little activity. I got to the house and showered. As soon as I was dozing off the house phone rang. I answered it. It was Doris she asked me if I missed her and the kids and if I've had enough time to think about everything. I told her yes, of course I missed her and the kids and that I've thought about everything and that lately shit has been hitting the fan. She promised me that if I give her another chance that she will never argue with me again and she will stop with all the questions and nagging. She said that she will forgive me for cheating on her and all she wanted was me back so we could be a family again. I told her that I don't know, I got my job, plus I'm handling some other business out here. She said that if I loved her and the kids then I would send for her, quit my job so me and her could drive to Cali while her grandmother watches the kids till we get back.

I thought about how I didn't feel cool around Jason and his girl and how I just shot my other New York nigga because he and his girl smoked up my dope. So I figured that maybe I should just chalk up my losses and take my ass back home to Cali.

I really missed my kids so I told Doris to call and book a flight and I'll let my job know that I had a family emergency and that I have to quit and move back to California so they could have my last check ready as soon as possible. Then we can pay a couple of months on our storage and drive back to Cali.

Doris was so happy that she hung up the phone, called and booked her flight, and hit me back with the flight information so she could fly out the next day.

I got to work the next day and I talked to my boss, he was disappointed. He told me that my last check would be ready by the next morning. He wished me luck and he told me that if I ever came back that I was always welcome to come work for him again. I thanked him and then I left to go get Doris from the airport.

We made up all day at a hotel because she refused to go to Jason's apartment where I had been with another girl. The next morning I got my check. I went to my bank, cashed my check and closed out my account. We went and paid three months on our storage and then we drove straight to California, my true Home Sweet Home.

CHAPTER 19

Paybacks a Mutha!

But Karma's a Baby

When we got back to Cali, we moved back in with Doris' grandmother and Doris uncle Johnny "Guitar" Watson. They lived in Los Angeles close to USC College on 22' and Budlong. It was a terrible part of Los Angeles for me to live in because it is an all Blood neighborhood. But I knew a few of them from being in and out of jail a couple times and from being out there in them streets. They knew who I was and where I was from. It was all respectful so I never had any problems. It was rough for a minute and hard for me to find a job so I got back with my "P.I.C." Troy was my true "Partner In Crime." We started back going out at night breaking into cars making money off selling sound systems. We stole from those rich kids that were going to school at UCLA College. We would go to Westwood and break into every car that we saw with the nicest rims on them. They stuck out like a flawless Diamond in the dark. We loved breaking into Honda's because those Asians had the best sound systems but the most challenging alarm systems, but nothing would stop us, we were the best at what we did. There was no alarm that we could not get passed. Vipers, Pioneer, Kenwood alarms those were the top of the line alarms and we were by passing them like we designed them ourselves, even the alarms with the alarms on the remote that would sound off if your car was being broken into. By the time you got to your car we would have stripped it of all its valuables. It would be sitting on bricks if you had some nice ass rims on it.

Doris didn't like me being out all night breaking the law so she asked me to please try harder to find a job. I loved my hustle. The sound system in my car at that time was the best that money could buy and me and Troy stayed with the best rims in the market. But I didn't want to stress my pretty little wife to death, so I looked a little harder for a job and it was just my damn luck, I found one.

One day I was in Compton over by Chester Adult School selling my boy a radio and some speakers.

He mentioned that he just became a supervisor for a security company. I told him to put me on.

I started my job at the post on 83rd and Figueroa and everything was cool. The building I worked in was a cool spot. My job was to click people in the building that lived there and to make sure no illegal activities was going on. Only thing though, I was the one doing all the illegal activities up in there.

Once I got to know the people in the building and I got cool with them, I'd pop my trunk and sell their asses some radios and speakers too or maybe a Fosgate amplifier or some bass tubes. Once I found out who all the smokers were, I bought me a quarter piece for one hundred and twenty five dollars and I started serving the local smokers in the area.

I had it popping up in that building for a minute. I had a good thing going on until one day I left to go take a break. By the time I got back and pulled into the apartment building my supervisor's boss was parked in my spot. I pulled up and she got out her car, and stuck her hand out. I gave her my walkie talkie and my security jacket and the security shirt. That was all of the uniform they issued, oh and that little punk ass clicker. The black shoes and the black Dickies was mine, and my 380 pistol that I always kept in my pocket, just in case some shit popped off.

I got home and told Doris what happened. She was disappointed but she really didn't like me working over there securing some ghetto ass building in that dangerous ass neighborhood anyway. Truth is Doris didn't like me working there because of my friends I was making that lived in the building; male or female.

***

New Year's 1993 came and for some dumb ass reason I felt like celebrating it by walking up the street to Budlong and Adam's and buying a bottle of champagne. I popped that bottle all by myself at midnight in our front yard in all blue.

By 12:09 I had emptied my bottle of champagne and I was lit!

I had the empty bottle in one hand and my drunken ass had my .380 in my other hand shooting it off into the air yelling "Happy New Year, Cuzz!" Once my gun was empty and Doris felt it was safe, she came outside and after about fifteen minutes of pulling on me, she finally got my drunken belligerent ass in the house.

***

Everything was going good, and then one day I got a call from my dad. He told me that he didn't trust his wife anymore and that it seemed like she was up to something. He said that he didn't trust being alone at home with her so he wanted me to come to Arizona for a little while and watch his back. My little brothers were in Tennessee living with my mom at the time. My dad told me that he wanted her to leave and he didn't know how to get her to go, so he wanted me to figure out a way to drive her out the house and back to California.

I told Doris that my dad needed me so I had to go now and that I would drive back on the weekends to check on her and the kids. Then I jumped in my car and I drove straight to my dad's house in Apache Junction, Arizona. When I got there my dad was relieved and he seemed very happy to see me. I told my dad that I loved him, and that all he had to say was that he needed me and I was there to help him any way I could. He thanked me and told me to let him know if I see anything suspicious or out of the ordinary with my stepmom. He said not to let my stepmother find out what I was up to because if she was to suspect something then there's no telling what she might do to us.

Once I got settled in, I grabbed the phone and I called my Arizona best friend, Juan. I hadn't seen

Juan since we were at Apache Junction High School together about five years prior. I hooked up with my boy and caught up and laughed all night reminiscing about the good ole days when me and him used to do some wild and crazy stuff.

I remember I stole a Volkswagen Beetle for Juan so we could fix his VW up, we really tricked his little bug out. Let's just say Juan was my P.I.C in Arizona.

When I got to my dad's house my dad asked me if I figured anything out yet. I told him no but I'm working on it. As I was lying on the couch that night thinking of a plan before I fell asleep, it came to me. The idea that I had would make my stepmother mad enough to move all the way back to the Philippines. I smiled at my devious plan and I fell right to sleep.

The next morning when I woke up the house was empty so I went to work on my plan. I walked into my dad's room and I went straight to my stepmother's jewelry box. It had a lock on it but all I had to do was pick the little cheap thing that was clear only meant to keep out toddlers. As soon I opened that night stand sized jewelry box, all I saw was diamonds everywhere. It was loaded. I only took a couple pieces out at a time. I took them to the pawnshop and I got cash for them that way I was able to survive while I was out there for my secret mission in Arizona. I was emptying the jewelry box piece by piece and ocking it back so when my stepmom finally goes in her box she'll be mad enough to leave.

After a few weeks of executing my daily mission and driving back to Cali on the weekends there were still no signs of my stepmother knowing anything about her jewelry missing. One weekend I was headed to LA for my weekend turn around trip to go see my wife and kids and I asked Juan if he wanted to roll out there with me. I told him that there's money to make out there because me and Troy go out at least one night while I'm there and hit a few underground parking structures.

When we got there, I greeted my wife and kids and I introduced Juan to them. I told Juan to wait here in the living room with the kids, watch a little TV, make himself at home and unwind from our six hour drive while me and

Doris run upstairs for a second. I couldn't wait to get my sexy ass wife upstairs.

We got upstairs to our room and we did our weekly ritual of "Ten Toes Up and Ten Toes Down" only this week there was something that felt very different and I knew it as soon as we started. So I stopped immediately while in mid stroke.

"What's wrong baby?" She had a scared look on her face. I looked her in her eyes.

"You cheated on me!" I said.

"What?"

"You fucked some other nigga Doris I can tell! Don't fucking lie to me! You cheated didn't you?"

"No, why would you say that?" I pulled out, got up, and put my clothes back on.

"You're a mutha fuckin lie! You cheated and I know you did! I'm outta here!" Doris begged me not to go. I tried to leave the room and she jumped up and blocked the door and she said, "Please don't leave me!"

"No Doris I'm leaving now move! You can't even tell me the truth!"

"OK I'll tell you the truth just sit back down on the bed!"

I sat down on the bed and Doris began to tell me that she went out to a male exotic strip club called

"The Right Track" it was over on Slauson Blvd, and prolly still is.

She said that she went there with a few of her friends and one night she got so drunk that she left with one of the strippers and they had sex. Not only was I mad about her cheating, but I couldn't believe she was taking money that was for my kids food and clothes and using it to tip some male exotic dancers.

As she confessed and told me what happened it was killing me from the inside out just from the thought of some other man touching my beautiful wife. I couldn't take it. I started asking her dumb ass questions that I shouldn't have ever asked her, but I had no idea that twenty years later those answers would still be burned in my head and that they would affect every relationship I would ever have after that.

Imagining life without her at the time was the furthest thing from my head so I had no idea, so I wasn't thinking about that. I just wanted all the facts on the table so I could deal with it and we move on with our marriage if possible. From that day on I have been damaged goods. I needed to get as far away from her as possible and go think this through.

As I was about to go downstairs and kissed my kids goodbye I looked at Doris eyes as she was hugging me, crying, and begging me not to leave. "You just had to pay me back didn't you? You're so fucking vindictive that you had to get even didn't you?" Then I said "I hope you feel good about yourself, now get out my way so I can go say goodbye to my kids."

When I said that it was like life left her body. Her arms released from around me and they fell to her sides.

She fell down to her knees and she started crying uncontrollably. I walked out of her room leaving her lying on the floor crying her heart out. I don't know why it still hurt me seeing her hurt like that, but it did.

But I still had to leave.

I went downstairs and I said my good-byes to my children.

I told Juan "Let's go! We out!"

He looked at me confused then he saw the look on my face and he knew that something was seriously wrong. So he hurried out the door. We got into my car and my boy asked me what was wrong. I told him that Doris cheated on me and I started punching the steering wheel. I grabbed the top of it and I pulled it and pushed it. I was yelling and cursing as tears came flowing out of my eyes. Poor Juan was leaning into the passenger door not knowing what to do or what I was gonna do and he was looking at me like I was crazy.

Once I finally stopped, my steering wheel was warped and crooked and all beat up. I finally started the car and drove us all the way back to Apache Junction Arizona in complete silence.

***

A month later, Doris paged me 911. I was at Juan's house. I called her back to make sure there was nothing wrong with my kids.

"What's up Doris? What's the 911?"

"You have to come home. We have to get back together."

"Oh really, why?"

"Because the kids miss you, and I miss you. Don't you miss us?"

"Yeah so?"

"So come home we want you back home with us."

"Oh so because you took me back after I cheated I'm supposed to take you back?"

"No you should take me back because I'm pregnant."

I sat up with a big smile on my face. "Are you just saying that to get me to come back home, or are you really pregnant Doris?"

"No I'm really pregnant. Now will you at least think about coming home?"

"Yeah I'll think about it but I have unfinished business out here. I'm still helping my dad so we'll see, but I might at least drive down this weekend."

I hung up the phone and my pager went off again. I looked down at the number and it was my dad's house number, he was paging me 911. I thought, Oh shit! The stepmother from hell must have tried to take him out or something and he needed my help. I called my dad's house phone and he picked up on the first ring.

"Hey dad, what's up? Are you alright? What's wrong?"

"A lot is wrong; I need to come home as soon as possible!"

"OK dad I'm on my way!" I hung up and I told Juan that I had to leave because something was up at my dad's crib. I gave my boy dap and I headed to the house.

I pulled up at my dad's house and everything looked normal. My dad's truck was in the driveway and so was my stepmother's car. I walked in, my dad and my stepmother were both in the living room watching TV. As soon as I walked in my dad turned the TV off and told me to have a seat.

My dad looked me straight in my eyes and he asked me if I stole the jewelry. I looked at him then I looked at my stepmother and I said "Yes."

"See, I told you Edsel! I told you he did it!"

"Little Edsel, why would you steal from your mother like that?"

I had a crazy confused look on my face and I said "Because that was part of the plan that we discussed."

My dad still straight faced and serious as hell asked me, "How could you do that to your mother? Some of those items are irreplaceable. Do you know how much you hurt her by stealing from her like that?"

"Dad but we talked about this! Why do you think I'm out here in Arizona? I have a wife and kids in

California I could be at home with!"

My dad looked me in my face and said that he knew nothing about our plan and that he never wanted me to run off his wife.

In-fuckin-credible! I could not believe what I was hearing.

My dad totally flipped the script and turned his back on me, and all in the same breath he asked me how soon I could be out of his house because his wife didn't feel comfortable with me being there any longer.

I gathered the little things that I did have there, I looked my dad in his eyes, and I apologized for ever coming out there.

Morning came and I said goodbye to my Arizona partner in crime and I headed back to Cali. On my six hour drive back, all I could think about was my unborn baby. I love kids, so I was very welcoming to the chance of having another one or two. I loved Andre and Poche' like as if they are my own and I never treated them any differently than I did my daughter. If anything I've known them longer than my daughter so our relationship was stronger. I really wanted Doris to be with baby. I wanted a brand new baby boy!

Hell if possible, the twins I always wanted.

My whole ride back to California I was smiling and dreaming of what my new little babies would look like and how they would be and what would I want to name them. As I pulled up to Doris' grandmother's house, I realized that I had not called to tell Doris that I was on my way. I was praying she was home as I walked up to the door. When I got to the door, it opened and Doris was walking out. It looked like she was going somewhere. I walked up and startled her when I was all of a sudden right up on her as she was locking the door on her way out.

"Hey!" Doris turned around and she gasped.

"Jesus baby you scared me!"

"My bad, you alright?" Then I asked her if she was heading somewhere. She said that her grandmother was gonna watch the kids while she headed to her doctor for her official confirmation on the baby.

"Well I'm just in time for my baby's first appointment!"

"Yes you are, I wasn't expecting you till the weekend." I explained to her how my dad's situation ended up and she just shook her head and said that the whole thing sounded crazy from the beginning.

"Yeah but it was all for nothing! It could've ended a lot worse, thank God it didn't. If that lady would have pressed charges on me I'd be in the Arizona State Prison right now! All because I had my dad's back and now look, he's turned his back on me! Anyway what time is your appointment?"

She said it was at three thirty. I said hop in I'll get you there in plenty of time Doris thanked me and she asked me for a hug. It was my first contact with my wife in over a month. She felt great in my arms. Her little 5'3 110 pound frame was very small and petite. We fit perfectly. We had been through a lot in such little time. I guess that's what made our bond so tough to break.

As she stood in my arms, holding me tight I looked down, she had her face buried in my chest. Then she looked up as I looked down and our eyes met. I was mesmerized by her beautiful smile. I was so much in a trance that she stole a kiss. After our long passionate kiss, right there on her grandmother's front porch for the world to see, we were back to normal like I had never left. We held hands as we walked to my car, hopped in and I hurried to her doctor's office over on Pico off La Cienaga Blvd. We got there with fifteen minutes to spare.

Doris signed in and ten minutes later her name was called for her to go into that little room where my wife had to strip naked for her male doctor. She pulled me in there with her and I sat on the stool off to the side until her doctor walked in. He has been Doris' doctor through all her pregnancies since she was a teen. He still held a slight grudge with me because we didn't need him for my daughter's birth because I delivered her myself at home. He understood that it was very unintentional but I'm sure he missed out on a nice check because of it.

At the end of the visit, her doctor told Doris the baby's due date. I heard the date and I started to do the math in my head. I calculated that the conception was around about the time that Doris was too drunk to resist that male stripper. From the look on my face and the smoke coming out of my ears, Doris looked at me and knew that something was wrong. She quickly asked her doctor to excuse us for a moment and he left the room. Doris asked me if I was alright and I said hell no.

"When your doctor comes back, ask him when the time of conception was."

"Why what are you trying to say?" and tears started to flow.

"I did I the math Doris, and you know I'm good with numbers, so just ask him, right here, right now, while we're both here." Doris sat there in shock from my assumption. Then her doctor walked back in and she asked him the question. The approximate date that he gave her was the exact time of her sexual encounter with Mr. Right Track. I was infuriated. Doris was speechless.

I walk out of the doctor's office and I waited for Doris in the car. I thought to myself here we go again. Just as we were about to make up and recover from the last piece of drama, here goes some more complicated shit! I was so pissed I had tears in my eyes. I was done! It's over! I didn't wanna hear shit she had to say, and I didn't have shit to say to her! It's a wrap!

Doris finally got into the car. I started driving her straight back to her grandmother's house. Doris tried to convince me that the baby she was carrying was mine and that she knew for a fact that the baby was mine. She told me that I would see for myself when the baby was born. I told Doris that she can't guarantee me that because she already told me that she was so drunk the night she was with Mr. Right Track that she could not remember if he used a condom or not. I told her that if she thinks I'm gonna sit around with her and go through all the emotional crazy mood swings, cravings, and pure living hell that she put me through while she was pregnant with my baby for nine whole months to find out that the baby she was carrying ain't mine! It's some stripper niggas baby! Then she must have bumped her head.

"Hell no! I'll see you in nine months and we'll go from there."

We got to Doris' grandmother's house and I went inside just to be with my kids. Seems like every time I've came here lately, it's been some bullshit ass drama that pissed me off and I leave. This time, even though this the worst possible scenario, I stayed downstairs and spent some quality time with my kids for a while.

The next day I got a page from Doris. I called Doris back, she told that she wanted me back and for me to come home. I told her that as long as she's carrying somebody else's baby I'm not even cool with being around her.

"Just please come home I have something important to ask you."

"Doris you are pregnant with a man's baby that you cheated on me with! What makes you think I wanna be anywhere near you right now?"

"You don't know that for sure."

"I'm supposed to wait around and find out?" Then I said. "We've been having unprotected sex our whole relationship, it's funny after all this time, you end up getting pregnant after you go out and fuck the next nigga! I'm not buying that it's my baby! I'm so cool on you right now, not to mention we gotta wait a week for your results to see if he gave you HIV and if you've got it, guess who else probably has it? Me!"

"That's what I wanted to ask you."

"What! What is it? Just ask me now cause I ain't coming over there."

Then Doris said that the same day that she goes in to get her HIV results she made an appointment to get an abortion. She said that she was doing it for us to save our marriage and to get our family back together so that we could get our life back on track. Then she asked me if I would go with her and hold her hand to be there for her because she's never been through that before.

Doris was a Christian girl so it totally shocked me to even hear the word abortion come out of her mouth.

There was complete silence on the phone while Doris was waiting for my answer. I took a deep breath and my jaws got tight as my back teeth bit down into each other, the muscles on the sides of my face bulged out and you could see my heart beat in the vein that ran over them. Then all of a sudden I broke the silence and yelled loudly into the phone.

"See Doris I told you that ain't my fucking baby! Because if you had just one percent of thought in your head that the baby growing inside you right now was mine, there's no way in hell you would even be asking me to come with you to sit there and watch the massacre of my unborn child, and possibly the twin boys I've always wanted!"

Doris started crying, she had exhausted all remedies as to how to put our family back together again, but at this point it was so much damage done that it was not looking too promising at all. She yelled into the phone as she was crying her heart out.

"Well what am I supposed to do?"

"I dunno Doris maybe you should have thought about all this before you decided to do what you did to get where you are right now. A single, married woman, with three kids, pregnant with some stripper nigga's baby, and possibly could be HIV positive." And I hung up the phone.

I thought long and hard for days, this was the toughest decision I had ever made. But I thought about my kids and the family life that I used to have. I kinda missed my family life. For the last three and a half years Doris completely took care of me at home. Everything from washing my clothes to washing my ass. Literally, it would be days I'd come home from working my twelve hour shifts too tired to lift my arms to hug my kids. Doris would run my shower and hop in there with me and scrub me down, then feed me her good home cooked meals then tuck me into bed because I had to do it all over again in just a few short hours.

***

I picked her up the next morning and we drove to the doctor's office in complete silence. Doris signed in, this time we were called into a totally different room than the ones we usually go into. This room was in the back of all the other rooms. We walked in and Doris began the ritual of disrobing and putting on the hospital styled gown and she sat in the big crazy looking chair. The room itself looked more like an operating room. It had a lot of hoses and tubes and a weird looking machine on the side that was see through and connected to the hoses that I was just looking at. I figured that it must be the baby killing vacuum machine that I'd only heard about up until now. It was a lot quieter back there besides a room that we passed to get there with the cry of a young girl's voice that came screaming from underneath the door along with a loud suction sound that I heard too. It was also very cold in that very morbid room as well.

Doris' doctor finally came in, he said he was sorry that we were going this route but he assured us that it would be a very quick procedure and that Doris would only feel a pinch. He asked if we were sure, then he asked Doris if she was ready.

He sat in his stool between Doris legs as they were positioned wide open and up high in the air. The doctor's assistant was a young pretty Latino girl about the same age Doris. She passed the doctor a giant needle and some type of clamping sort of tool. Before he touched Doris he stopped one more time.

"It's still not too late if you two don't want to do this." Doris had tears rolling down her face as she laid there. She said that we were sure and to please continue. Her doctor looked at his assistant. The pretty little Latino girl hit a switch and I heard that same sound I had heard coming from underneath the door from that room that we passed that next to us. Doris reached out for my hand and I accepted hers. I grabbed my wife's hand with both of my hands and then the doctor went diving in with that giant needle and that crazy looking clamping tool. All of a sudden I heard a sound that left a dreadful sound bite in the sound catalog of my brain. I saw a vision that's burned in my already damaged mind that I will never ever forget in my life. As I saw what was possibly my twin boys being crushed by that tool the doctor had in one hand and then being sucked out through a small hose that was in his other hand. The baby parts all collected into that c-thru machine that was right next to me. Doris was squeezing my hands while the endless tears rolled down into her ears.

The procedure was over. The machine was switched off. But that sound continued ringing in my head for days and days.

I was at Doris' side nursing her for as long as it took, until the bleeding stopped and she was just spotting. I had empathy for what she went through. I knew her only motive was to ensure that now I would stay around knowing that there was no mystery baby growing inside her. Rather the baby she terminated was my baby or not she knew, I was not gonna stick around for nine months to find out. She did not want to risk the chance of losing me for good.

I guess will never know if it was or wasn't my twin boys' lives that were ended that day nor does it matter now. What matters now is that I'm back, and it's now time to start our path to recovery.

CHAPTER 20

Locked up in Los Angeles

I spent as much time as I could out in the streets making money. Me and Troy would stay out all night stealing everything that we had a market for. Then we would spend all day selling the goods. At this point we had a fence that wanted all the Honda interiors that we could bring him. So we ran a little chop shop theft ring right out of Doris' grandmother's garage in the backyard.

We would steal two cars a night then strip all the interiors out of them and sell them for a thousand dollars each. Then we would drive the cars totally stripped just a few blocks away and leave them. Then we would sell whatever items that was in the trunks, laptops, leather jackets, etc. Everything was going very good, nice and smooth.

One night, as I was trying to leave to go out and put in some work, Doris started an argument. I told her to chill and we'll talk about everything when I got back because to me it was bad luck to argue with my girl and then leave the house. Sure enough that night me and Troy were breaking down a white Acura Legend for its sounds and rims right there in an apartment building on Bundy and Wilshire and we had six guns pointed at us as they yelled, "Freeze assholes! Put your fucking hands up and don't you fucking make a move!"

We were trapped and couldn't run so we both just put our hands up. I remember as the cops got closer they told us to turn around and face the wall. I looked over my shoulder as the cop was two feet away from me. His pistol was pointed right at my head and it was shaking like crazy. He asked me if I had any weapons on me.

"Yeah I gotta .380 in my back pocket." Oh shit what the fuck did I say that for? Three of the officers were right behind me with their pistols pointed at my head.

"You better not fucking move asshole. Now that I know you're armed I have every right to blow your fucking head off!"

I looked straight ahead with my hands up high. "Yes sir! I'm not even breathing right now sir!" Me and Troy got cuffed and stuffed. We were caught dead bang. They never hit me with that gun charge.

But they sure as hell tried to stick every auto burglary and grand theft auto on us in that entire area. Even though 90% of them we did do. We held our mud and only copped to what they caught us red handed for.

On May 10, 1993, I was sentenced to 270 days in the Los Angeles County Jail. The LA County Jail is the most notorious, dangerous, dirty, and flicked up ass jail in the United States of America.

Since I didn't have any violent charges after doing a couple of months in that raggedy ass LA County Jail, I was asked to be a trustee at a police substation.

Next thing I know, I got transferred to the Firestone Police station in south central Los Angeles on the Eastside.

It was hella cool there. We got contact visits. They had a little bench press and some dumbbell weights there. Best of all, we were taken to the Metro Station up the street in Watts. I washed the policemen's cars and made cash money. Then when Doris would come visit with the kids, I'd give her whatever I made that week which was around three hundred dollars, tax free! I had her use that money to furnish our new apartment that she found for us in Long Beach. She and the kids moved there while I was in the County jail.

I got to know the Metro station so well that I had Doris come up there visiting me on the low. It was all good until one day I wanted my wife so bad that I had her come to the Metro station and park the car and come in the building for a special little contact visit.

I left the side door cracked open for her to sneak into the Metro Police station while I waited for her at the elevator. She walked in and we got on the elevator by ourselves, I had blankets and I laid them on the floor of the elevator once it closed. Once the elevator started going up I pulled the emergency stop button. I got on my knees and I pulled Doris sundress over my head and I pleased my wife.

When she collapsed and slid down the elevator wall and I quickly told her to get up and shake it off because I heard the cops pressing the buttons and radioing trying to get that elevator moving again. It was risky but exciting. We always did public things like that and we got a thrill out of it. It is definitely because of Doris that I am a big exhibitionist today.

We hurried and regrouped then I pressed the button in, and the elevator was once again moving.

When we got back to the ground floor and the door opened there was about nine cops waiting for that elevator. Me and Doris played it off like we didn't even know each other. When the doors opened she was on one side of the elevator and I was on the other. Her legs barely had life in them and she drove off smiling and happy as hell. For some strange reason the next day my name was called to go back to the LA County Jail to finish doing my time. I was never told why, but I'm willing to bet there were probably cameras in that elevator, we were probably being watched. I wouldn't be surprised if me and Doris had a sex tape out there floating around somewhere.

I did two more months in the LA County Jail at super max out in Wayside right after Valencia, California. I got released at a beautiful September twilight hour. When those last doors opened up, I ran straight passed all the payphones that were right outside the jails release tank, all the way down the street towards the 101 freeway to the Denny's. I used the payphones way over there far away from that damn jail and then I called Doris to come get me. I wanted to get as far away from that place as possible as quickly as possible.

When I called Doris to tell her I was out she couldn't believe her ears. She woke right up and since it was so late at night she let the kids sleep while she sped as fast as she could to come get me, all the way from Long Beach.

I was too nervous to even order any food from Denny's. There was no way I was worried about food when I had my beautiful wife on her way to pick me up and finally take me home. She pulled up in the parking lot and jumped out the car and right into my arms. We kissed so hard we almost knocked each other's teeth out our mouths. That's when I knew it was real. That was the moment that I knew it was no longer that dream of me getting out that I've been dreaming for the last four and a half months. At the very moment that I could hold, squeeze, smell, kiss, and taste my wife. That's when I believed and realized that I was finally a free man, I thanked God because I was finally out of the Belly of the Beast. We hopped in the car.

I wanted to get as far away from that jail as possible. I drove as Doris gave me directions to our new home in Long Beach that I hadn't even seen yet.

As I was driving me and Doris couldn't keep her hands to herself, she directed me to pull over on the side of the Hollywood Freeway. Long Beach was only a thirty minute drive but it was far too long for me and Doris to wait. I followed my wife's orders and pulled over and next thing I knew we we're getting it in on the Hollywood Freeway. At least we wouldn't disturb the kids when we got home.

When we finally got to the apartment, I looked around our new place as Doris gave me a quick tour.

It was very cute and cozy; it was a perfect little family environment for us and the kids. Doris always had great taste. She ended the tour at the kids' room. I woke them up one at a time, they all thought they were dreaming. It was too cute. All I remember them saying as they were rubbing their eyes was "Daddy is it really you?"

Doris got them dressed and ready for school and daycare while I took a long hour shower to get that La County crud off of my body. I wanted to use some Ajax and a Chore Boy, but Doris thought that it would be a bit extreme. You just do not understand how dirty you feel after coming out of that place!

Doris joined me at the end of my shower. She gave me a good scrubbing, then we got down and dirty again in the shower, then we washed ourselves off and got dressed.

Doris had to be at work and I had to go check in with my probation officer. Doris had a job working at a print shop in Venice Beach. We dropped the kids off in Carson. Andre went to Annalee Elementary School while Poche' and Kristin stayed at a daycare right across the street from Andre's school.

I got Doris to work in just enough time. Damn haven't even been out six hours and I was already feeling the pressures of the free life. But I'll take a bad day on the streets over a good day in jail any day!

I gave my wife a kiss, she told me to be careful and to have a blessed day. She also told me how happy she was that I was finally home. She told me what time to pick her up then she turned to walk into the little print shop on Lincoln Blvd then I left to go meet my P.O. at the Carson office on the Del Amo Block. My P.O. was pretty cool. I told him that I lived in Long Beach. He said that he could transfer me to the Long Beach office on Cherry Street if it would be easier for me. I told him "No!" I wanna stay with this office because this is where I'm at all day everyday anyway.

I hated being at those damn probation offices. You never know what might pop up in their computer system on your ass as your sitting there, like an old warrant or any damn thing. The probation and the parole offices are like roach motels. You check in, but you might not check out! So as soon as we were done I was outta there. Since I was already in my hood I slid thru and hit the block to check in with D.A. homies.

I love my homies. They are my extended family. My big homies were like father figures that weren't always around in my life. There's no bond like that bond from the streets of the hood that really raised you and taught you how to survive out there in them streets in a full-fledged gangbang war with the "Enemigos " Of course my niggas was happy to see me and it was good to be back in my hood. My homies had much love for me. They knew I took on a family at a young age and they respected the fact that I was taking care of my responsibilities and basically the next man's too. So my big homies told me to make sure

I chill and lay low because I just got out and now that I'm on probation I could easily catch a violation and be sent back to jail. I kicked it with my niggas till it was time for me to start heading over towards Venice Beach to pick Doris up from work.

I got to Doris job I was a little early so I parked the car and I walked into the shop to let her know that I was there. When I walked in, Doris came around the counter and gave me a big hug and a kiss. She was excited to see me because she had some good news to tell me. She told me that there was a position open at the shop helping out with customer service plus they needed a delivery driver. Doris said that she spoke highly of me to the owner and if I was interested then he wanted to give me a quick interview for the position.

"Auight, fuck it! I'll at least talk to the guy and see what he's talking about," I said

I took the interview and the owner liked me, so he hired me right on the spot. He asked me if I can start in the morning. The next morning me and Doris showed up for work and I got started. I really needed the job because my car note was a little too high for Doris to keep up with while I was away on that black man's summer vacation, so the dealership from Tennessee contacted Doris and notified her that they wanted five thousand dollars in back payments to catch up the car note or they wanted the car. We definitely didn't have five-G's so once I'd been working this job for a couple months I stopped at a lot that was only a mile away from our job.

I walked on the lot to check out this car that I had my eye on since I started working at the little print shop. I would drive by it at least twice a day. Then one day, in the middle of my shift, I stopped by. I asked the car salesman about the pretty little red Porsche. He gave me the price on the car and he asked me if I had good credit. I told him that I had great credit. Then he asked me how long have I been on my job. I looked at him then I looked down at the beautiful little red Porsche that I'd always wanted. It was used and a little too small but it could fit all three of my little kids in the back so I wanted it. I looked at the salesman and I said, "Oh about two years."

"OK well let me get an application on you and have a look at your credit and maybe we can get you rolling off the lot by the end of the day," he said.

"OK but I have to hurry because I'm on the clock. I work as a manager for that little print shop a couple blocks up the street, "I said.

"Yeah I know that place. OK well let's hurry so you can get back to work and I'll work on getting you approved," he said.

"OK cool! That sounds perfect!" I said. I finished the application and as I was walking to my car he said "Hold on!

What's your bosses name so when my sales manager calls to verify everything they know who to ask for."

"Tell them to ask for Doris. She's my boss and she's known me for years. She can answer all their questions about me no problem."

"OK buddy, well you'll be hearing from me as soon as I have an answer for you."

I hurried back to the little print shop just in time to take Doris to lunch. Doris and I used to walk across the street every day and eat at the hamburger stand that was adjacent to the little print shop.

They had the best sandwiches in Venice Beach. I explained to Doris what I did and she was shocked and kind of upset because I lied and now she was gonna have to lie for me. Truth is, she was actually mad

I went over there without her. She knew how bad I wanted that car because I spoke on it every day we drove by it, wishing and praying that it was still there. I told her that it was only a matter of time before our Lexus was gonna be repossessed. So we needed a backup plan right now. By the time our lunch break was done Doris was over it. She said that I was right and she knows how bad I want that car so she wished me good luck and gave me a kiss.

"Thank you baby now come on let me hurry up and get you back in there before they start calling to verify my two years of employment," I said.

Doris laughed as we stood at the curb waiting at the crosswalk for the light to change. I was still fresh out and on probation I was not about to jaywalk, I was scared straight.

As we were clocking out and about to leave work the phone rang. It was for me. It was the used car salesman calling to congratulate me on purchasing my little red Porsche.

"What? Are you serious?" I said.

"Yes sir! It's all detailed, washed and waxed, and waiting for you to come sign your life away."

"You talked to my boss?"

"Yep sure did, she's a very nice lady! She assured me that I wouldn't have any problems with this purchase because you weren't going anywhere anytime soon. Plus you're right up the street so if I do have any problems I can just walk to your job and pick up my car."

He started laughing, I gave him a fake laugh then I told him that I'll be pulling up in two minutes and two seconds. I looked at Doris she was smiling, "Congratulations baby."

"You little stinker, you didn't even tell me they called." She just gave me her beautiful smile and we hurried out the door to go get my Porsche.

I got to the lot and signed all the paperwork and did the whole car buying process, which normally takes all damn day. Since I came in earlier that saved us a lot of time. Next thing I know, I was driving off the lot happy as hell, in my little red Porsche.

CHAPTER 21

One Argument Too Many

Tension between me and Doris started building. I don't know if it was because we worked together so we were always around each other or what. But we started arguing all the damn time about nothing! It could be the dumbest shit or something little, it didn't really matter. Doris would end up picking a fight about it and we'd be arguing all day long, for days at a time. It got old quick. I went to Bally's gym in Long Beach in the traffic circle. We lived right around the corner from it, so I got a membership. Doris started an argument about that. Saying that I was meeting girls there or something. So I stopped going and I started jogging.

We lived close enough to jog to the beach so I did that every morning at five. Then Doris said I was going to go mess with a girl and that I wasn't going jogging. The arguing got so bad that it started to show at work.

It interfered with our job performance. Next thing I know our boss called us both into his office. He made up some bullshit ass story about how it's December and it's his slow season and that he's sorry but he's gonna have to let us go. We were both shocked!

We left our job for the last time to go pick up our kids. Then as soon as we got in the car Doris wanted to argue about us losing our job and how it's all my fault.

"Whatever Doris! I don't want to argue, let's just go home and try to figure something out!" I said.

We drove in silence most of the way to Carson to pick up the kids. Then as we were exiting the freeway, Doris broke the silence by saying she'll just get back on AFDC, they'll give her a couple months back pay, plus a few hundred dollars in food stamps then we'll be good for a minute till we get another job.

It was two weeks till Christmas so we needed to figure something out quick.

"OK we'll go down to the county building first thing in the morning."

As soon as we walked in the house our phone rang. I picked it up. It was the repo man, he wanted the Lexus. He said he knew where we live all he wants is the car. He said he was going to be in our area tomorrow and asked if he can come pick up the car.

"Yeah no problem. I'm tired of hiding that shit anyway! I'll clean it out and it'll be parked in front of my apartment complex."

"Great! We'll be there tomorrow and thanks a lot! I'll be sure to tell the creditors so they can make a note in their system that you were compliant with us. It'll look better on your credit report then just a regular repossession," he said.

I hung up the phone and I let Doris know that the repo man was coming to pick up the Lexus tomorrow.

She instantly got sad because she loved that car; she drove the Lexus while I drove my Porsche. I went outside and I pulled the Lexus around to the front of our complex and I commenced to cleaning that car out. The next morning, Doris and I got the kids situated at school and the day care then we hit up the county building right there in Compton off Sante Fe and Alameda. We spent the whole damn day there but it paid off. It always did. See those county checks was what kept me and Doris alive in times like these.

Especially them "Og Food Stamps!" You know the ones in the booklets. They were paper and the cashiers would wanna tear them out the booklet or they would trip about accepting them from you.

You could stand outside the check cashing spot and buy up everybody's food stamps for half the price they were worth. We never sold ours though, shit we had three little ones to feed. Doris walked out with a fat check and a stack of food stamps. By the time we got out of there it was time to pick up the kids. We literally spent that whole damn day in that county building. But it sure paid off! We stopped by Nix Check

Cashing to bust that fat ass twenty-five hundred dollar county check so we were good! Then we picked up the kids and headed home.

When we got home Doris started cooking dinner. I was in the living room playing with the kids.

While I was wrestling on the floor, beating up on Andre and Poche', the house phone rang. I answered the phone. It was the repo man. He was out front repossessing the Lexus and boy was he pissed! He told me that he's been waiting for a flatbed tow truck for two hours and that it was not a good neighborhood for him to be hanging out in. He said that he was shocked when he got here and saw that the car was on bricks.

Then he said he looked inside and everything was stripped out of the car, he said it was totally cleaned out radio and everything.

I told him yeah you wanted to come pick up the car so I cleaned it out and I took everything off of it and out of it that wasn't on the car when I bought it. "You got your car so get off my phone and don't call this number again, bye!" and I hung up the phone. I went in the kitchen and told Doris about my conversation I just had with the repo man and we both busted out laughing. Doris had no idea I had stripped the car clean of the radio, rims and everything of any value out of that car.

The phone rang again; I thought it was the repo man again so I answered it with a serious attitude.

"Dang son! That's no way to answer your phone"

Hey mom! I'm sorry; I thought you were somebody else. How you doing?"

She said that she was good and that everything was fine, she just missed the kids and wanted to talk to them. I put the kids on the phone. They loved talking to my mother, and my mother really enjoyed being a grandmother. While the kids were on the phone Doris was telling me that school was out for the Christmas holiday for the next three weeks. Then she asked me what were our holiday plans because there's no school and we were not working so we might as well not take Poche' and Kristin to their day-care so we can save money, but we had two weeks till Christmas so what did I want to do.

"I don't know. I just talked to my mom for a brief second and she said that she really misses us."

Then I said, "Too bad we're not in Tennessee for another white Christmas."

Doris looked at me with that spontaneous Aries look. "We could be in about two days."

I looked at Doris like she was crazy. "Are you serious? Do you really want a repeat of that Christmas road trip from hell?"

"No, it won't be like that this time. We know to take interstate 10 this time instead of 1-40. Plus this time we can stop off in Beaumont, Texas and visit your Uncle Keith's family on the way and be in Tennessee in time to surprise your mother for Christmas."

Me being an Aries too and also a very spontaneous person I agreed. That night Doris packed everything we needed and got us all ready for our road trip to Tennessee to surprise my mother for Christmas.

The trip took us three days because of our stop off to visit my Uncle Keith's family. I missed my little cousins; they had gotten so big so quick. A trip to Beaumont, Texas isn't a trip if you do not stop off and get yourself some Boodan. That food out there is so good I almost hurt myself eating all that Boodan while we were there.

When we got to Tennessee my mother had no idea that we were there. I called her when I was thirty minutes away in Chattanooga. She moved since I left and I didn't know where she lived so when called her I told her that I needed her address to mail her some Christmas presents. Doris wrote down the address and thirty minutes later me, Doris, and all three of our kids were knocking on my mother's door.

When she opened it we yelled, "Merry Christmas!" My mother burst into tears as she bent over and hugged all three of her grandbabies. My mother was always so emotional. She's a very loving lady; just don't ever get on her bad side. She hugged Doris then she gave me a hug and a kiss on the cheek and she said as she was balling like crazy with crocodile tears flowing down her lovely face, "This is the best Christmas present that I could have ever have wanted."

My mother took Doris and the kids inside to show them her Christmas tree and to give Doris a quick tour of her new house. I stayed on the front porch and I took in the beautiful country scenery and I inhaled that one of a kind country damp wooded area smell. I could literally smell Christmas coming.

I looked at rooftops of all the houses and you could see smoking chimneys. They gave off an unforgettable hickory and oak smell that was priceless. My three little brothers came running out onto the porch to see their big brother. They were super excited to see me and I had definitely missed them too. My little sister Michelle was right behind them, she was the prettier little female version of me. I'm the oldest of us five, then it's my brother Joey he's under me, then my little brother Mikey who is B*K*A* Little Suave, then it's my only sister Michelle, then my baby brother Denver, 'Tiny Suave. I hugged my little brothers and my little sis; it was really good to see them all. I really missed them and it was obvious that they missed me too. My mother's house was filled with her kids and grandkids; she loved it and wouldn't have had it any other way.

We had a beautiful white Christmas. My mother cooked a delicious Christmas dinner and Doris helped out, everything was great. Doris went to the super market with my mother so she could stock up the shelves and fill the fridge since my mother had all her unexpected guest. We contributed with those good old food stamps we brought with us from Cali.

We made it out to my grandparents' house for a visit. My grandmother threw a welcome back dinner for us and everybody showed up. My Aunt Joan and Uncle David, and four of their kids came, Ki-Ki, Corey, NeNe, and Kevin. My Aunt Pat was there and her daughter Jasmine. Jasmine had her two kids there too, my little cousins Avery and his little sister Shauntae. My Uncle Charles was there. My cousin Ki-Ki and I we were so happy to see each other. My big cousin Jasmine was still looking nice and healthy, no visual signs of HIV. She even had a new boyfriend and everything. He said he didn't care about the HIV because he loved her. Jasmine was a very lovable person, she was always smiling, and she was a very loving and happy person. Doris used to hate when Jasmine would see Kristin. Jasmine would grab Kristin and pick her up and give her a bunch of kisses and love. Kristin was such a pretty little two year old baby that you had to just pick her up and kiss her. She had the most precious little smile too, with her big ole pretty eyes. I used to call her Gizmo. Doris would elbow me as soon as Jasmine would bend over to pick Kristin up. I would be smiling as Kristin would be laughing and smiling while Jasmine would have her up in the air just kissing her big ole chubby cheeks like crazy. Jasmine didn't mean no harm she was just showing her baby cousin some love. There was no way I could've told my big cousin not to kiss my daughter without destroying her, so I just let it be. But I did understand where Doris was coming from because this was in1993 and the whole HIV thing was still very new and we didn't know much about it then.

New Year's came and we brought our guns, alcohol, and a bunch of fireworks out to my grandparents' house to celebrate New Year's and to bring it in the only way we know how, "Cali Style."

Since my grandparents' house was far out in the country it was all legal. We drank all we wanted and popped off all the fireworks, M-80's and Cherry bombs we wanted, hell we had some Disney World

Fireworks out there! They sale Fireworks year around out there, they have big ass Firework Super Markets everywhere! That shit blew my mind when I first saw it! Then we would pull out our pistols and shot up the country side till we ran out of bullets. I liked shooting off my grandfathers all black pistol grip pump 12-gauge shotgun. It was beautiful, sleek and sexy and it fit well in your hands, but when you pulled that trigger she had nice little kick to her. It was made just like a Black Panthers Riot shotgun. He had the barrel shorten a little too. At night a three foot flame shot out the end of the barrel with every shot. It was a fireworks show all by itself.

When the yard thinned out from the little ones I'd grab my little brothers and my little cousins and we'd have a big ass war with the bottle rockets. We would have fun shooting them at each other the rest of the night.

Sometimes I would light my rockets and hold it then throw it right in my little brothers and cousins direction. I would even grab a Roman candle and shoot those at their asses too.

Jasmine was the oldest grandchild. But I was the oldest grandson. So I always felt like it was my job to make sure that my little brothers, and my little cousins, even my little sister, wasn't no punks! I used to always rough them up and whoop on them. They couldn't walk passed me without me socking them in their chest or if it was a girl I'd sock her in her arm or on her shoulder. I've been terrorizing them by doing that to them Since they were little, way back when we all lived in Carson because that's where I learned it from, my Uncle Keith and his homies would whoop my ass like that every day to toughen me up and to keep me on my toes to make sure I was never slipping. So I carried on the tradition. I remember at my Junior High School in Carson we would play a game called Right Hand Knockout. This meant, if you were carrying anything in your right hand then one of us could come and slap it right out of your hand. It could be anything from books to a warm fresh giant chocolate chip cookie that you just bought during nutrition break. If you slipped up and was carrying any food through the lunch tables or just left the cashier paying for something and you turned around with it in your right hand then that lunch tray with a nice cheesy slice of pizza or a cheese burger with fries would end up on the ground and you couldn't get mad about it.

Some dudes would pick their food up off the ground and kiss it up to God and bite right into it, then offer you some. See in my hood they were training us to use your left hand as well as your right. Good thing I was a lefty. After the bullets were gone, and we had popped off all the fireworks, and drank up all the liquor it was about 3 a.m. and time to head home. We were really enjoying our time in Tennessee with all my crazy ass family. There are a lot of us out there and we went hard, especially with that liquor.

We were going to stay little longer but tension between me and Doris started building again and Doris started that arguing shit again. It went on for about three days straight. It started to get embarrassing and definitely disrespectful to be doing that all in my mother's house. I told Doris that I was tired of the arguing shit all day every day. I told her one more argument and I was going to take her ass home and drop her off.

Doris didn't last five minutes; I couldn't take anymore of her and her mouth. I told her to pack everything up and for her and the kids to get in the car. Then I told my little brother Joey to ride with me.

"Where?" he asked.

"Imma take Doris and the kids home and drop them off and come back. Do you wanna roll with me so I don't have to ride back by myself?"

"Are you serious?" he asked.

"Hell yes! What's up are you rolling?" I said.

"Hell yes!" I said.

Doris packed everything up while my mother was saying goodbye to her grandbabies. Doris was crying, the kids were crying, and my mother was crying. Doris tried to apologize and said she didn't want to go, but I was tired of her smart ass mouth and her funky little attitude. That shit was embarrassing and it was disrespectful to be showing her ass like that all in front of my family. What happened and what we went through in the privacy of our own house was one thing. When it becomes a public scene then it had to stop. I truly believe that's why we lost our job at the print shop, she needed to learn to choose her battles and battle grounds. This wasn't happening right now because of this out here in Tennessee, this has been a progressing situation that's been building since we were back in Long Beach. From back when I would be trying to go to the gym and workout or go jogging so I could stay healthy and get in shape. It was uncalled for and I was tired of it. Doris needed to learn to stop all this damn arguing and realize that she's risking the chance of losing me.

I don't know how all six of us crammed into my little red Porsche but somehow we did and we headed back to Cali. Halfway back to California we stopped at a little truck stop diner somewhere in the great state of Texas. Home of my favorite football team, America's team, the Dallas Cowboys!

When we sat down at our table, I noticed the news was on and everybody's eyes in that diner were glued to it and what was at full attention as to what was going on. So when our waitress came back I asked her what was going on. She said that a major earthquake just hit southern California and a lot of people died and there was major damage all through the Los Angeles area. Doris jumped up and ran to the payphone. She used our calling card from our house line to call her mother in Carson to make sure everybody was fine. She came back as our waitress was bringing our food and said that everybody was

OK, including her grandmother in south Central. Her mother told her that most of the damage was in Northridge, that's where it had hit the hardest. I had no idea where the hell Northridge was, I was just glad to hear that her family was OK and not hurt from the big quake.

We didn't realize how big of an earthquake it was until we walked into our apartment and it was a wreck. Pictures had fallen off the walls and off the entertainment center. Dishes had fallen onto the kitchen floor; broken glass had covered the entire kitchen floor. We had to keep the kids out of there. I've always kept a fish tank ever since I was about ten years old, actually younger than that. The fish tank that I had in Long Beach was a nice little 40 gallon octagon tank. The light fixture had fallen into the water, half of the water had rocked the tank out from the quake and all the fish were electrocuted and floating in the little water that was left. They stunk up the house so I took their little stinky cadavers and I flushed them.

Doris and I walked around our whole apartment with our mouths open in complete shock. Even our water bed was empty. Yes we had a water bed. It took us all day and night to get the apartment back to being clean and safe enough for the kids to run around and play in again.

I must admit after putting your house back together again after a natural disaster like how the Northridge earthquake had wrecked ours was enough to make any couple bond again. So after we were done straightening everything up and things around the house were looking back to normal again, Doris asked me if I had to leave. I told her, yes I did. True, this had drawn us close again but I knew that it would only be a matter of a day or two before we would be back to arguing again. Plus I had my little brother with me, so I needed to get back to Tennessee. I told her that we should take a break and in the meantime imma be in Tennessee looking for a new job and stacking some money. Then once I felt we were ready then I'll send for her and the kids. She wasn't trying to hear it. Doris was crying and trying to understand why I was still leaving but it was something that I felt needed to be done. I had just gotten out of jail going through all that bullshit. I did not get out to have to be stressed out in the company of my wife every time she felt like arguing, that shit wasn't me. I made love to my wife then we fell asleep the next morning I kissed my kids, told them I loved them and that daddy was going back to Tennessee to get a new job. I promised them that I was gonna move them back out there as soon as I got everything together for them to come out there. "Promise?" They all said.

"I promise." I hated leaving them. I loved them so much but I will have my family back in Tennessee with me as soon as I can. I bought a cheap little CB radio to play with on the way back to Tennessee to help me stay awake because I had a bad problem with falling asleep at the wheel. I hooked it up to my car battery. I had a big antenna that I bought and me and Joey hit Interstate 10.

We stopped off in Arizona to see our dad. Of course he wasn't too happy to see me. I didn't even go in his house. I basically stopped by so my little brother Joey could see him. I waved to him while I was sitting in my little red Porsche. He came out and said hi to me and admired my car. He said it was nice, and then I showed him the CB radio. He showed me how to use it a little, then me and Joey said our goodbyes and we got back on the highway.

We played with the CB all the way back to Tennessee. We talked to the truckers to give us a heads up on smoky or the Bears that was trucker code for the highway patrol. I learned a lot by buying that CB and bringing it on that trip. I learned that there was a lot of drugs and pussy being sold over those airwaves.

Me and my brother would just listen in and laugh as soon as we heard some lonely trucker trying to hook up a date with some working girl on one of the channels. We pretty much kept it on channel 19 the whole ride out. That radio was quite a learning experience. I had no idea what went on behind the scene of a truck driver's life. Now I have a pretty good idea of how it all goes down. After that little two day road trip, I had a new found respect for the life of those truckers out there that help keep this country in motion. They're on those highways risking their lives driving long hard hours, making deadlines and drop offs and pick-ups all day every day, every minute of the day.

CHAPTER 22

I had to Get'um

We got back to Tennessee pretty quick and in one piece thanks to that CB radio. That was a wise little investment. Lord knows I would've ended up going off a cliff or off the road into a ditch if it wasn't for that bit of entertainment during that trip. My mother was happy that we made it back safe and sound. She said that she's been on the phone with Doris and the kids every day.

I hurried up and got busy trying to find a job. I started off going to a couple temp services out there.

I applied and in a matter of two days, I was getting called to go work little odd jobs for two or three nights a week at different factories doing back breaking ass work, but I was young and strong so it was nothing, I actually enjoyed it. I would even get jobs that were last minute and only for that day. Every hour of work I could get I worked it, I took every job that temp service called me for. I was number one on their go to list because I was so willing and ambitious. I was trying to stack all the money I could, especially after my cousins called me talking about a big weekend party that goes down in Atlanta every year called the FreakNik. I had no idea what the hell a FreakNik was nor have I ever been to Atlanta. Atlanta was only an hour and a half drive from Cleveland and the way my cousin Pete and his brother, Charlie was talking about this shit I had to go check it out.

They assured me that it was something that I did not want to miss.

I told Charlie that all that sounds good but I wanted to know where we were staying the weekend. My cousin said that I didn't have to worry about that because his boys have a house out there and we were welcome to crash there all weekend. Then he explained to me that there won't be much time to sleep the way it goes down out there. I really wanted to go check out that function so I took in all the hours I could, but the work was still kinda slow and inconsistent.

One night I decided to go out while I had a Friday night off. I went by myself to the most popping ass club in Chattanooga, Tennessee that there was back then called Whole Note. But everybody called it the Swole Note because the party up in there use to Swell Up and be Cracka-Lackin.

I walked up in the club and I immediately stuck out like a sore thumb. Those bama ass country niggas knew as soon as I walked in that I was not from nowhere near there and their bitches knew it too.

As soon as one girl came and asked me where I was from, all the hoes were in my face. I grabbed a drink and posted up. I got a few numbers and kicked it for about an hour then I had one last drink and I bounced out before the club let out.

I'm smart enough to know when I'm somewhere by myself that I've never been to, that you should always be the last person to get there and the first person to leave. That's shit you learn growing up in the streets of

Los Angeles, especially the way their bitches was all in my face once they found out I was from California.

If I would've stayed a little longer it was bound to be some shit!

I was buzz driving on the way back home but I was cool. I made it back to Cleveland just fine but when I got off the freeway, those Long Islands I had was running right thru me so I had to piss like a Mutha Fucka.

Little Suave's girlfriend was the manager at the Mr. Zip gas station that was right off the freeway exit so I stopped off in there to use the bathroom. I parked and went inside but she wasn't working, it was somebody else's shift but I knew him too so it was no problem. Everybody in Cleveland knew each other. Hell we're all mostly related.

"What's up homie I don't want anything I just have to take a quick piss." I walked in and said

I was still buzzing like shit, but I was I cool and walking fairly straight. He said he had to front the coolers so he'll be working if I needed him.

"OK thanks," and I walked towards the bathroom. The bathroom was behind the counter so when I was coming out the from taking my massive piss, I saw the little cigar box that little Suave's girlfriend told us about, she said it was their drop box.

I looked for the worker; his ass was way in the back of the store inside the cooler working. He couldn't even see the front counter so I had to get'um! I bent down and I crawled over to the cigar box and opened it; JACKPOT! It was full. I reached in it with my big ass hand and I grabbed everything that was in it in one big scoop. I didn't leave shit. I stuffed it all in my pocket and I went back into the bathroom. I opened the door then I slammed it shut so the worker could hear it. "Auight homie thanks, goodnight."

"Bye," he said and he didn't suspect a thing because I'm so suave and it happened so fast. I got into my Porsche and quickly drove to my mom's house, with my FreakNik party money in my pocket. I counted it out....two racks! There was a blank two hundred dollar money order in there too, that was cool for that little easy lick.

When I got to my mom's, I showed little Suave and I broke him off because that's what we did. We always looked out for each other, that's what brothers are supposed to do. We both laughed when I told him how I put that simple little lick down. It was too easy and very random. But that's how spontaneous I was if I see an opportunity, I would take it.

The next morning little Sauvé's girl came busting into my mom's house. I was in there talking with little Suave about the club I had went to the night before and how the girls was acting up in there. She came up to me shaking and clearly nervous as hell.

"Big Suave, please tell me you didn't rob my store last night!" She was damn near in tears and scared out of her wits because she had to confront me about something so serious and risky.

"Hell no! I just went there to take a quick piss!" I said.

"Swear to me you didn't! Look at me and swear! Please!"

I looked her dead in her eyes. "I swear I didn't rob your store last night sis." She took a deep breath and she hugged me.

"Oh my God thank you! I believe you," she said. "My employee is saying that the money was there when you came in last night then after you left it was gone."

"What money sis?"

"The money that be in that drop box I told you about!"

"Oh OK, well I didn't see no money Cuzz! Maybe your employee took it."

"Well if you didn't take it then you shouldn't have a problem coming to my store and talking to the detective. My employee said that you were the only person that it could've been so the detective wants both you and my employee to come meet him at my store at noon to get both of your stories."

"Sure no problem! I'll be there at noon sis."

She took another deep breath and let it out and she gave me a hug. "Thank you big bro, I'll see you then."

"OK cool no problem, see you then." Then she grabbed my little brother and asked him to walk her to her car.

I got to the store at high noon. Me and the detective were there but the employee never showed up. I gave the detective my side of the story and he did his little report and he seemed to believe the shit I was feeding him. It was looking good for me because at least I showed up on time and I gave him my little story. We were finished and the employee still hadn't showed up and it was his job on the line. I knew exactly how to play that shit and for now my plan was working like a dream. The detective thanked me for my time and he gave me his card and I got the hell out of there looking clean as a whistle. They don't call me Suave for nothing.

I headed back to my mom's house. As soon as I walked in my mother told me that Doris needed to speak to me and she was saying that it was important. I called Doris and she told me that the storage payment was due in Georgia. She was having a panic attack because all our stuff was in there from other house. I told her not to worry and that I would mail out a payment today. I talked to my kids and I told them that I would send for them soon and to be good and listen to their mother. After I hung up with Doris and the kids, I went into little Sauvé's room and I grab my money from my little stash spot. I went through it and grabbed that two hundred dollar money order. I filled it out to the storage company and addressed an envelope, put a stamp on it and I took it out to the mailbox. I raised the little red flag on the side of the box so the mailman would know to grab its contents. When I walked back inside my pager went off. It was one of the temp agencies. They had a job for me that they wanted me to rush over to right now and it was only for that day. I've been faithful to them for about three months straight but now that I hit my little lick last night, I wasn't so pressed to just jump up for any little odd job right now. So I declined the work and I told the lady on the phone that I've been busting my butt and proved myself to be trustworthy so it's time for them to hook me up with a Temp-to-Perm position. The lady understood and she agreed and said that if I save her today and go to work then she promised that I will be at the top of her list for the next temporary to permanent position that comes across her desk. I sat there holding the phone thinking about how shitty my day started off but I was not really feeling like working, but a true hustler never turns down an opportunity to make some money, no matter how much you got tucked away.

"You're promising me the next permanent position you get, right?" I said.

"Yep! I sure am! You've got my word," she said with her strong country drawl.

"OK, what's the address and the contact name, I'm on my way."

"There's my boy, thank you very much! I really appreciate cha!"

A week later I went to the temp office to pick up my check and Betsy Lou called me into her office. She said she had some great news for me.

"Great! What's up?" She told me that the Coca Cola Plant was hiring and they called them to send over a few good men. She told me that I was the first person to know about it just like she promised.

She explained to me that I have to go over there and apply with them through the agency and if they wanted me then

I'll work for them and if I last ninety days then I'll become permanent with full benefits and I'll get a big pay raise.

"Perfect! I'll take it! When can I go apply?" She asked me if knew how to drive a forklift because it was a forklift position. "Hell yes! I'm a very good forklift operator." I told her that I use to drive a forklift for LAX airport when I was eighteen years old and that I had my forklift operator's license and everything.

"Great!" She said and she asked me if I was available to go apply first thing Monday morning. I told her that Monday was perfect and that I will be there on time no problem. She was happy for me. Then Betsy Lou gave me my check and the address and contact name and she shook my hand and wished me luck. I told Betsy Lou that I don't need luck, I've got God on my side. She smiled and I left the office feeling good knowing that this was an opportunity of a lifetime in a little small town like this to have a job offer like the Coca Cola Company. I went straight home and called Doris to tell her the good news. I told her that if I get this position then I'll be sending for her and the kids real soon. Doris was very happy. She said that she missed me and she was glad that I was out there in Tennessee doing what I was supposed to be doing by staying busy and staying out of trouble. My pager went off so I told Doris that I had to go because it could be my temp service calling about some work. She said goodbye and that she loved me and that she hoped to be in my arms soon. We hadn't used the "L" word in a while because of everything that we've been going through with all the arguing and stuff. So it was kinda good to hear that word come out of Doris' mouth. I told her that I loved her too and I could tell Doris was smiling from ear to ear. We hung up the phone and I grabbed my pager and I called that number back. It was Charlie. He was checking on me to make sure I was still going to Atlanta for the FreakNik weekend party. I told him "Hell yes! Ain't nothing stopping me from going to check that out Cuzz!"

"OK good! I'm just making sure." He told me to be ready because we only have two weeks left.

"Aye Cuzz, I'm ready right now!" He started laughing and he told me that he'll call me next week, then it will be countdown till FreakNik '94!

I hung up the phone and it started ringing. I picked it up.

"Hello?" and a voice that I've heard before but I couldn't remember where from asked for me by my government name. Not having a clue as to who the hell this could be calling my mom's house looking for me I said, "This is he, may I ask who's calling?"

"Yes this is detective Dick from the Mr. Zip case calling."

"Oh, how can I help you Dick?" He explained to me that he spoke with the employee and that now some new information has come up and he would like to see me down at the station. He told me with the new information he could just get a warrant and have me picked up but since I showed up to Mr. Zip's that day then he's gonna give me a chance to be at his office tomorrow morning at ten in the morning. I told him that I appreciated that and I asked him if he thinks I should have an attorney present when I come tomorrow and he said that he highly recommends it. I hung up the phone and I started shitting bricks wondering what that snitch ass nigga could have told him to make him all of a sudden believe his story over mine or was this new evidence that popped up. I grabbed the yellow pages to look for a lawyer. I called the number with the biggest and fanciest ad in the book.

I spoke to my now new attorney and he said for me to bring five hundred dollars with me in the morning and that he'll go over all the information I just gave him. I also gave him Detective Dick's number from the business card that I still had. I hung up the phone feeling a lot better now that I had a representative for my early morning interrogation. I talked to little Suave and I told him what just happened. His eyes got big as hell and he asked me what I was gonna do. I told him that they don't have shit on me besides some snitch ass employee and that not enough to arrest me on. It's his word against mine so I'm straight. Then I told my little brother I was going in there denying that shit till the wheels fall off.

The next morning I got to the police station at ten sharp. I walked in and I saw a guy that looked exactly like Perry Mason.

He looked at me and he said, "Mr. Dugais?"

"Yes sir!" I was smiling from ear to ear. I knew with this guy I didn't have anything to worry about.

I handed the Perry Mason look-a-like an envelope with the five hundred dollars in it that he asked for and all I could think was that if this guy is half as good as the real Perry Mason then I'm walking out of here, if not then I could kiss my little Atl FreakNik XXX Weekend festivities goodbye. But more importantly, my chance at working for one of the best companies in Cleveland, Tennessee and then being able to send for my wife and kids so I could have my family back.

We sat down on the bench and he briefed me before we went inside to talk to Detective Dick. He informed me that he's been at the station since eight o'clock that morning talking to Mr. Dick. He told me that the new information that they had was evidence linking me to the robbery and they've pulled my record so they believed the employee's story and not mine because he's been with Mr. Zips for so long with no problems and also because he didn't have a record. Then he asked me, me between me and him did I take the money.

"No."

"Come on, I'm your attorney, you just paid me so this is lawyer to client confidentiality." This is when I knew I was fucked because then my lawyer asked me if I had a storage in Georgia. The look on my face was priceless.

"Yeah, how in the hell do you know that?" He said because Detective Dick just showed me a copy of a two hundred dollar money order that was faxed to him and if they do forensics on your handwriting it would probably be a match, now wouldn't it?"

"Damn is Detective Dick's last name Tracy?"

"So you did do it?"

"Yeah man fuck! Now what?"

My lawyer explained to me that they have enough evidence plus the employee's testimony to convict me. He said they have a pretty solid case built against me so when we go in there; they're going to arrest me. I thought about my five hundred dollars back from him and running to my Porsche and driving my ass all the way back to California. He saw the look in my eyes and he knew that I was contemplating something.

"But if we go in there and give them a full confession then I will talk to them about letting you right out on your own recognizance as soon as they book you in. Then since you're pleading guilty and admitting your wrong doings when we go to court next week it will look good before the judge."

I asked him if I were to do all that then what kind of time am I looking at. He said he'll try to get me the lowest sentence possible but I'm at least looking at a year. I told him that there's no way I can do a year right now because I just got out of jail, plus I have a very good job right now at Coca Cola.

"Well you could always pay me another five grand and we can take it to trial and I'm sure with your record the prosecutor will shoot for a five year sentence and with your record he's gonna get it. Not to mention they will contact California and they will be here to pick you up the day you're released from here to expedite you back to Los Angeles to violate you and give you more time. It's up to you, as of now they're not calling California, they just want their conviction. Give them their conviction and do my best as far as your time and keeping LA County out of this," he said with arrogance.

I told him that I was just worried about my job. He said that there is something that he can check on but right now we needed to get in there and give them what they want while it's on the table.

"Can you make sure that I can get that O.R. before I go in there?" I asked him.

"Yes, hold on lemme go confirm that for you." He was dumb enough to go in there and ask them about the O.R. and leave me waiting on that bench.

I was thinking that very about bolting out the door but my lawyer walked back out realizing what he had done. "Why don't you just come in here with me."

Damn! What is this dude a mind reader or something?

I ended up getting booked in by Detective Dick Tracy and getting that O.R and released right out.

Getting booked in and all that wasn't the hard part. The hard part came as I walked into my mother's house and walked over to the phone to call Doris and fill her in on all this bad news. She's gonna fucking trip out!

I picked up the phone and dialed my home number in Long Beach, California. I told Doris the whole damn story from the night at Mr. Zips up until the very moment I left the police station. She asked me a million and one question. I told her that's all I knew that point until I went to court on Tuesday. She started crying, I hated hearing my wife cry and

I wasn't there to hold her. That was tearing me apart. I told her to calm down and to just stay focused on her and the kids right now and that I'll be fine and that I'm still fighting to get her and the kids out here as planned, but of course this is gonna be a major setback in that plan, but I was still gonna make it happen somehow because I wanted my family back.

I told her that it is very important for her to please make sure she filled out my green probation slips and send them in for me every month so this case does not catch up with me out there in California and I get violated and more time out there in that raggedy ass LA County jail again. Doris assured me that she's got that and for me not to worry and that she'll make sure that get done because that's the last thing that she wanted too.

I told Doris that I was stressed out about all this, especially about my job at Coca Cola. I told her that I'm still going to my interview Monday and to pray that everything goes well and to really pray that Tuesday a miracle happens.

I told Doris that I was hungry and I needed a drink so I was about to get off the phone and go over to the "Corner Pocket" to eat have a drink and shoot some pool to take my mind off this horrendous day I just had. I hung up with my beautiful wife and I hopped in my little red Porsche and headed up to the corner pocket. As I was driving up there I was trying to wrap my head around possibly going back to jail for another year, missing out on one of the best jobs in Cleveland, TN, and missing the party of the year in Atlanta, GA.

Monday came; I got sharp as a tack and headed to Coca Cola for my job interview. I pulled up with a lot on my mind but I was determined to stay positive. When I got out of my car, I noticed an old white man staring at me as he was getting out of his car. I just stood there looking at him as he was now walking up to my little red Porsche with his mouth wide open and he complimented me on my nice car. I thanked the man very much for the compliment but on the inside I was thanking him for not being some red neck hater that was just walking over assuming that I was in a stolen car. As we both walked towards the giant Coca Cola plant, the old guy told me that he always dreamed of buying a Porsche but his family grew faster than his bank account and by the time his kids moved out and went off to college he kinda figured he was too old for a car so powerful. I told him that was nonsense and that it's never too late to live out your dreams.

He thanked me for the memorable flashback of one day driving his dream car. He was smiling like a teenage boy that had just lost his virginity. I held the door open for him as we entered the giant building. He walked in and straight through and went on about his day while I stopped at the front desk to check in with the lovely little secretary. I gave the beautiful brunette southern bell my name and what company that sent me and she gave me a beautiful smile and she handed me a clipboard with the Coca Cola application clipped on it and a bright red Coca Cola pen to fill it out with. She told me to fill it out and bring it up to her with my driver's license and my social security card with it.

I filled everything out and I gave it back to her with my credentials that she asked for. She made copies of them and handed them back to me and she said that the plant manager would be with me in a few minutes.

Fifteen minutes later the old man from the parking lot walked in.

"Edsel!"

"Yes sir!"

"Now isn't that a very distinguished name?" he said.

"Yeah I guess you can call it that." We went into his office and took a seat and the old man proceeded to give me my interview. We seemed to hit it off pretty good. He got up out his chair.

"I feel like we've already met because of our little run in this morning." I told the old man that I felt the same way. We both let out a little laugh, mine was superficial but he couldn't tell.

He offered to give me a tour of the plant.

"Absolutely! I always wondered how all this stuff worked."

"Well let me show you Edsel." I felt like I was on that Willie Wonka movie because this old dude was about as old as Gene Wilder. He gave me a grand tour of the Dallas stadium sized Coca Cola factory.

He explained to me that the soda is made and bottled right there and then shipped out on the big Coca Cola trucks that I would be loading up if I had what it takes to drive a forklift. I assured him that I was more than qualified to operate a forklift. I told him that I drive a Porsche everyday so surely I won't have any problems driving his little forklift because I was practically a pro. We stopped walking then the old man pointed to a forklift that was parked off to the left of us and he said, "OK then, let's see whatchu got kid."

"Right now?" "Yeah, go get on that forklift and drive it up to that rack of two liters, then go all the way up to the top shelf of that rack and bring down that pallet of two liter Cokes without dropping them." I looked up at the pallet that was at least forty feet up on that rack and I walked over to the forklift and cranked it up. I drove up to the rack and I raised the forks to the pallets opening. I drove in and picked up the pallet, I tilted it back a little, backed up, and I lowered it to the ground without wasting a drop.

I lowered the forks till they were flat on the ground. Then I turned off the forklift and hopped off and walked over to the old man. He stuck his hand out. "If you're available to start Monday then I'm willing to at least try you out for the ninety day probation period. After that who knows."

I shook the man's hand and said "Yes sir!"

He smiled and he said "Welcome to Coca Cola son."

I was so excited I didn't know what to do, so I hurried and got out of there before I made a fool of myself. I rushed home to call my wife and give her the good news. She was happy for me, but then she burst my bubble and she asked me, "What about tomorrow? What if they lock you up?" I had that question in the back of my head but I remembered Perry Mason saying that he was gonna check on something so I was trying to stay positive about tomorrow. So I got off the phone with my little depressing ass, joy killer, Debbie Downer ass wife.

As soon as I got off the phone with her my pager went off. It was Charlie hitting me up about the Atl trip. I called him and I told him that I'm prolly gonna have to cancel on the trip because a lot has happened since I last spoke to him. I told him that I had caught a little case, and that I have court tomorrow and that I'll prolly be getting locked up and the only way I would not be getting locked up would be an act of God. If I didn't get locked up because of an act of God then I just got hired at the Coca Cola plant and I would have to work Monday thru Friday from eleven a.m. until seven p.m., so it would be cutting it really close to try to make it to Atlanta after all of that.

Charlie told me that if I'm not in jail then we can just roll out as soon as I get off work Friday evening, and it was no problem because it's only an hour and a half long drive. I told him that if he don't hear from me tomorrow then to have some fun for me too next weekend. My big cousin told me to just think positive and not to worry because a lot can happen in a weeks' time. I got off the phone and grabbed little Suave and

Joey and we went to go eat a nice little meal before I had to possibly go to jail in the morning.

I got to court the next morning. It was May 10, 1994, exactly one year to the day that I got sentenced to 270 days in Los Angeles California. My lawyer had a quick sidebar with me to let me know that the prosecutor is being cool about his little thing that he checked on for my sentencing and now all we needed was for the judge to go for it and I would be a happy man. "Really? Why what's this thing that you checked on?" He started to tell me how he had to call in for a favor with the prosecutor and how the fact that I worked for Coca Cola helped me a lot because that job held a lot of weight in this town. Then the judge called my case so me and ole Perry Mason went up to the podium. I just watched him work his magic, and work his magic he did. He was really like a real live Perry Mason up there the way he buttered up that judge into exactly what he wanted him to do. Only thing I had to do was keep my mouth shut so I wouldn't fuck shit up.

In the end I got sentenced to a year and a day with work release and I have a split sentence. I had a million questions because I had no idea what all this was, but I had to keep my mouth shut and trust Perry Mason on this, but it was hard because I didn't hear anything after the judge said a year and a day. Once the judge was done with his whole spill, my attorney finally explained it all to me. I had to surrender myself starting this Sunday to serve the split sentence with the work release, which meant that I turn myself in from Sunday till Thursday. I get to go home on the weekends, plus during the week I get released to go to work. I couldn't believe my ears!

Perry Mason explained to me that all I had to do was stay out of trouble, be on time every day turning myself in and pay back every dime that I robbed Mr. Zip for, plus pay all my court fees. He said once I paid all that off then we could come back to court and I could possibly get released on probation. I told my Perry Mason looking attorney thank you for everything and I told him that I was very happy with the outcome. He wished me luck and told me to make sure I stayed out of trouble. I told him sure thing and I left that court room a happy man.

On the way home I was thanking God. I started counting my blessings because the sentence that I just got meant that I could keep my good job at Coca Cola and it meant that I could also go on my trip to Atlanta to go check out that FreakNik. After what I just went through I needed a vaycay.

I got home and the first call I made was to the wifey. I had left my pager in my car so the judge wouldn't judge me on my appearance and assume that I was a drug dealer. So when I got back to my car it was vibrating like hell from everybody that knew I had court that day. I called everybody back and I told them all the good news. Then I took my little brothers out to go eat and celebrate a little. Everybody was happy for me, especially my cousins Pete and Charlie. They were happy that I was going to be able to make their

Atlanta trip after all. They told me to be ready because it's coming soon. It was time to start counting down the days; ten days till FreakNik '94! Sunday came quick, it was the first day that I had to turn myself in to the jail. The work release went like this. I didn't have to be there until eleven p.m. because I told the judge that I worked from 9 a.m. to 9 p.m. so he gave me two hours before work to get out of jail every morning and two hours after work to turn myself in every night. So when I checked in at eleven p.m. that night, I was clear to leave at seven the next morning.

Then the split sentence part of the sentence went like this. When I left for work on Thursday morning at seven a.m.; I didn't have to go back to jail until Sunday night at eleven p.m. That was the easiest time I ever had to do.

When I got to the jail the first night I didn't know what to expect. I pulled into the jail parking lot and I took off my watch and my pager and I left all my money locked in my car because I figured they were gonna strip search me and take all that anyway.

I walked inside the jail and the deputy at the desk said that I needed to go in the inmate entrance on the side of the building. He said that I would see a steel door with a doorbell. He said to just ring it and the jailer would come let me in. I walked back outside and I saw the grey steel door, I rang the buzzer and the jailer walked out and let me in. He told me to sign in, to go upstairs, grab a pillow and a blanket, and find a bed.

"That's it? No search or changing clothes?" I said.

"For what?" he said.

"I don't know I was just asking. "I signed in and I walked up the dark, creepy, little staircase. It was eerie and quiet. I grabbed one of the blankets and a pillow that were stacked by the door at the top of the steps. Then I opened that big solid steel door and it was pandemonium in that place. Once I opened that big steel door all the noise came blasting out of that place. It was loud as hell, the TV was blasting, there was about six guys, black and white, sitting on a picnic bench on the left when I first walked in. They were playing poker. Money was flying, they were smoking cigarettes and everybody was in street clothes with their watches and gold rings and gold necklaces on too. It was going down! The dealer stopped dealing and asked me if I wanted to get in on the action. I declined and I asked him where my bunk was. He pointed to a doorway that was on the right and he said to just go in there and pick one. I went through the dark doorway and I tried to focus my eyes in the dark dormitory room. Once my eyes adjusted I could see that the dorm had wall to wall bunk beds in it. It looked like the Carter building on New Jack City where crack head ass Pookie was smoking all his dope at. Nobody was asleep. People were moving from bunk to bunk whispering and staring. The bathrooms and the showers were all the way in the back of the building.

The tiles in there were piss stained yellow and lime green. I found a bunk in the front corner of the dorm closest to the entrance because I wasn't staying long anyway. By the time I finally dozed off, the jailer woke me up and he told me to get up because it was six thirty and he didn't want me to be late for work.

I jumped up like a fireman. I had slept with all my clothes on anyway. By 6:35 a.m. I was downstairs waiting for seven a.m. to sign out to leave. The jailer asked me what I was waiting on. I told him that my sign out time was seven a.m. He looked at me and he waved me out the door.

"Thanks!" I said. I signed out and was at my mother's house stretched out on her couch going back to sleep by 6:45 a.m. My shift didn't start until eleven am. I couldn't wait to get to work I was very excited about my new job. Coca Cola was a very well-paying job and it had the best benefits in town.

I got to work thirty minutes early, my supervisor was already there. I was in the break room on my second cup of coffee when he walked in. he introduced himself and we shook hands. He showed me how the time clock worked. He explained to me that we had to punch in using our social security number to clock in and out. We had to punch the clock no sooner than fifteen minutes until our shift started and if you clocked in later than five minutes after that then you're considered late. You only had three times to be late and then you're fired. That goes for your lunch breaks too. You cannot be late clocking back in from your lunch breaks either. He explained to me that if I was ever caught on the clock or off the clock with a Pepsi or any kind of Pepsi products or even eating at a fast food establishment that served Pepsi instead of Coke then I would be fired on the spot. We couldn't even be caught with an empty Pepsi can in our car. I listened and learned all the little do's and don'ts about my new company that I was now a part of. There was a lot them but it was all good because I'm a very loyal person so I didn't have a problem with any of the little idiosyncrasies of the company.

My supervisor was a black guy around thirty five. He seemed to be a cool dude. He continued to run everything down to me as we walked through the gigantic plant until we got to the work location that we met at Monday thru Friday to start our shifts.

He grabbed the invoice papers for my assignment and he showed me how to read them and how to find the product that they were referring to. He handed me a walkie talkie radio. I instantly thought about my recent road trip from Cali with my fun experience with my CB radio. We both hopped on a forklift and he told to follow him while he showed me where every single soda or juice was at on that invoice. Then he pulled a pallet and he showed me which pallet to pull then we drove both of the pallets back to our work area. We broke the pallets down and built them to the exact numbers that were on the invoices, then he showed me how to shrink wrap them. He showed me where to put the pallets after its been built and shrink wrapped.

Then he gave me the next invoice and he told me to have at it. I went and found the product, brought it back to the work area, built it, and shrink wrapped it. Then I loaded it into the empty bay next to the one that he had just put a pallet into on the big Coca Cola truck that was parked inside the plant.

My supervisor started smiling and told me I was doing a great job. He handed me a whole stack of orders and he told me to go ahead and do as many as I could. He said it was a lot of work and he did not expect me to finish them all so just do as many as I'm able to do. That sounded like a challenge to me and I love to be challenged. I take all fades and challenges.

He told me if I had any questions or needed any help then to just hit him on the walkie talkie. I told him no problem and I got to work. Three hours later I had the whole truck loaded all by myself. I hit my supervisor to let him know that I was finished. He told me great job, then he told me to go ahead and take my well-deserved lunch break.

My first day went good and I really liked my new job. My supervisor was cool as hell so were the other guys that helped keep the big plant going seemed to be cool peoples too.

I got a chance to meet a lot of the other plant workers while I was in the break room taking my precise thirty minute lunch break. I started to make some of my special motor oil rocket fuel coffee. But I figured maybe not on my first day that would probably be too soon. Then as I thought about my special brewed coffee I had a flashback of bitch boy Jason and his snitch ass little white girlfriend.

That week flew by. Next thing I knew, it was Thursday night. Less than a day before we take off for FreakNik '94. I didn't have to turn my ass in tonight so I was at home packing a small bag for the trip.

I talked to cousins Pete and Charlie; they wanted to meet me at Mr. Zip because it was by the highway. I had to explain to my big cousins that I had been banned from Mr. Zips forever and if I were to ever even just as much as to pull onto their property then I would be right back in jail on a violation. They both got a kick out of that shit and said that they'll just meet me at my job. They said that they'll be parked by my car so I'll see them when I walked out after I clocked out.

CHAPTER 23

XXX Weekend

The day of Freaknik 1994 was finally here. That day went by so fast because I had such a busy day at work. I clocked out and walked out to my car. My cousin, Charlie, was posted up and sitting in his clean ass Biretta. It was looking real nice. It was one of those Pace Car editions. My cousin Pete, was chilling in his brand new Corvette, that was sparkling and shined up real nice and clean too. And here I was getting into my little red Porsche, we are gonna kill dem hoes down there in Atlanta this weekend!

I walked up and said what's up to my down ass country niggas.

"What's up Cali are you ready for Atlanta?" They said

"Shit is HotLanta ready for me?" I said. We all started laughing and I got into my freshly washed and waxed Porsche. Both of their cars looked were just as clean.

We hopped on that 1-75 and because all three of us were in sports cars we raced the whole way there. Our hour and a half long trip only took us an hour. The whole way there I was bumping my new Too Short CD, "Shorty the Pimp." My pimpin ass nigga Too Short goes hard! He's a true playa! That hour drive was nothing compared to the two hours it took us just to exit the freeway once we got into the Atlanta area. Cars were backed up on the freeway so much that we were blasting our music and having girls dancing outside of our cars on the freeway. It was out of control, the partying had started already. Then once we got off the freeway it still took us another hour just to get to Charlie's boy's house. As soon as we got there I took a shower, got dressed, and within thirty minutes I was ready to hit the streets.

We all made drinks for the drive over to the party scene. Charlie's boys had also packed a cooler full of liquor, beer and ice that we put in the trunk of his Biretta so our cups would stay refreshed. We hit the streets and in a matter of minutes we were in a shit load of traffic again. The first night was hell, we finally got to one of the parties but it was impossible to park. If we would have conquered the task of finding somewhere to park, it looked even more impossible to get into the party. So we just pimped the parking lot.

Shit we had the nice rides with the music bumping and a cooler full of liquor, we were set up real nice right where we were. It wasn't hard for us fly ass niggas in our fly ass cars to snatch up our first victim of the Atlanta trip.

One beautiful ass lady walked up to me while we were all stuck in the gridlock traffic. She just hopped right in my car.

I looked at her and I said, "What's up girl? Where you going?"

She looked at me with her beautiful green eyes and her golden chestnut complexion and she said, "I'm going where ever you're going."

"Fasho!" I said then I asked her if she had any friends because there are five of us.

"No I don't have any friends with me, but I have my twin sister and three of our cousins with me."

"That's even better! Where they at? "She told me she'd be right back and she made me promise not to disappear.

"Where Imma go green eyes? I'm kinda stuck mommy, but you might wanna hurry back in case these cars start moving, feel me?" I pointed at the gridlocked traffic and said.

She hopped out the passenger's seat and she left giving me a sexy little back shot visual of a perfectly round ass as she sauntered off to go get her family. I hopped out my car to let my posse know that we on! But by the time I got out my car cousins Pete, Charlie and his two boys were at my door asking me who in the hell that bad ass bitch was. "Just some little car hopper."

They asked me why she hopped out my car. I told them because I have four of my niggas with me, so she went to go get her identical twin sister and their three cousins. Those niggas went berserk! I told them to chill out and let's have a drink until she came back with them and see what they all look like before we started celebrating. I told them the rest of the crew might be busted and bitches be sending the prettiest and most finest chick in their little squad to get all the fat ass busted bitches in, and the busted bitches be the ones that drink up all the liquor, smoke up all your Chronic. Then they have the nerve to ask you to take their greedy fat asses to go eat some at Denny's at the end of the night, knowing good and goddamn well they ain't worth two tacos for ninety nine cents at a Jack in the Box drive thru.

I was halfway done with my drink and my buzz was kicking back in real nice when all of a sudden a wall of beauties came walking up to me. All five of the ladies were fine as hell. By this time I couldn't remember which girl was the one I had originally met, nor did it matter. All of these girls were cut perfectly. They all had some sexy ass hazel eyes and their bodies were sculpted into a exotic fusion of a

California dream girl, a Texas Stallion, and a Atlanta Georgia Peach body all in one. They were definitely some of God's greatest work ever.

I said what's up to the girl that was closest to me and I gave her a nice firm hug and I said, "Damn baby what took you so long?" I asked her.

"Oh you must be talking about my twin sister Hazel. She's the one who came and got me and my cousins? I'm Bridgette." The beautiful lady blushed and said.

Hazel walked up as I was holding Bridgette in my arms. I was punch drunk by their stunning beauty. They looked like those Brooks twins from Carson that are in that Round of Applause music video but with green eyes.

As I'm standing there with Bridgette still in my arms and Hazel by my side my boys walked up and I introduced them to the twins, then the twins introduced us to their equally beautiful cousins.

I called Cousin Pete over and I said, "Aye Cuzz, I got somebody that I want you to meet." Bridgette reached her hand out and I said, "Pete meet Hazel, Hazel meet my cousin Pete."

Bridgette dropped her hand and Hazel looked at me in shock as she turned to Pete and she said, "Hi I'm Hazel."

Pete was all smiles. He was more than happy to meet Hazel, and why not, she was fine as hell. I told Pete to let Hazel ride with him and we'll all caravan back to the house. I looked around and Charlie and his two boys had coupled up with the three cousins. We all got in our cars and started them up. It was looking like traffic was starting to be in our favor.

With Bridgette in my passenger seat, I followed Pete as our entourage carpooled back to the house.

The house was a nice four bedroom, three bathroom house that was furnished very nice. Everybody beat me to the bedrooms so me and Bridgette were left in the living room. The living room was cool with me because I was close to the kitchen, that's where the all alcohol was. I told Bridgette to go in the kitchen and make us a drink while I find some music to play while we sip on something and chill. Bridgette came back with our drinks as I had selected the Above the Rim soundtrack. I took a sip of Bridgette's little alcohol concoction and it was exactly how I needed it after a long night of driving in gridlock traffic after working a hard day's work and then traveling to another state to party. I asked her if they have been living in Atlanta all their lives. Bridgette told me that this was her and her sister's first time in Atlanta. She said that it was actually their first time away from home period. She told me that they were all from Columbus, Ohio and that her and Hazel were nineteen years old and had been sheltered all of their lives. The only reason they were able to make the trip to Atlanta, Georgia for the FreakNik was because they came with their older cousins that were twenty, twenty one, and twenty two, or their strict parents would not have let them come.

Then she said she feels weird being down here with me because her sister seemed like she really liked me and that's why they all came with her to meet up with us. She said that she was surprised that her sister didn't say something because she's not used to not getting her way because she always get what she wants.

I told her that her sister's a big girl and that she'll be alright. Besides, I did not want the car hopping bitch! I told her to drink up and the little weird feeling will fade away as she made her drink fade away. I told Bridgette that her sister can't always get her way, that's just that spoiled ass upbringing that her parents tainted her with.

Bridgette finished off her drink in one last swig, then she got up off the couch and she started revealing that sexually deprived body one article of clothing at a time. She walked up to me wearing a pink bra and panty set that was embracing a truly heavenly body. She had some nice b-cup titties and an ass that was big and juicy yet firm and round like Roxy Reynolds's ass. "You're right! I'm feeling better about this already," she said.

I stood up and she grabbed my shirt and pulled it over my head and threw it across the living room. Then she dropped down and started undoing my pants. My pants hit the floor and Bridgette reached into my boxers and pulled out my semi hard dick. She gently licked around the head of my now fully erect penis.

Then she used her teeth to carefully bite just past the head of my dick. She pulled her head back slowly grazing the head of my dick all the way to the tip. Then she put her luscious Meagan Good sculpted lips on the very tip of my dick and slowly but firmly sucked it till she got past the head. She stopped and sucked nice and hard and pulled her head back fast and her mouth made that popping sound like she was enjoying a big stick ice cream pop from off the ice cream truck up in the hood and was teasing her twin sister with it because she wasn't gonna share it with her.

My dick was as hard as penitentiary steel bars as I reached down to retrieve a gold foiled wrapper out of my front right pants pocket. I tore open the packet and I pried those Meagan Good lips from her tasty big stick and I rolled on my latex protection. Bridgette stood up and I spun her around and I slid her sexy little pink panties down her upside down heart-shaped ass and I let them fall to the floor. She stepped out of them then I kicked her legs open like a policeman about to do a search. I folded her in half and she grabbed the back of the couch and held on tight.

With the kitchen light behind me I stepped back to let that perfect lighting shine through so I could get a look at this beautiful heavenly body that my God created for me. I looked over what was some of

God's best work and I licked my lips, especially when the light shined on her tight little pussy that was perfect. I noticed a sweet drop of nectar that was starting to drip from her little opening. I reached down with two fingers and I caught the juices that had built up from the enjoyment of her sucking on my dick.

My fingers came up with her juices on them. I rubbed her swollen clit as it glided between my two fingers then I slipped one finger into her tight little honey pot. She moaned and gyrated her hips and then she looked back at me with those sexy green eyes that reflected like a cat eyes, from the light in the kitchen. I slid my second finger in her tight little love box. Her eyes were squinting and her Meagan Good lips were open and her teeth were clenched together tight. I could hear her sucking air thru her teeth as the thick knuckles of my fingers slid in and out of her tight pussy. I flipped my hand so that my palm was facing the floor. With my middle and ring finger deep inside her very needy pussy, I put my thumb on her clit and I worked my magical fingers and she started going insane. She was gyrating her 42 inch hips, and now that beautiful Roxy Reynolds's ass was rolling in a figure eight.

She stopped and her body locked up and she squeezed the back of the couch. That's when I pulled my pussy dipped fingers out of her and I tasted her sweet juices then I rubbed the rest of her organic lubrication all over my latex covered dick, easing the head in. I have both of my hands on her twenty-six inch waist line. As I'm going in she took her left hand and she reached back and squeezed my arm, but it's too late, I'm in!

I started fucking my Ohio princess and as my rhythm got faster the harder she started to squeeze my arm harder. Finally, I grabbed her arm with my left hand and I held it back there as I was flicking her. As I'm holding one arm back like she's being handcuffed she's still holding onto the back of the couch with her right hand with her face lying to the side resting on her hand. Finally, I let go of her left wrist and I gripped her sweaty little waist and I held on and thrust my hips forward as I'm pulling her tiny little waist back to meet, my every motion as I fucked the shit out of sexy little Bridgette.

As I'm fucking her, I looked down at that Roxy Reynolds's fine ass booty, as waves of ass roll up, then back to my dick with each pounding thrust. The faster I fucked, the rougher the sea of waves got, the average nigga would have drowned in the ocean of ass. But not me I was all up in it, handling every crashing wave of that big ole booty!

Bridgette's body locked up, her hot creamy juices coated my throbbing dick as it pulsated inside her spent little love box that I had just thrashed. I wasn't finished but with her head still resting on the back of that couch and me still slowly and consistently sliding my rock hard dick in and out of her dripping wet pussy, her legs gave out and she dropped to her knees and her left hand started waving behind her and she said, "I'm done. I can't possibly cum anymore, no way! I'm done, please no more."

"You're done? I haven't even came yet!"

"I'm sorry, I can't. I tap out!" I started laughing as I was standing there with a hard ass dick still ready to do some more flicking.

"Damn, I guess I just wasted a condom?" I said. I snapped the condom off and I went into the bathroom to piss and flush my empty condom. As I'm walking out, Bridgette went in and she shut and locked the door. With my dick barely staying in my boxers I went to the couch and I laid on my back looking up at the ceiling as I listened to Jodeci play on the stereo. I'm exhausted from the session but I am also sexually frustrated at the same damn time. My dick hadn't gone all the way limp as I started dozing off as Kc, JoJo, Dalvin, and Davonte Swing serenaded the living room. Then out of nowhere Bridgette pounced on me. Her hair was wet, curly and smelling like peach scented conditioner. Her skin was soft and she smelled as if she was fresh out the shower. She told me that I looked tired. I told her after that little session we had just had I was a little tired. I told her that my little buddy was still wide awake and that she owed me one. She told me that she really didn't owe me shit but she's got me.

She told me to just lay like this and she'll do all the work. She was still straddling me and she sat up. Her back was to the light that shined from the kitchen but I was still able to see the silhouette of her shapely body. She put both her hands on her head and she started grinding my on dick like she was on a mechanical bull. I reached up for her bra. I had to see her beautiful titties. I unhooked her bra from the front clasp and her B-cups were all of a sudden some voluptuous Double D's. She had some pretty caramel colored nipples. Her breasts were round firm and sat up on her chest like Lacey Duvalle's breasts do, perfectly!

I completely removed her bra and I squeezed both of her breasts. I gently pinched her nipples with my thumb and index fingers. She rose up and eased her panties off then she went back to grinding on my throbbing dick. I told her that her shower sure gave her a strong second wind. She put her fingers to my lips to shush me. She slid back and she reached into my boxers and she pulled out my blood engorged penis.

She went to mount my buddy and I told her to hold on while I grabbed my protection. I reached and grabbed another gold foiled packet out of the front right pocket of my jeans. I tore it open and I handed it to

Bridgette. She gently rolled on the latex shield, leaving a little space at the tip like she's done this a few times before. She quickly slid down my dick, she was even wetter than before and her pussy was much tighter in this cowgirl position and she seemed to like the fact that she was in control this time.

I squeezed her beautiful perfect titties as she rode my dick like a stripper worked a pole. The way she was working her hips and how tight her pussy was had my senses peaking in a matter of minutes. I kept my dick in check as she continued to bounce up and down in a consistent Jamaican style rhythm. Her Lacey Duvalle titties were bouncy but still firm.

Then she reached up and she cupped both her breasts, she arched her back, looked at me with those sexy hazel eyes and she nutted all on my dick. I could feel the warm squirts as she skeeted her hot love butter covering my penis as she came, and kept gumming. She stopped but her orgasms didn't.

Once she was fully spent and could move again she squinted her angel eyes, leaned over, and put one of her breasts into my mouth. I sucked on it and rolled my tongue around her very sensitive nipple. I licked around her areola and I switched and nursed her other yearning breast. I nursed her beautiful titties with my tongue as she moaned in my ear from the intensity of the eroticismic pleasure, while she was still very slowly riding my still hard dick. Then she asked me in my ear if I came.

"No, but I'm cool, I'm a pleaser so don't worry about me. I'm totally ok that I pleased you mommy.

The way you cum drives me crazy! I love that shit!"

"Fuck that! I want you to cum daddy!" Then she laid flat on my chest and arched her back. She whispered in my ear for me to look over her shoulder at her ass. I raised my head up and I saw an ass that was identical to PinkyXXX ass. It was a golden color. It was big and beautiful and smooth with no spots or blemishes on it. But oh my God. Her ass did have those sexy fucking tan lines that drove me crazy, that's some sexy ass Brazilian shit! She popped that ass on my dick as she laid flat on my chest. Her big beautiful ass was popping up and down twerking on my dick like a Nicki Manaj video, while her tight little gash swallowed my dick with every pop. All I could see as the kitchen light shined perfectly on her ass was those sexy ass tan lines. They had me hypnotized. Her ass was popping that tight pussy onto my dick and it was driving me crazy. It was a beautiful, sexy, visual masterpiece of God's work.

It was all I could take as my balls were so swollen from being denied for the last two hours of flicking

Bridgette's tight little pussy, then all of a sudden they exploded and emptied into my dick. My dick unloaded about a gallon of cum into the empty space that Bridgette left at the tip of the condom. I wrapped my big strong arms around Bridgette's little petit waist making her stop the riding because the sensitivity of my dick was at its highest point, and now I was tapping out. I reached down and pulled my dick out before it went limp and lost the condom and its contents inside Bridgette's tight little pussy.

She had her arms around my neck while she was still laying on me chest. She picked her head up and put her cute little nose to mine. Then she smiled and I noticed for the first time the little dimples on her face.

Now that I'm thinking about it she really did looked a lot like Laura London and now that she was smiling I noticed that she had some deep dimples on both her cheeks. Then I told her how cute they were and how I'm a sucker for dimples. I confessed that I didn't notice them earlier and then I told her that she should smile more often.

"That's the difference between me and my twin. I have the dimples and Bridgette doesn't."

"What the fuck!" I laid there feeling baffled and I said "Well that would explain dem titties too then?" I said.

"Yep, mine are bigger," she said. "Your ass tried to play me earlier by shooting me to your cousin

Pete. Hell naw! I wasn't having that! He's upstairs right now mad as hell, sexually frustrated laying there with his dick in his hand," she said. "I came downstairs to check on my sister and I saw your yummy looking ass lying here, so I had to have what was mine in the first place. Hazel always gets what she wants."

"Yeah I heard," I said.

We noticed the sun was starting to rise. Me and Hazel got up to go check on her twin. The bathroom door was still locked so I told Hazel to go and get me a butter knife so I could pick the lock. I popped the door open and Bridgette was laid out in the bathroom floor bucket ass naked passed out snoring with her mouth wide open. Hazel and I helped her sister up and into the living room where I laid her down on the couch. I covered her up with a throw that was lying across the couch.

I told Hazel to look inside the fridge for something to cook because I was hungry. She grabbed the eggs, pancake mix and she started cutting up some potatoes. I told her that she might as well cook for everybody because once they smelled the food cooking they were gonna start coming from everywhere to eat. Once she got to cooking and that god smelling aroma started flowing through the house, they started coming to the kitchen two at a time, well except for cousin Pete. He was a little upset but he quickly got over it.

Besides, he didn't even know which twin to be mad at. Only I knew the difference between Bridgette and

Hazel personally and now that I've had them both I'm thinking that I like Hazel a little more, for a couple of reasons. Either way it went, that was just out first night of FreakNik '94. We still had all day until about noon tomorrow then I'd better be getting my jail bird ass back to Cleveland, Tennessee.

Nothing else compared to that first night but we did have some fun all day Saturday after we dumped the twins and their cousins off at their hotel. I gave Hazel my pager number and I promised to meet up with them later on that night. But I already knew that wasn't happening with all those girls running around the streets of Atlanta that weekend.

After we dropped the girls off, we headed to the nearest gas station so we could get some gas and a bag of ice for our cooler of alcohol. As we were creeping along the gridlocked streets, at a snail's pace, and sometimes even slower, we were at a standstill about fifty yards away from the gas station. Charlie hopped out his car and walked up to mine and he passed me a joint. I tried weed before but it wasn't my thing, it didn't even get me high. I got out my car as we were in this standstill traffic and hit it a couple more times just because of the scenery, also because of the fact that I knew that it wouldn't faze me. As I'm passing the joint back to Charlie, a jeep that was now next to us rolled its front and back passenger side windows down and they said, "What's that I smell?" We just looked at them like ya'll know what it is. Next thing me and Charlie knew, the five girls that was in it were now outside in the street with us passing our joint around to each other.

They said they were from the Chi and they asked us where we were headed. I pointed to the gas station that was right in front of us and I said, "We need some petro and a bag of ice for our drinks." One of the little sexy ladies said that they had some ice in there jeep. I grabbed my cup and I asked her to fill it up for me.

She came back with my cup full of ice and some Bacardi and coke in it. "Fasho baby! Good looking out!"

By then Pete and Charlie's boy came walking up and they started introducing themselves. After a couple sips of that Bacardi and coke, and another hit from the joint, I was feeling really nice. I don't know if it was because I was working off of no sleep or if I had finally gotten high off weed, but by the time we got to the gas station I was loaded and not giving a damn about that bumper to bumper traffic because I was in slow motion anyway.

All I remember after leaving the gas station was that little mama that had made me my drink was now riding with me in my Porsche, or should I say on my Porsche. She stood up through my sunroof and sat on the top of my truck. We cruised at about twenty miles per hour all the way to the park where they were having a big ass festival. We parked and walked over to the park. They had three stages of different genres of music going on at the same time and the park was packed! There must have been at least five thousand people in that park. Police were everywhere but they wasn't tripping off of nothing. The only thing they were worried about was fights or shootings and I didn't witness either one that entire trip. I had never been around this many of my people and nothing jumped off. The police was so cool that we had all went walking passed about five cops with alcoholic drinks in our hands. I had a joint in my ear and Charlie passed me his lit joint and I was hitting it as we walked right passed the officers. We had a blast that day.

Some girls were walking in front of us and I yelled, "Whatchu got under that sundress baby?" She turned and faced me and my niggas and picked her dress up over her head showing us and everybody at the park that she had nothing on under that dress.

We walked from stage to stage checking out the scenery. Everything was cool until somebody let their pit-bull off its leash and stampedes of people ran in every direction. I didn't run, but I knew it was time to go when a police officer ran past me, plus my cup was empty so it was definitely time to get back to the car. We took the Chicago girls back to the house. I relived the night before with lil mama that was making me drinks all day. I am going to call her Lisa Raye because now that I think about it that's exactly who she could pass for. She had her exact beautiful face and that perfect soft complexion skin. Little Miss Lisa Raye put it on me all night too. She really showed me what that Chi-town business is about. We flicked until we both passed out. I finally got about four hours of sleep. I woke up the next morning with her legs all wrapped up in mine, with her pretty little face laying on my chest. It was quiet as hell in the house as we crept downstairs. I heard some music in the backyard so we walked to the sliding glass door that led to the backyard where the music was playing.

I pulled back the blinds and opened the door, Pete, Charlie and his boys were back there with the other

Chicago girls, they were BBQ'ing, swimming and having a good time without me and my friend so I decided that we should crash their little party. I picked her up and I walked straight to the pool and I jumped in with her in my arms bucket naked; in the nude.

After we ate up all the BBQ the girls loaded up in their jeep. I gave my new little friend a kiss goodbye on her nice soft perfectly shaped lips. I gave her my pager number then they headed back to their hotel. After they pulled off, me, Charlie, and Pete hopped in our cars and raced back to Cleveland, Tennessee after experiencing probably the best FreakNik Atlanta ever had, FreakNik '94.

CHAPTER 24

My Family's Back

Between working all day almost every day and jail, time was flying by. I only had a week left until my ninety day probation period was up and I could possibly become permanent! The better I got at work the more hours they offered me. The more hours I worked the more money I made. The more money I made, the more I was able to pay on my restitution and court fees. I was almost done with all my fees, so I decided to contact Perry Mason. I told him to set a court date so we can try and get me released based on me doing good and having no run ins with the law and also because all my fees were paid in full. The day I had court I went in early and I paid my final payment that was owed to the courts. The judge was glad to see that I've stayed out of trouble and working hard at my job. He was more pleased to see that I had paid all my fees. He released from my jail sentence and continued me on probation.

I got home and I called Doris to tell her the good news. She was happy about the outcome and very eager for me to send for her and the kids. I told her to hold tight because one of my co-workers that started a couple days after me was cut loose yesterday for no apparent reason. I heard that they do that kinda shit right before your ninety days so they don't have to make you permanent and give you your full benefits and raise. But I told not to worry and to just pray on it and that I should know something by next week at the latest.

When I got to work that day, our secretary at the front desk told me that my plant manager wanted to see him in his office. I walked over to his office and I knocked on the door. I heard him tell me to come in, so I entered his big, spacious, nicely furnished office.

He told me to have a seat. My plant manager told me that he called me into his office to let me know that he was making some changes around the plant. Then I thought about my co-worker from last week getting canned, and I was waiting for the ole fart to drop the hammer on me and give me my walking papers too.

Then he went on to explain to me that he wasn't too happy with my supervisor's work and that he might be letting him go soon. He explained to me that he was gonna be looking for someone to replace my boss. He told me that at the pace that I've learned my way around the plant and with my take charge attitude that he's seen me progress at Coca-Cola, he said that's just the type of employee that Coca-Cola needs. Then he said that I may be that supervisor that he's looking for in the near future. He told me to keep up the good work around there and that I'm doing a fine job. He told me to go back out to the secretary because she's got some paperwork for me to fill out. Then he stood up, extended his hand and he said, "Welcome to Coca-Cola Edsel, I'm hiring you on permanently, and I'm willing to promote you to a supervisor's position based on your performance over the next six months," he said. "Go out there and fill out your forms for your full benefits and your tax forms so you can be officially on board!"

I thanked the man a hundred times before I left out to go do my paperwork. I was very happy because this was a dream job. I could stay here and one day retire from this place and still be young. This also meant that I could send for Doris and the kids because I have a permanent and stable job now.

I filled out the forms and I ran upstairs to the payphone in the break room. I called Doris and I told her the great news. She was so happy, she was in tears. She asked me how soon was I gonna send for her and the kids. I told her I can send for them when I get my next check on Friday.

She said that now she's about to have a yard sale starting tomorrow to sell everything so they will be ready to fly out by Saturday. I told her to sell it all and when they get out to Tennessee we'll look for a place together and when we find one we'll just furnish it in one day through Rent-A-Center. We both started laughing then I said bye to my wife, told her that I loved her and that I couldn't wait to see her and kids.

Then with a big Kool-Aid smile on my face, I clocked in and hopped on my forklift.

***

Doris and the kids flew in Saturday night. I borrowed my grandparents' family van to go pick them up from the Chattanooga airport. The next day me and Doris spent that whole Sunday going to open houses to find our new home. We applied at two of the houses we saw. I liked both of our choices, but one of them was a lot cheaper but it was far out in the country. The house that was closer was in a very expensive community and the rent was almost double.

That Wednesday after work Doris picked me up at the end of my shift. She was all smiles when I got in the car and I immediately found out why. She had a set of keys in her hand. "We got it!" she said.

I instantly knew what she meant but I didn't know what house we had gotten. I was really hoping for the cheaper of the two. The house out in the country was fine with me; I like to drive so the commute wouldn't have bothered me. Then Doris asked me if I could pick one of the houses which one would I picked out of the two we applied for.

"The cheaper one." Her smile disappeared.

"Why? That's the house that's way out in the country with no one or nothing around for miles." I told her because it was a lot cheaper and I that I didn't mind the commute. "Well that one is taken, but we got the approval for the one in that nice little neighborhood that has that nice fireplace in it, plus it's a corner lot with lots of yard space for the kids to play in," she said. "But I don't want to move there if you don't like it."

I told her to stop pouting before she tripped over her bottom lip. I told Doris that it wasn't that I didn't like I was just hoping for the cheaper house so we wouldn't have to struggle. I explained to her that once I got that promotion in six months then the house would be more in our price range. Then Doris asked me a question that made a lot of sense. "So we should wait till you get your promotion and move again?"

"Hell no," I said because I hated moving and Doris knew that.

"Well babe let's just move in here now, we can afford it we'll just have to budget to keep the place and get the essentials we need until you get promoted."

"What if I don't get the promotion? Then what?"

"Didn't you tell me that you and your plant manager are hitting it off and that he seems to like you?"

"Yes, but nothing is guaranteed, plus we're doing this on one income." Doris offered to get a job because that's how bad she wanted that house. She knew I didn't want her working. I wanted her raising our kids, not some daycare that's going to cost us more then what she'll be making at some job for all three of our kids to go to.

I thought about it and I said, "We'll take it, but we're really gonna have to sacrifice and cut some corners for these six months to keep that house." So I told Doris if she down with that then we can give it a shot, and if not then let's not even set ourselves up for failure.

"Yes! Whatever it takes!" She reached in her purse and pulled out the leasing agreement that was already filled out and signed by her, all it needed was my signature. Then she pulled out a receipt and she said, "I'm glad you finally said yes because I already paid for our move in and I've already had the lights and gas turned on."

"Where did you get the money for that?" I said. "I hope you didn't write them a check because I don't have enough money in the bank to cover that Doris Jean!"

My little manipulative wife told me not to worry because she paid for it all with cash out of her own pocket. Then I asked her where in the hell did she get the money from. She told me that she got it from the money she made from selling our apartment full of furniture in Long Beach that I had helped furnish while

I was washing police cars in jail last year. She also said that she had saved a couple of months of her county checks, and she cashed them and brought that money with her too. Then for the grand finale she reached back into her purse and she pulled out a brick of those food stamps booklets and she said we have over five hundred dollars in food stamps so we'll be good as far as food goes for a while.

I smiled and I kissed my wife and I said, "That's why I love baby."

My wife smiled and gloated for a minute while I signed the lease. She knew what she had done today was very risky by her getting that house without me approving it first, but she also knew that whatever we both put our minds to we always got it done. By the end of that weekend we were all moved in.

I was in the front of the house doing some work on the yard when a car drove up and honked its horn. The driver rolled the window down and said, "Hi Edsel! Welcome to the neighborhood!" I looked up and I saw an old white man in a brand new 911 Porsche Turbo. The old dude was my plant manager at Coca-Cola.

"Thank you sir! Nice car! You just picked that up?"

"Yes, just now, thanks to you!"

I started laughing and I said, "What are you doing over here?"

"I live up the road here."

"Oh OK, we're neighbors."

"Yes we are. Apparently I'm paying you too much." He started laughing and then he said, "Monday morning I'll race you to work, loser buys lunch!"

I pointed at his hundred and twenty thousand dollars,-triple black Porsche 911 Turbo, with the bright red calibers and I said, "I have no chance against that car. I might as well pay you now for your lunch on

Monday," I said. "By the way, it fits you fine. You look twenty years younger sitting in that driver's seat.

Welcome to the Porsche club sir." His face lit up as he hit the gas pedal. I had buttered him up so good, I could see him smiling all the way up the road until he turned off my street.

A few months had passed and winter time was coming again. I had some firewood delivered for our fireplace. Me and Doris couldn't wait to fire that baby up; it was so nice and sexy having a fireplace in our living room. I had to go buy one of those fireplace sets to cover the front of it for the safety of the kids, especially baby Kristin.

My daughter was always into something around the house. One day Doris noticed that Kristin was being a little too quiet around the house so Doris went looking for her. She found baby Kristin standing inside the refrigerator with a whole pack of hot dogs stuffed in her mouth. Her big ole cheeks were full.

She looked like a little chipmunk, it was too cute. Then one morning I went to get a movie that we rented so I could return it to the video store. I hit the eject button on the VCR and the VHS cassette pushed out a whole stick of butter as the tape came oozing out of the machine, destroying not only the movie that we had rented, but also our brand new VCR. I knew exactly who did it because when I turned around to look at Andre, Poche', and Kristin as they were playing on the floor and watching the early morning funnies. Kristin's eyes got big and she jumped up and ran to her mommy in our bedroom.

***

Thanksgiving came and me, Doris, and the kids spent it with my supervisor. He invited me to bring my family over to enjoy Thanksgiving dinner with him, his wife, and their two bad ass kids. I took him up on it because it's always good to be in decent standings with your boss. I kind of felt bad because he was about to lose his job to me, but that's life if you're slipping and messing up be prepared to lose your position, that goes for anything in life. Plus none of us liked his ass anyway, not even the old white dude, his own boss.

But that day I saw him in another light. He was different as a family man compared to how he was at work.

I didn't know if it was because of the holiday spirit or if it was because that's just how you have to carry yourself at work when you're in a position of power. If I'm lucky, I'll soon be finding out. We tried to enjoy that meal but the food had no flavor. I guess I was just spoiled by Doris' cooking. My expectations are very high between Doris, my mother and my grandmother's cooking, those ladies were definitely no comparison.

But we were nice about it, we thanked them for their hospitality, and he and his wife thanked us for coming. My boss said that we should do it again sometime. Doris hurried up and told them that next time dinner will be at our house, so she would be able to cook for them to kind of show them how it's done.

They agreed and we headed home.

By the time we pulled into our driveway all three of the kids were knocked out. Doris went to go unlock the front door, while I started carrying the babies in one at a time. I tucked the kids in while Doris popped the cork on a bottle of wine. I started the fireplace, then Doris laid a blanket down and we enjoyed our bottle of wine. We made love right there in our living room in front of the fireplace then we passed out.

One night Doris let me go out to a party in Chattanooga, I went with my cousin Charlie and two of my coworkers. We had a lot of fun. It was my first time going out since I had my family back with me. I couldn't believe Doris let me go. She was cool with it, she even said that I deserved to go out and enjoy myself with the fellas. So I hurried up at the chance to get out on the town with my boys. Doris just had a couple of rules for me before I left. "Just don't drink any Sisco, and don't stop at Mr. Zips on the way home." I gave her a sarcastic look and said, "Ha ha very funny."

Everything was going nice and smooth until we were on our way back to Cleveland. A state trooper got behind us and hit his lights. I looked in the rearview mirror and all I saw were that infamous flashing light that's been haunting me since I was a little boy. He got me for speeding. He came out of nowhere. We all had been drinking our asses off, I was just doing a little buzz driving, I was good at it. My big problem was that my California driver's license had expired and since I work so damn much I hadn't been able to get down to the D.M.V to get my Tennessee license yet. So as I'm pulling over I say, "Somebody give me their license real quick before the trooper gets to my window!" My cousin slid me his license from the backseat. I rolled the window down and the trooper asked me that infamous question. "Do you know how fast you were going?" I told him no. I actually wasn't paying attention.

"Just let me see your license and registration and give you a quick ticket and let you fellas get home."

As I was handing the officer with the big dumb ass hat on my cousin's license, my drunken ass coworker that was in back of the passenger's seat yelled out. "Why we getting a ticket? Is it because we're black? Black men can't be in a Porsche?"

The trooper ignored him because I turned around to hush my drunken ass co-worker by saying "Yo Bobby!

Chill my nigga, he's just gonna write me a ticket and we out Cuzz, so chill out!"

As the trooper was about to turn around to go write the ticket and then let us go Bobby yelled again, "No! Fuck that! I'm tired of these racist ass pigs!" When that country hillbilly ass Tennessee state trooper heard that, it was all bad. He told his partner that was in the police car running my plates to go around to the passenger side. Then the trooper told Bobby to step out of the vehicle. I started shaking my fucking head, and then I looked at my cousin like if to say why didn't you shut that fool up? Charlie didn't say a word. I woke my co-worker up that was sleeping in the passenger's seat so he could let that drunken ignorant ass Bobby out of the backseat. Then the trooper on my side said, "Why don't all of you step out of the car." I thought to myself Aw shit, here we go again. I stepped out of the car, and then I let Charlie out of the backseat. I told him that he's gonna have to start speaking up because the trooper has his license. Then I looked at my cousin's eyes and I realized why he hasn't said a word this whole time. He was the drunkest person in the damn car.

"Damn Cuzz! Yo ass is twisted! Can you straighten up for five minutes then we'll be headed home Cuzz. Can you please do that for me cousin? Get your life together real quick, Cuzz!"

He just nodded his head as I pushed him towards the back of the car where my other co-worker was. He was looking better than my cousin. I guess he slept some of the alcohol away during his little power nap while we were on our way home.

Both of the troopers put drunken ass Bobby in the back of the police car because he would not shut his mouth. The trooper with my cousin's license came walking up all in my face with that big dumb ass round hat they wear. He looked at me then the license and he said, "Now which one of ya'll boys were driving?"

Thank God all us black folk look alike.

My cousin who was trying to pull it together raised his hand. The state trooper walked over and got all in his face and he asked him if he'd been drinking. Charlie shook his head. Then the trooper asked him if he could walk the line for him. He told my cousin that if he could walk the line from the back of my car to the front of his cruiser then he'll let us all go and they'll just run in the idiot that's cuffed in the backseat of their squad car. As my cousin was leaning on the back of my car the trooper asked him if he was ready. My cousin nodded his head; and as he raised his right foot he slid sideways; and fell into the highway face first and he didn't move. I just put my head down into my hands and I shook my head. The troopers threw my cousin in the backseat a belligerent Bobby. Then the trooper asked me if I could walk the line.

"Yes sir, no problem!" I said, even though I drank just as much as them two in the back of the police car. I knew I was straight enough to pass any test they threw at me, except maybe that ABC shit, I can't do that shit sober.

"OK, I'll tell you like I told sleeping beauty. If you can walk that line from car to car then I'll let you drive off no questions asked."

I got to the line and I didn't think too much about the task at hand I just looked down at the line, took a deep breath and walked it nonstop until I got to the front of the police car. I did it with ease. The trooper said, "OK, you two gentlemen have a goodnight." I told my co-worker to hop in so we could roll out. We both got into my car and buckled up making sure to follow all the rules. I started the car and as I'm about to put the car in gear the trooper wrapped on my window with his flashlight. I rolled the window down.

"Yes officer?" He asked me who does this car belong to/ "It's mine officer."

"Could you please step out the car?"

I unbuckled my seat belt and I stepped out of the car. I asked the officer what was wrong. Then he asked me to please turn around and interlock your fingers. I turned around and all I heard was a clicking sound and I felt two ice cold bracelets tighten around my wrist.

"What's the problem officer?"

As he escorted me to his police car he explained to me that Tennessee state law is if you allow somebody to operate your vehicle and their drunk and they get arrested for DWI then I face the same exact fines and legal punishment as they do, jail time included.

"What the fuck kind of law is that?" I asked.

"It's the law of the great state of Tennessee, you're not in California Mr. Hollywood," he said.

I couldn't believe what was happening. They stuffed me in the back seat with sleeping beauty and belligerent Bobby. They made my co-worker walk the line. When he was done the trooper said "Thank goodness you passed! I was running out of space in my squad car." They let me tell my coworker what to say to my wife. Luckily, his car was parked at my house. I told him when he got there to have Doris come up to the Chattanooga city jail with my check book to bail me out.

We all got processed into that shit hole ass jail so now I was waiting for Doris to come and spring me up out of there. I was cussing ole Bobby Brown acting boy out while we were in the drunk tank. I told him that if he would've just kept his fucking mouth shut we'd be at home right now and not in this fucking throw up smelling drunk tank. He apologized after he started sobering up. I told him that this was not a good look because I'm about to get promoted to the supervisor's position and I'm not trying to mess that up.

"What supervisor's position? We already have a supervisor." Then I told him how the plant manager is not feeling our current supervisor and that he's already asked me to take over as soon as they fired his ass. As soon as I said that, the bailiff came and called my name. He said that I'm being bonded out and to get ready. I told his ass that I was ready right now.

"You gonna leave me in here Cuzz?"

"Hell naw as soon as I get to my wife I will have her bail you out too."

"Us two? Thanks man!" Bobby said.

"Hell naw nigga! It's because of yo ass we in this bitch! At least my cousin had my back and tried to get us out of the situation, yo ass fucked that all up running your drunk ass mouth. You a grown ass nigga and can't even hold your liquor homie! Besides my money ain't like that, Cuzz! Call yo peoples my nigga. I'm sure they'll come get you out."

The jailer came and popped me out. I told Bobby that I'll see him Monday at work. He didn't even look my way. I walked out and kissed my wife and my cousin Charlie came soon after.

At work on Monday Bobby was acting like a little bitch about the other night, but fuck'em he brought that shit on himself. He'll get over it and we'll be back cool again. He knew he was wrong so that shit was on him, get over it!

By the end of the week I started to notice that my supervisor was acting kinda funny style. He always knew that me and the plant manager were cool so I think that always intimidated him. I think he saw me as a threat to his position because he knew that I was next in line to fill his shoes if he slipped up.

But what I didn't know at the time was that Bitch Boy Bobby had told our supervisor about our little conversation in that drunk tank. I guess he was all in his feelings because I didn't bail his ass out that night.

Ever since then I noticed our supervisor being all standoffish and he wasn't as friendly to me anymore. He even wrote me up for being nine minutes late to work the day before.

At this point I realized that he was starting to ride me and getting on me for every little thing I did. He even made a comment about me being three minutes late coming back from my lunch break. He didn't write me up but he made a slick ass comment about it. I let it slide but I was getting really pissed at the fact that this dude who broke bread with me at his dinner table on Thanksgiving with our wives and kids was now trying to fire me. He knew I had a family to support. The more I thought about it the madder and madder I got! As my fucked up mind got to thinking, I started plotting on doing something really bad to this dude because in my mind he was trying to interfere with my money that I needed to feed my family with.

So I thought to myself I'm gonna get his ass and I was too, until one day I slipped up and I spoke out loud and threatened to smoke his ass. Bobby heard me and he asked me if I was serious. I looked at Bobby not realizing what I had just did and I said, "Serious about what?"

"About what you just said?"

"What are you talking about Bobby? I was just rapping a NWA song homie!" But I knew at that point that if anything would've happened, I would still be in jail right now because bitch boy Bobby would've snitched me out. That's when I started to rebel at work and then I came up with another plan. I waited for one of the busiest days of the year. It was around the New Year's holiday. I went to work; we had a serious deadline to make. There was a lot of pressure on everybody especially my supervisor. We really had to get these big major orders out by a specific time or it would have looked bad on our entire plant. So

I went into work knowing all this and I twisted up all the invoices, load about twenty trucks with the wrong orders and I walked out the plant leaving my incompetent ass supervisor to try and figure it all out and fix it all in time to make their deadline that night. That was an impossible job for anyone to do. I really screwed that shit up in hopes that it would be enough to get Bobby and my bitch ass boss fired too.

CHAP TER 25

Traded the Married Life for Prison Life

By the time my birthday came around there was nothing to celebrate about. By this time we had lost our house and we were staying with one of my boys in his little two bedroom apartment, while I worked odd jobs to try to save up to get us our own place again. I could not land a consistent gig, let alone another permanent one. The stress was starting to put a lot tension between me and Doris again. There was a lot of pressure building for me to get us another place, which led to daily arguments with me and my wife. It was so much pressure that one day in front of my homie and three of his boys, Doris got all in my face as we we're arguing. Things got real heated Doris called me a punk ass nigga and she pushed me. I snapped! All I remember was that I was on top of Doris with both my hands around her neck. Then I remember looking down at her face and I had a flashback of how my mother's face looked when I was a little boy and my dad did the same thing but worse to my mom. At that point I realized what I was doing and that it wasn't me.

This incident had taken me totally out of my character and things needed to change instantly.

I remember looking to my left and my little four year old baby girl was standing at the door looking all confused as she stood there crying for her mommy. I jumped off my wife and I picked up my daughter. I held her and kiss her as I called little Suave to come and get me.

He said ok and he was on his way. I grabbed my duffle bag. I packed what I could in it, leaving everything else behind in Tennessee including my family and I caught the next Greyhound bus all the way back to California.

Once I was back in Cali I didn't waste any time contacting my best nigga Troy. When I called Troy to let

him know that I was back and ready to put in some work he told me that he had just the thing for us to do. I was happy to hear the good news. I told him that my Aunt Joan and my Uncle David had a house in

Downey and that they were letting me sleep in their garage until I get something going out here. Troy told me to give him the address and he'll be on his way.

Troy came by and he told me about his newest venture. He said that he wanted to start a chop shop and now that I'm back we can go out and get the cars and take them to a location and break them down. He said that he already had buyers lined up.

"Cool what are we gonna be looking for?" I said

"Porsche," he said.

"Oh shit! That sounds like fun!"

We went out that night and every night for about two months straight. Some nights we would bring back two Porsche's at once. We would be racing back to Downey coming down the 105 freeway doing about 160 miles per hour. It would be about two or three in the morning so we would be the only cars on the road. We were making at least five thousand a week, each. That was good money for 1995. We had a full proof system. We knew how to disarm the cars of all factory and non-factory alarms and or theft tracking devices, we were professionals. We knew how to locate and remove those Lo-Jack and Tele-Track vehicle tracking devices.

As soon as we pulled the car into our shop we'd locate the orange, light blue or green box and disconnect it and have someone drive it up the 110 freeway and out onto the freeway miles away. Then we would disassemble the entire car. Then we had air compressor power tools to take all the valuable resale parts off the car. We would take our power saws and cut it up so we could sell every part of the car as possible, which was 85%. We would drive the car into our shop, and then a few hours later we were carrying the car out, piece by piece. We loaded all the scrap pieces that we weren't able to sale and go dump them miles away then come back and load up all the things we could sale and lock them safely in the U-Haul truck. By the time we'd be done with all of that it would be about 6:30 a.m., so then we would take a quick power nap and be back up by 9 a.m. making calls and making deliveries until every bolt from that car was gone. Usually by noon that day, the U-Haul truck would be empty and our pockets would be full. Business was booming and we loved doing what we did, but of course all good things must come to an end.

One afternoon, Troy needed me to ride with him to move a stolen car that he had went out and got the night before without me. He saw a Porsche Turbo slipping so he said he had to get it. I told my homie no problem, let's roll. We hopped in the stolen Porsche and as soon as Troy started it, an unmarked police car pulled up behind us and hit the siren. I looked over at Troy as he sat in the driver's seat.

"What do you think I should do?" he asked.

"This is a Porsche 911 Turbo so punch it!" So he did. We were both excellent drivers and we both owned a Porsche. We raced each other every day on the freeways of Los Angeles practicing for this very moment. Troy drove his ass off as I navigated us through the streets of Los Angeles. Our shop was by Century and Prairie Ave. We went flying passed the Hollywood Park Casino, then passed the Los Angeles Forum where the Lakers once played. We were doing over 100 miles per hour.

I looked back and I remember seeing at least fifteen police cars behind us, but they were no match for that Porsche 911 Turbo. With Troy behind the wheel and me navigating we were the perfect team and there was no way we were gonna be caught. Troy listened and executed every command I said as I called out our route.

"Turn left! Go right- right here! Hold up, red light, OK clear, run it!" The sirens got quieter and the police lights got dimmer. Nothing could catch us now, except that damn police radio. Little did we know there were police cars in front of us heading our way with a description of a white Porsche 911 with two black male suspects in it traveling at a high rate of speed. We hit a side street and hopped out the car as it was still rolling. An unmarked cop car recognized us from the description on his radio and he turned on the street right behind us. Troy was a little skinny dude so as soon as his feet hit the ground he was gone. As I hopped out I heard "Freeze!" I looked at the back of the Porsche and there was a guy in plain clothes with his big ass gun pointed at my head. At the time I didn't know if he was a cop or some vigilante or what. So I ran like hell! Problem was, I weighed almost 300 lbs., I was a big Samoan looking black dude with long hair that was running for his life, especially if this guy actually was an LAPD officer because them mutha fucka's are known to shoot first then ask questions later. It was also next to impossible for me to get away because it was broad daylight and I had half of the Los Angeles police department chasing my ass. I ran around a building and back towards the Porsche, but by then all the other police cars were pulling up to a screeching halt as I got back to the Porsche. Next thing I knew I had two dozen pistols and shotguns all in my face. The police officer that was chasing me ran up and jumped on my back as I was following their orders to lay face down on that hot ass asphalt. I'll never forget the feeling of that cop's gun. He was shoving that cold steel into the back of my head. He used the barrel of his gun to pin my face to the ground.

While he was breathing heavy in my ear, he told that if it wasn't for all these witnesses out here he would not have had a problem blowing my fucking head off for making him chase me. He handcuffed me and handed me other to an officer in one of the black and white squad cars. They threw me in the backseat and tried to play good cop bad cop but I was too seasoned in this jail shit to fall for that. The two officers in the car told me to just sit tight as I complained of how my cuffs were way too flicking tight around my wrist. I told them that my fingers were getting numb, they told me that they knew I wasn't the driver and as soon as they catch my buddy then they were gonna let me go.

"Good luck!" I said laughing. Then they tried to tell me to just let them know where he might have went and as soon as they arrest him they'll release me. I told them to go fuck themselves. They took me to the station. After they booked me, they gave me my free phone call. I called Troy's cell phone. Our phones weren't in our names anyway so it didn't matter. Troy picked up on the first ring.

"Sup my nigga," I said.

"Hey! Where you at? I'm on my way!"

"I'm in the worst place."

"You got caught?"

"Hell yeah! Where was my fat ass about to go with all those damn police officers on our bumper like that? That police radio is a mutha fucka!"

"I know trust me," Troy said.

"I'm straight though they already said that they know I wasn't the driver, they also told that as soon as they catch the driver they're gonna release me."

"Yeah right! You know that ain't happening." We both started laughing our asses off.

I told Troy that I'm good and that I'll ride this out just get me a good lawyer, and I should beat this little shit because they knew I wasn't the driver. "Fasho my nigga, I got you."

The police was mad at me because I wouldn't snitch my boy out. The next thing I knew I was in court being charged with a felony evading the police and grand theft auto. My high priced lawyer I had couldn't even get me out of this one. Those crooked ass cops took the stand. The judge asked them if they saw the driver of the stolen white Porsche and all three of their lying asses pointed at me. I couldn't believe them lying ass crooked ass cops just lied like that on the stand while under oath and before God. Even the off duty cop that chased me around the building was on the stand in his full uniform pointing me out as the driver too. The judge slammed his gavel, found me guilty, and sentenced me to three years in the California State Penitentiary. I had been to jail about five times by now, but this was gonna be my first trip to the big house, prison.

***

Prison was a whole new world. They loaded us up in the back of an eighteen wheeler tractor truck like cattle. We were all in cages back there with two deputies that had shotguns in their hands. They were talking big shit and mad dogging us the entire five hour ride.

We pulled into Delano State Prison Reception Center in Central Valley California. As I'm shackled from head to toe the first thing I saw as I got off that cattle truck was the guard towers. That's where the trigger happy ass correctional officers standing up all day pointing their AR-15 sniper rifles down at us, longing itching for some shit to jump off so they can have a reason to squeeze off some rounds, and trust me, they don't miss.

Nervous as hell, I was shaking like Muhammad Ali as I walked into a prison compound for my first time at the young age of twenty three years young. As the officers hurried us inside the facility the first thing I noticed as I was walking into the first miniature sized holding tank were the words "NO WARNING SHOTS!" They were painted on every wall in there so there's no excuse, you were warned. There were about one hundred of us, blacks, whites, Mexicans, and a couple of others. They always kept us separated because of the constant racial tension between the blacks and the Mexicans. They had about thirty of us in a cell that was made to only hold about ten men. We had to strip butt naked while we got screened and medically cleared. There was everything from crack heads to rapist to murders in that cell. It was a very unforgettable experience.

As soon as Doris found out I was in jail, she quickly moved back to Cali. She took this opportunity to get back on my good side by using my daughter to come visit me in hopes that I would take her back. Of course I could never deny my beautiful little girl, so in the long run Doris plan ended up working. Doris and the kids were making the weekly trip to come visit me for hours at a time on the weekends. It was good to be able to play with Kristin and the boys. Me and Doris would sneak kisses the whole visit and hold hands while we would eat the microwavable meals together from the vending machines in the visiting room. They had a bunch of different microwavable foods to choose from. They all tasted like cardboard but even that was an upgrade from the food the prison served us three times a day.

Getting those weekly visits really helped make those weeks and months and years go by fast. I'll never ever forget that day in September of 1996.

I was walking the yard with one of my homies and I heard on the radio that Tupac got shot. My heart dropped at the thought of the world losing the best rapper ever. Tupac was somebody that I'd never got the opportunity to meet personally but thru the lyrics of his songs I felt very connected almost like we lived a similar life and had a lot of the same experiences in life. Everybody I know that knew Pac personally said that if he was alive we would be the best of friends because we are similar in our lifestyles as far as the Hollywood shit and the women.

Everything was all good because the next day they were saying on the radio that he was still alive at a Nevada hospital. By the third day he was still alive in the hospital, so I'm thinking he's on his road to recovery because when you're locked up you're only getting the partial information through the little bit of radio and TV news. So I was thinking positive and figuring that Pac had once again escaped death. So I started talking big shit with my niggas saying that Pac lived through five more shots and that now he's just gonna get out the hospital and get back into the studio and drop some more heat and be talking big shit.

Because that's what Pac did. He had been through everything from shooting the police to getting shot at least five times. He was on trial with Snoop "Dogg" Lion Two of America's Most Wanted they were in there like some straight G's and he walked up out of that shit, it was all good, so this will end up all good too!

Until Friday the 13th

September 1996. I was buffing iron on the weight pile on the yard when I heard the tragic announcement that Tupac Shakur had died. Everybody on that yard and in the entire prison period could not believe it was true. I hurried to the phone and called Doris to confirm what I did not want to believe. But it was true Pac was gone, I could not believe it, and sometimes I still don't. I still believe that

Tupac is out there somewhere reading this book and smiling. But I know one thing for a fact, if Pac was still alive, I know he's somewhere out there raising hell and talking big shit about a lot these sucka ass rappers that's out here knowing that if Pac was still on the scene they wouldn't even have a rap career.

January 1997 came and I got approved for the halfway house. I got there Super bowl weekend. It wasn't completely freedom but it was halfway there. The halfway house I ended up at was in the city of Van Nuys, in the San Fernando Valley. It was called the Orion House. It was on Orion and Roscoe Blvd. I liked it there. I got a little freedom to be able to get out there and see some girls. They would give us daily passes to go to the store and come right back. They would only be for an hour but that's all the time I needed to step out there on the scene so I could see what I could see. I was a nigga fresh out on swole and ready to explore my options with the ladies. I met a few ladies that lived in the area just from going on those daily passes. I even bumped into Lisa Bonet walking back to the halfway house one day and she gave me her number. She was looking sexy as hell while she was waiting at a red light on Roscoe and Sepulveda smoking on a Black and Mild. So I had to holla!

One morning as I was walking to the store I heard Theo the DJ radio personality for 92.3 The Beat make the announcement that Biggie Smalls was shot and killed last night while leaving a Los Angeles night club. I just stopped in my tracks, put my head down and I said a quick prayer for his mother, his daughter, his son, and for Faith Evans who I knew was somewhere taking it very hard. That was another one of our senseless tragic losses from that East coast West coast Hip Hop feud. Now two of the best MC's to have ever touched a mic was gone. God bless their souls.

I was getting so much play from the ladies that a bitch made nigga that called himself my friend started hating on me. Of course I didn't find this out until after I had been released from there.

Anyway, he told Doris that I had a few girls that I was seeing in the area and that they would come visit me at the halfway house. He just wanted what I had so he figured if he worked with Doris to help get me caught then he could have her. I guess he thought Doris would find out about my girls and leave me for him. Yeah right bitch nigga, you only exposed yourself to being the hoe ass nigga that you are. You should've kept it player and just hollered at my wife and kept my name and business out your mouth, then at least you'd still have your dignity.

There was one girl that I met during my fourth month stay at that halfway house. She conveniently lived on the next block over from the Orion house. I used to walk over on my job search days and pay her a little visit. The halfway house would give us four to six hours to go anywhere we wanted to look for a job.

So when I could get away with it I would walk to the store at the corner and buy a box of condoms, then walk over to her apartment. She would greet me at the apartment's security gate and walk me up to her place. This girl was an angel. She looked a lot like Jasmine Cashmere. Even the way we had sex was the same way me and Jasmine have sex when I see her now that I think about it. They both have that same Butter Pecan complexion with a nice slim waist and some full beautiful breast, except this girl had inverted nipples. That was my first experience with inverted nipples so I'll never forget that girl for that reason alone. I used to play with her nipples with my tongue. I would suckle on them then I'd gently blow on them and watch each one pop out. My little Angel liked it nice, slow and gentle. I can't say that we were making love because there was no love involved other than the fact that I loved having sex with her and I'm pretty sure the feeling was mutual.

Our sessions were very passionate. It's was like our body meshed together perfectly, her little petite frame fit like a glove with my big boned body. Her apartment was nice. I really liked her bedding it was always clean and soft just like her skin. Everything was all white. She had white sheer drapes. She kept the windows open so a nice breeze would blow through keeping our bodies at a perfect not sweating temperature. It was like we were up in the sky on a bright cloudy day. The slow and passionate way we would have sex was very elegant and erotic. We would be in missionary position. I would have her soft dainty little hands in mine up over her head. As I would slowly and deeply grind she would bite her bottom lip and stare at me with her eyes squinted. Because of her exotic bi-racial mix she had the longest eyelashes

I'd ever seen. They were definitely some Angel eyes. We would go at a slow but even dance as our hips met at a consistently perfectly matching rhythm with each other's, over and over again. Each gyration brought us both closer and closer to the ultimate goal of reaching our pleasuring sexual peaks. We would go and go as it built and built. I knew when she was climaxing because she would bite her bottom lip and start this faint yearning sound as she whimpered in my ear. It would get a little more pronounced as I would gyrate, never changing my rhythm, as I pumped and pumped. Then as we both reached our orgasmic explosion at the same exact time she would squeeze her intertwined fingers with mine and Angels back would arch. I would keep gyrating never breaking my stride making sure I kept that rhythm going so Angel could ride her orgasmic wave until she was completely spent. Then after the orgasm aftershocks stopped Angel would slowly open her eyes and look into mine, then she would slowly open her mouth and start licking her bitten bottom lip. Then we would slowly release our hands and I would lay there with my little Angel feeling that nice cool breeze like as if we were up in the heavens suspended on her cloud like bed.

CHAPTER 26

My Introduction

to Porn

The day came for me to parole for that halfway house and go home to Doris and kids. I explained everything very clearly to Doris about how it's very different being on parole than it was being on probation. I told her that now that I'm on parole if I have any contact with the police then they're taking me to jail. So absolutely no arguing. We lived in an apartment so if our neighbors called the police and they came to our door then I'm going back to prison, no questions asked. So I told her once again, no arguing!

Well that didn't last long at all because next thing I knew me and Doris were yelling at each other about something that I can't even recall to this day. So before it could escalate into something unnecessary I walked out the house. I couldn't believe it. I had only been home for a few months and here we go again. I was not about to have a repeat of our last Tennessee incident, that shit wasn't me. I walked to the nearest payphone and I called Angel but she didn't pick up so it was on to the next. I went through my pager and I got the number to my six foot one and a half inch tall one hundred and thirty seven pound model type valley girl. I call her Jessica because she was tall with that slim little model type body. She had that beautiful brown complexion like the super sexy and beautiful Super Model Miss Jessica White.

I dialed Jessica's number and she picked up on the first ring. She already knew about the wifey so when I told her what had happened she quickly said, "Come here and stay with me!"

I said "What about you're live in boyfriend?"

She told me to hold on. While I was holding the line I heard Jessica call her boyfriend's name. Then

I heard him say "What do you want?"

"Get out! You gotta go! Pack your shit and leave now!" She got back on the phone and she it was all good and for me to come now. She said not worry because by the time I got there her boyfriend would be gone. She gave me her address and some very brief directions because I knew nothing about the San Fernando Valley.

I hung up the payphone and in an hour I was pulling up at Jessica's house with my shit and moving in! Me and Jessica hit it off real good. She was an alcoholic like me. We both drank gin and juice and we both liked to fuck. But alcohol and sex was pretty much all we had in common. But I was more than cool with that because I was fresh out of prison so that's all I needed at the time. But even fucking Jessica Whites look-a-like eventually got old too.

Her brother had a good job at Sony Studios in Culver City. I asked him to hook a brotha up with a job. He had some pull up there so he did. He set it up for me to go apply for a set builder's position. He put in a good word for me so they hired me no problem. It was a real good job and a very interesting one too. Being on that lot I never knew who I was going to run into. In between jobs I would wonder around the Sony and Culver studios lot checking out sitcoms and movie sets while they were filming. I met a lot of cool people working that job; it was another great opportunity for longevity at a job with possibility of retirement. I lost that job because Jessica didn't want my little brother hanging out at her house while me and her went off to work so I had to start taking my little Suave to work with me. I would sneak him onto the Sony lot with me and he would hide out inside one of the prop houses or just wonder around the lot all day long until I'd find my little brother and we'd go eat what we could off whatever little money I have for us for lunch. Working a regular job doing things legal and the way society wants you to live means that a lot of times your ass is broke. So a lot of days me and little Suave didn't eat, because I didn't have any money to feed us. This was my little brother that I sent for to come stay with me for a better life but some days he would be so hungry that when I'd find him he would be somewhere in one of those prop houses balled up in fetal position crying because he was so hungry. That would make me feel bad as a big brother and his sole provider. I would be just as hungry but I stayed strong for my little brother. When times got desperate like that I would go into the studio workers break room and raid their refrigerators to put some food in my little brothers stomach. He was my responsibility so I would do anything for my little bro! After a while the Sony lots security started to catch on to me sneaking my little brother onto the property and before I knew it I was fired. Once again I lost a very promising job that I could have one day retired from but I was still young so I didn't realize the loss of such a good job nor did I beat myself up about it. It was a fun job and I enjoyed it while it lasted. Now it was gone and I needed to figure out my next move. Losing my job caused some friction between me and Jessica. Not to mention the fact that I had just sent for my little brother from

Tennessee and moved him in without even asking Jessica. That caused even more friction and a lot more responsibility and pressure on me. I sent for my little brother for a reason and I was not about to let him out of my sight.

One day my mother called me crying and she said that my little brother Mikey was in the hospital. I asked her what happened. She said that she thinks he tried to kill his self because of his wife. I instantly had flashbacks of my mother's multiple suicide attempts from when I was a kid. Little Suave has always followed in my footsteps. He dropped out of high school, like me. He got married at a woman that already had children who was much older than him, like I did. She was also very manipulative and controlling like my wife was.

Little Suave was also in trouble with the police and in and out of jail at a young age, like me as well. He pretty much looked up to his brother and followed, exactly in my footsteps and I've hated myself for years because of it. I wish I would've showed my little brother, that I love so much, a better way of life. It's my fault my little brother was shot seven times in Las Vegas Nevada in July 2004.

He was shot because he was doing something that I taught him to do. I was in prison at the time it happened. But before I got locked up I took little Suave on his first robbery lick. He saw more money than he had ever seen in his life, not to mention the rush you get from putting a major lick down, it's very addictive. But from that day on my brother was addicted. That was the day I got my little brother hooked on the same drug that I have been addicted to all my life and to this day I wish I would have never introduced my brother to the worse drug in the world "MONEY!" Little Suave survived those seven shots. I thank God every day for sparing my brother's life, but I feel like the worse big brother in the world because it's my fault, that right now, little Suave is serving a forty four year sentence in a Nevada State Prison.

One day my boy called me and said he had an audition in Hollywood to go to and he asked me if I wanted to ride with him so afterwards we can go hit the gym. I told him hell yeah because I was home bored as hell and to come get me. The audition was at a photography studio off Sunset Blvd. on Las Palmas. My boy checked in and was taken into one of the rooms for his audition.

While I was hanging out waiting for him to return so we could go hit the gym a man named Ron Ellis approached me. He introduced himself as the head photographer and the owner of the studio. Ron told me that he had someone that would definitely like to meet me.

I said "OK, who is it and what is it about?"

He said that his friend was only five minutes away and he would explain everything when he gets here.

I said "OK cool!"

I looked around at the pictures on the walls while I now waited for this mystery person to arrive.

Ten minutes later a man walked up to me with purple hair smiling and extending his hand out. "Hi my name is Eddie Pierce, are you Suave?"

"Yes, are you the guy that wanted to meet me?"

"Yes I am!"

"OK, what's this about?"

The man with the purple hair was clearly gay, so my fag flag instantly went up. I was worried about where this conversation might be going, but I was willing to at least hear the man out. There was no telling who this guy was or who he might know. This man could make me the next Denzel Washington. Eddie wasn't that type and he got straight to the point. He asked me something that I've never been asked before in my life. Eddie looked at me with a little smirk on his face and he asked me if I've ever thought about doing porn. I gave Eddie a once over look because I didn't know how to take this line of questioning. I thought I was being tested because I had never been approached by anyone like the Fierce Mr. Eddie Pierce before and I had definitely never been approached about no Porno shit before either. Being from the hood you don't run into no Homo shit, or at least not in my hood! But I had already heard about the Hollywood scene so I didn't take offense to what he had just asked me, but I had to make sure this wasn't no gay shit.

"Excuse me; did you say porn, as in porno movie?"

"Yes I did!" He explained to me that he was a make-up artist for the porn industry and he also doubles as a talent agent. "Excuse me for saying, but you are gorgeous and you have a very exotic look to bring to the industry." Then he told me if I was interested then he was sure that he could get me my first scene as soon as I wanted to start.

I was looking at this dude as he was talking to me with his over the top metro sexual look, and with his purple curly top hair. I stopped Eddie and I told him I'm not with no gay shit so if that's what this is about we can end this conversation right now.

"No, no! Don't go off of my appearance and preference, although you would make much more money doing gay movies, but it's clear that you're not gay. I'm referring to straight porn."

Once that was cleared up, I tried to wrap my head around the offer that Eddie had just presented to me. I really couldn't believe my ears. I just got out of an eight year serious relationship with a wife and three kids and now I was in Hollywood standing in a photography studio being asked to do straight Porn by a gay guy. How random was that? I didn't know what to say. I told Eddie that I didn't know about doing this Porn thing. I told him that I've only watched one porn movie in my life and that was when I was fourteen, and now you're asking me to be in one?

"Yes! What do you think?" I told Eddie that I would think about it. Eddie smiled and said that was good enough for him. He gave me his card and he told me to call him when I was ready.

My boy came out from his audition just as Eddie was walking out the studio. I told him what just happened and he almost ran out the door to chase Eddie down. I asked him what he thought I should do. My boy was like, "Do that shit!"

When I got home that night, I sat my girl down so we could have a much needed talk. I told her that I've noticed since I moved little Suave in that it's been a lot of tension between me and her. Then I told her that also since I recently lost my job that it's been even more tension. She said that it was true and she apologizes for her slight change in attitude, but it's just been a little overwhelming lately. I told her that there was no need to apologize and that I totally understood. Then I told her that I was going to relieve the tension between us by moving out and finding a place for me and my little brother so that this tension stops, so that me and her can continue at least being friends and so she could also have her space back.

Then she asked me how I was going to pay for my own place and I'm not working. I told her I got a job offer and it's been heavy on my mind all day and night ever since I got the offer and that I'm just now making the decision to take the job. Then I asked Jessica if she would be surprised if she was to ever see me in a porno. "Hell no! The way you fuck the shit out of me, you need to be doing porn! You're the only guy that's ever been able to keep up with my demanding sexual appetite!" Then she said, "Go for it!" I was still kicking it around in my head but at the same time I figured it was time for a change and if I was going to be able to afford an apartment for me and little Suave plus utilities and to be able to feed us so that we would no longer be starving to death, then this might do it. Plus I needed something that's going to keep me busy enough to keep me out of trouble and out of prison.

So I thought to myself, since I would be having sex with the most freakiest, kinkiest, nastiest, and possibly the most beautiful and sexiest women on the planet then porn might just be the answer.

Jessica was very cool about it too. She even helped me look for my new place. Since she knew the valley and I didn't, she took me around till I found the right spot for me and my little brother to live. It took us about two weeks but we finally found a nice apartment in Chatsworth. It was on De Soto and Parthenia, and they had a "First Month Free", move in special. That was just what I needed. Plus it just so happens that Chatsworth, California is the Porn Capitol of the World! So that worked out perfectly! Me and little

Suave moved in our new apartment and me and Jessica parted as friends, with benefits!

I got on the phone and called Eddie. He was happy to hear from me. I told him that I've thought about his offer to do porn. He asked me if I was ready. "Yes."

"Great! When do you wanna start?" I asked him how soon can book my first scene.

Eddie was thrilled and he told me that he would have to call around to see who's shooting and then he would call me right back.

"OK cool! Thanks clot! Hope to talk to you soon. "I said.

An hour later my new agent called me back. He told me to go over to Star World Studios in North

Hollywood and ask for Rob Spallone. Eddie gave me the address and told me to be there at 10am the next morning. I told him I'll be there, then I thanked the purple haired man and I hung up the phone.

The following morning I walked into Star World Studios in North Hollywood California. When I walked in

I saw a group of guys gathered around an office table looking like they were right off the set of Soprano's.

They were in a deep conversation, but when I walked in they all got quiet and looked up at me all crazy. I asked which one of them is Rob Spallone. The main guy that was sitting behind the desk in the big fancy chair said, "Are you the guy Eddie sent?" "Yeah, I'm here for the "Go-See."

"Go over to our clinic and take your AIDS test. If you pass it, then be here Tuesday at 9am." He said and looked at me as he took a long drag from his fifty dollar cigar.

"Is that it?"

"No!"

"What else?"

He sat up in his fancy two thousand dollar recliner chair, took his cigar out of his mouth, then he pointed at me and said firmly, "Don't be late!

Epilogue

My First Porn Set Ever

On a Tuesday morning, in the first week of January 1998, I walked into Star World Studios at 9am sharp with my HIV test results in my hand. I had no idea what to expect. Only set's I had been on were the set of my previous job at Sony and Culver Studios, so I pictured maybe a few white people walking around the studio with headset's on carrying clipboards and people isolated in their dressing room practicing their lines for their scenes. So I made sure I was on my best behavior. I walked in the studio sober as a judge. But once I got inside I could not believe my eyes. It was totally opposite from what I imagined. The first thing I noticed when I walked in was the loud and distinctive smell of some bomb ass chronic! They were smoking so much weed I thought I was on a Cheech and Chong movie set. Everybody in the studio was black. The only white person that I saw was the man with the little Sony Camcorder in his hand. His name was Mitch Spanelli. Mitch was the cameraman, the producer, the director, and the writer of the movie: Black Avenger's 6. There was an area with a couple of couches around. That's where everybody was hanging out at. The first person I met was "Mr. Marcus." He was chilling on a couch with one of the girls.

This girl was butt ass naked sitting on his lap hitting the weed bong. There were more girls, they were all over the place coming from everywhere, and it was like a different one would pass by every other minute just minding their own business. For the first thirty minutes I don't think I saw the same girl twice, they were all walking around naked like as if they were in an all-girls college dormitory. Then I met Byron Long. He was sitting on a couch smoking some of the best weed I had ever smelled in my, life, he was hitting that shit out of a three foot long fancy glass weed bong. He was Filling his lungs and then blowing out the white cloudy smoke contributing to the cloudiness of the already smoked out room. Then Byron passed the three foot chronic smoking contraption to "Tony Eveready." Tony was sitting next to "Delvin Weed" they were talking while Tony was hitting that powerful ass weed, while Delvin Weed was sipping on a pint of Vodka. I met both of them as they were talking some gangbang shit they both seemed to be some cool as niggas. Weed continued drinking his Vodka while Tony was now chasing his weed smoke with some Tequila.

Then another naked girl walked out from the dressing room. She was light skinned and very pretty with a couple of tattoos. Her name was "Porsche." Porsche walked up and sat on Tony's lap.

She took a man sized hit from that chronic filled bong and coughed and choked till uncontrollable tears ran down her face. Then she picked up Tony's bottle of Tequila and she took a swig from it so big that Tony slapped the shit out of Porsche's ass. "Bitch, Don't drink up all my shit!" Porsche jumped up pouting and rubbing her ass, then she went back to go finish getting her hair and make-up done. Then from the back of the studio came a short little sexy ass lady with the sexiest lips and the cutest little nose with the body to match. She had the cutest little tight booty with a tattoo on it that said 'Lil Ass' on it.

I was praying that she was going to pop my porn cherry. I wanted her to be my costar so badly. She was my type! She walked up to me wearing nothing but a thong. She had some big beautiful titties with some sexy six inch come fuck me boots on, and she was still a tiny little sex kitten, small and petit. She was the first of the girls to greet me. She gave me a hug and she said, "Hi, I'm Little Ass, you're new. What's your name?"

"They call me Suave," I said. She pushed her perfect titties on me and stretched up and kissed me on the lips and she said "Hi Suave, welcome to my world, nice to meet you, hope to get to work with your sexy ass soon."

I just looked at her fine ass and smiled as I said, "Hopefully today!"

She walked away and admired that tight lit ass as she disappeared to the back of the studio where she had come from. Then a big dude with a belly like mine walked up to me named "Notorious D" he introduced himself and he pointed in the direction that the fine little lady had just went to and he said "I see you just met my wife?" "Damn! That's your wife? She's bad!" I said.

"Yeah, I know, thanks." He wished me luck on my first scene and he told me not to worry, to just focus on the girl. I told him that my focus was the money I'm getting once I'm done fucking the girl! He said, "there you go! You'll be straight I see you have the right attitude already."

I asked Notorious if he knows Eddie. He said "Hell yeah everybody knows Eddie Pierce!" Then he said "Come on he's right here in the make-up room getting these hoes together."

He took me to where my new agent was. Eddie had two chairs of girl going at once. He was doing their make-up and hair all at the same time. Eddie saw me and he said, "There's my new star!"

"What's up Eddie, I see you hiding all the girls in here with you." I said.

Eddie told me that he knew I was here because all the girls were coming into the make-up room asking who the sexy new guy is with the long hair. Eddie introduced me to everybody on set that I didn't get the chance to meet, including Mitch Spanelli. Mitch introduced me to the girl that I was going to be working with.

Once she realized that she was going to be working with the new guy she started bitching and raising hell.

Apparently working with new guys is not a good thing because they always have wood problems or worse, they never get a wood at all. So you can be shooting for hours and the dude just can't and won't ever get it up and the poor girl ends up spending hours trying to fluff the guy by sucking him and sucking him and his poor little dick is lifeless. Well this chick wasn't exactly my type either and with her bitchy ass attitude she was having I knew I was going to need a drink. I asked Tony if there was some Gin around.

"Yeah come on I'll show you where it's at, Cuzz."

I followed Tony; he took me to the back of the studio. There were about six different theme sets in this big building. One of them was a strip club set with a bar.

"Get whatever you want, Cuzz."

"This shit is real liquor, Cuzz?" I said.

"Hell yeah, this is a porn set, Cuzz! Not no Hollywood bullshit! So just help yourself." "Fasho, Cuzz! Thanks!"

I made myself a Gin and juice, and then I walked back around to where everybody was hanging out waiting to do their scenes too. I took in all the scenery as I took a sip of my drink and I was tripping off how super ghetto and ratchet it was and I thought to myself, shit I'm at home! I was on my second cup of Gin and Orange Juice, my buzz was just kicking in real nice because I made my drinks hella strong so I could take that nervous edge off my back. Then the time came for me to do what I came to do, My First Porn Scene.

Khai walked up to me wearing some lingerie, she was still acting all stank but by now I was buzzing so I didn't give two shits. She handed me her AIDS test and her driver's license so I could match the name on her ID with the name on her test. I handed her my test and ID and we both checked the dates on each other's test to make sure they were taken within the last thirty days. If not then your test is not current, you're unprofessional, and you would not work that day. Of course my test was current because I had just taken it the day before and so was my co-stars. But after all that she still insisted that I wear a condom for our scene. Mitch apologized to me and he asked me if I was cool with wearing a condom and he asked me would I still being able to perform. "Hell yeah! No problem." It's hard enough fucking without a condom in front of twenty people that you don't know. Plus with a white dude that's constantly sticking a camera up your ass and over your shoulder, breathing in your ear while he's trying to get the best shots and angles he could. Wearing a condom takes away any sensitivity you would have with no condom on and it makes my job as a porn star actual "work!" I agreed to use a condom and we went through the positions and expectations of me for my scene. It was now time for action!

We started the scene off as me being a homeless bum in an alley and I'm awakened by this sexy little petit chocolate lady with some nice firm B-cup titties that was wearing some sexy lingerie. She wakes me up, since she knows I'm homeless and probably hungry she feeds me her sweet little pussy. I licked her pretty little clit like a hungry baby lion licking the last drops of milk from its mother's

I took two fingers and I spread her pussy lips. I cheated my head to the right to give Mitch a good shot of the pink insides of her wet juicy pussy as I licked circles around her clitoris with the tip of my warm, soft but yet firm tongue. Then after fifteen minutes of me nursing on her pretty little pussy we transitioned to the blowjob position.

The scene was going nice and smooth. I've seemed to take her attitude away with my above -average cunnilingus skills. Her dick sucking skills didn't need to be superb; I was already fully erect from her squirming and moaning while I was eating her pussy like as if I was already a seasoned vet. Was obviously pleasing her with my oral expertise. Plus I love it when my dick is in a woman's mouth, she could be an amateur, as long as my dick is in her warm wet mouth and I could feel her soft tongue on the underside of my dickhead then my buddy is at full attention.

Just as she's getting into sucking my dick and forgetting that it's attached to the new guy, it's time for us to transition to our first position. I put the condom on and I go in for the penetration shot. I let the head of my penis slide in and out a few times so the cameraman can get that penny shot. Then I slid my dick into her tight little gash. "Damn this bitch is tight." I started to get my strokes in on her very wet but tight little pussy and it's feeling very good, almost too good. Just as it's starting to feel too damn good the cameraman tapped me on the shoulder as he's filming and he signals for me to transition to the next position. We had enough footage of that position so we switched to the second. Damn when I went for the penny shot it was like her little pussy got even tighter! I get going at a smooth rhythm during our second position and I could feel the sensation starting to build. Now we're about forty five minutes into the scene.

I'm pumping away as she's moaning and yelling to me saying, "Give it to me! Don't stop fucking this pussy you fucking dirty derelict homeless bum!" I'm waiting for the tap on my shoulder to change positions but nothing, so I kept going. "Damn! This bitch pussy is feeling so good!" Even through the condom my sensitivity was still through the roof! I'm all into her telling me to "Give it to her! Don't stop fucking her pussy!" that as I'm feeling her pussy choking my dick I almost slipped up. So just as it was feeling too fucking good I hurried and pulled out. As soon as I did her moaning and yelling stopped and she instantly sat up in full bitch mode.

"What the fuck! Why did you stop? That's why I don't like these new guys!"

The camera guy asked me if I was OK. I was now on my knees squeezing the hell out of my dick trying desperately to keep from cumming. I'm squeezing my dick and holding my breath while I'm looking at the tip of the condom, and then it happened. The entire condom filled up with cum.

I told Mitch that I needed to go to the bathroom. "Are you alright? What's going on?"

"He fucking came, that's what's wrong! He fucking came!" Then she got up and started going the fuck off. "I'm done with this scene or get me a stunt dick in here now! I'm not trying to be here all day while this new guy struggles through his first scene!"

Then Mitch said, "Damn Suave, you blew it. I guess I gotta get someone else to fill in and you don't get paid."

"I'm still good Mitch, just give me a second."

I told Mitch that I can still continue with the scene I just couldn't hold that nut any longer because that girl pussy was so fucking tight it was torture!

"So you can get wood again?"

"Yeah I'm still semi-hard right now."

He looked down and he said "But you already came, you blew "The Money Shot" that's the most important part of the scene! I need a cum shot!"

"No problem, I can cum again!"

"OK, I only need one more position and we're done. So if you can pull that off then that'll save you."

"OK cool. Go find her and let's knock this last position out Doggy Style, just ask her if I could do this last position without a condom so we can get through this scene and wrap this thing up."

Mitch left and came back ten minutes later after begging and pleading with that complete psycho bitch from hell, for her to please come back so we can finish what we had started. Finally after ten minutes of hell he was able to convince her to come back and let me do our last position without a condom. She came back at the same time I was walking back from the bathroom washing up. As soon as she walked up she was talking big shit. "I'm not sucking your dick to get you back hard! You better grab some lube and get it up yourself!" I grabbed the lube and I jacked my dick while she got down on all fours in Doggy Style position. I rubbed her firm little tight chocolate ass and I instantly got ready to knockout this last position. I wanted to get away from this chick. I needed a fucking drink! This bitch killed my buzz!

I told Mitch to grab his camera because I was ready. He told me to just give him another fifteen minutes, then this time let him know when I was about to cum, then pullout and then cum all over her face.

"No! No facial! He can cum on my ass, that's it!" Khai turned around and said.

I looked at Mitch and he just shook his head, threw his hands up and he said, "Whatever Khai, let's just get this scene over with."

I wasn't tripping because to me looking at her pretty little chocolate ass was the best view anyway. We were on the ground, Khai was on all fours and I'm on my knees. I grabbed my dick with my left hand and I spread her left butt cheek with my right hand giving Mitch a nice camera shot of her tight pink pussy. I was in full anticipation of how great her pussy is going to feel sliding up in it this time without a condom. It was so good with the condom that I couldn't fucking wait! I put the tip of my dick in the entrance of her pussy, in and out, in and out making all her pink inside disappear and reappear as I was setting up the money shot for Mitch.

I finally eased my well lubricated dick into her air tight pussy. "Damn this feeling should be illegal!" now I see what all this girls fuss is about, she's got some quality ass pussy. But what did I know, this was my first scene and at this point I had only been with a handful of women.

I've gotten my rocks off once already so I'm able to get into the sex a little more and actually get my fuck on now without having that urge to cum from her nice BJ and our first two positions. I was starting off fresh now and I'm finally able to enjoy my new job. Ten minutes into our last position Khai is starting to get louder and obviously more into the scene. I can tell because her pussy is now dripping wet and loosening up. I pulled out to give Mitch another penetration shot and I then I started flicking Khai with no hands, pulling out and then sliding my dick in hands free. I was really getting used to this new job as I started to feel that good sensation again as the urge to explode was starting to build. I held back the persistent urge to cum which only makes my load compile expanding my balls with every stroke.

I looked up at Mitch and he nods giving me my que. I get about ten more pumps in and I asked Khai if she's ready for me to paint her pretty little chocolate ass with my thick hot white cum. She looked back at me and she gave me a sexy little smile and she said, "Yes, cum for me you dirty little homeless bum!"

I pumped hard and deep, then harder and deeper. It was time for the money shot! I pulled out and I grabbed my fully engorged dick with my left hand, then with perfect timing I released my cum and I shot my hot, thick, massive load all up the side of Khai's ass. It was a big load, I painted both her cheeks, and I squirted and squirted and squirted. My second load was bigger than the first one. Mitch couldn't believe it. He grabbed his "stills" camera and he took pictures of me, Khai, and more importantly the money shot. Those pictures that he took with his stills camera were for the box cover of the movie.

It was finally a wrap. Khai got up smiling. "Thanks for getting me through that, I thought we were gonna be here all day." Then she walked off to go wash up. As I was putting my boxers on Mitch said, "Damn that was your second load in less than an hour, and it was huge! Some guys can't cum that much with three loads put together!" "Yeah, I guess I did pretty good for my first scene right?" I said "What? That was really your first scene?" Mitch said and looked at me.

"Yeah, I'm brand new to the industry." "If that was your fist scene then you're gonna make it in this industry. That girl didn't help you at all, she was a bitch!"

THE END

Suave is an adult film star who now wants to share his experiences after working 18 years in the industry, This hall of fame performer definitely has a story to tell, one book at a time. Take this new journey with him as he shows you another way he can entertain...Introducing Suave the Author..

To Be Continued...

Made in the USA
Monee, IL
24 September 2020